Ski Skating With Champions

"How To Ski With Least Energy"

By Einar Svensson

Library of Congress Publication Data

Svensson, Einar, 1926-
Ski Skating With Champions, How to Ski With Least Energy

Library of Congress Catalog Card Number: 94-92442
ISBN: 0-9641941-0-4

Copy editor, Text Layout:	Einar Svensson,
	Marlys Svensson
Text Design, Typesetting:	Einar Svensson,
	Laurie Figuly
Cover Design, Graphics,	
Illustrations, Photos:	Einar Svensson, except as noted *
Printer:	Dynagraphics,
	Portland, OR, USA

*Photo Credits:

Figs. 1-1, 1-2, 1-3, 1-4: From "Norske Skiløpere," Skiforlaget**
Fig. 1-4: Press photo, from "Längdåkning," Artur Forsberg**
Fig. 1-5: From "Skiing, a Way of Life in Norway," Einar Bergsland**
Fig. 2-1: Skarverennet by Jostein Sandsmark, Geilo, NOR
Fig. 2-12: Artificial Snow Making, Areco North America, Woburn, MA, USA
Fig. 8-1: Miriam Bedard, with permission of La Métropolitaine, Montreal, CAN
Fig. 9-1: Mikkelplass and Grünenfelder, by David Wheelock, Sun Valley, ID, USA

** Archival photos

Front cover photo:
From the 10 km Pursuit, World Championships, 1993,
Falun Ski Stadium, SWE, with 70,000 spectators cheering.

Bib #4	*Jelena Välbe, RUS*	Bib #3	*Trude Dybendahl, NOR*
#5	*Stefania Belmondo, ITA*	#9	*Anita Moen, NOR*
#7	*Marjut Rolig, FIN*	#8	*Katerina Neumannova, TCH*

Printed in the United States of America
10 9 8 7 6 5 4 3 2

Ski Skating With Champions
18405 Aurora Ave. N., Suite H-83
Seattle, WA 98133, USA

PREFACE

My intent is that the scope of this book should be broad; it is written to fulfill the cross country ski community's need for a comprehensive textbook on the sport, as practiced by the internationally elite skiers today. Its purpose is to educate young and old, newcomers and advanced level skiers on how to ski skate technically perfect, without excessive use of energy.

Ski Skating With Champions is the product of more than five years of my work. It is an extensive compilation from research, testing, practice, competition, international coaching clinics and photography of Olympic and World Championship racing, using my own equipment and under my supervision. The text demonstrates professionally, with hundreds of photos and illustrations of current world and Olympic champion skiers, how to apply the numerous different skate techniques.

The subtitle, "How to Ski With Least Energy", reflects one of the main topics that is repeatedly addressed throughout the book - that of how to ski most efficiently - applying the best technical movement solutions when skiing in the many variations of terrain and snow conditions - depending on the skier's available energy resources.

Within the time of compiling materials for my text, the cross country skiing world was electrified by the expanding application of ski skating. Its blending of enjoyable dance-like rhythms with relaxed movement of all the body's elements to produce increased speed, has totally captured the enthusiasm of athletes and the skiing public alike - it is fun. It is more fun when you have mastered a variety of techniques and can choose among them to suit the terrain and conditions in which you are skiing.

Chapter 1 on the "History of Ski Skating" technique points out that ski skating has actually always been an essential element of the traditional sport of cross country skiing. Although the technical aspects of ski skating were basic to Classic diagonal technique, dur-

ing the last 10 years there have been more advances in equipment and constant expansion and broadening of skating concepts (technique) than in all prior skiing history, resulting today in a much greater difference between ordinary cross country skiers and the international elite than ever before.

The author believes this gap is primarily educational (technical and physical) and therefore the next three chapters contribute to an understanding of the basic knowledge behind becoming a good ski skater.

Chapter 2 discusses the "Skating Environment" (a factor grossly ignored in America and in many other countries) and how it should be controlled and directed to make ski skating a pleasure for recreational skiers as well as serious racers.

In Chapter 3, "Criteria for Learning and Improving Cross Country Ski Skating", the four interdependent physical skills necessary for successful ski skating technique are explained, along with specific terminology that the author employs throughout the text.

What I consider to be the *real secret of rapidly improving* a skier's performance and speed is contained in **Chapter 4**. The new and original approach stresses the significance of "Understanding Neuromuscular Function And Control" to explain my special viewpoint on the "Sequence of Movement of Body Elements".

Chapter 5, "Learning Basic Skate Movements", begins the study of skating techniques which continues through Chapter 9. It illustrates basic on-snow exercises and introduces the use of simple, easy-to-follow, analytical bar lines and corresponding photographs of expert skiers to illustrate and sequentially explain ski skater's movements. The fundamental exercises help in the transition to the more advanced techniques The following chapters on technique systematically and gradually expand the skiers information, knowledge and skill levels.

Chapter 6, "Double Poling", provides the fundamental technique for the body and arm positions and movements which are used in most of the skate techniques.

The text then divides skating into two major groups - repetitious skating to one side, "One Side Skating / The Marathon Skate" in **Chapter 7**, and numerous new alternatives with skates out to both sides, "Two Side Skating / The Skate Dances" in **Chapter 8.**

The names identifying techniques are similar to or a translation of those used as the official language (terminology) of the Winter Olympics, Lillehammer, Norway 1994. The term "Dance" when applied to skating emphasizes the rhythmic, enjoyable aspects of the technique.

Chapter 9, the final discussion of skating technique, covers all aspects of "Downhill Skating and Turning" with elaborate sequential illustrations and explanations. It progresses from fundamental straight downhill motion to high speed skate step turns.

Chapter 10 is a systematic "Summary" of 17 variations of ski skating, to be used for comparison and references.

The extensively illustrated **Chapter 11,** an "Introduction to Ski Skating Mechanics" of movement, is another completely new contribution to the existing literature on ski skating. It is complemented with extensive wind tunnel testing data, documenting many of the statements and thoughts made in the text - namely that the current and future development of skating techniques will vary with speed of skiing and available energy resources of the individual skier.

I have devoted a lifetime to the sport of cross country skiing, both recreationally and as a competitor. My experience started as a kid having fun - tumbling on a pair of skis made from wooden tar barrel staves. Over the years, I have relished the continual changes in ski technology, which has unfailingly sought to make skis lighter and faster, and in ski technique, which is always trying something different, always adding new dimensions to the scope of skiing. The recent development of ski skating is truly unique and challenging. It has again provided a new inspiration to me - intriguing new physical challenges, new opportunities to study, and new knowledge - and I hope you, the reader, will enjoy joining me in exploring it in depth.

I dedicate this book to my family who has supported my love of skiing

Marlys, who patiently read, typed and retyped the text and guided me through the edits

John, who was a willing "test specimen" in the wind tunnel and companion on the ski trails

Marit, who edited the first drafts of the mechanics of movement chapter and gave me a layman's and an alpine skier's point of view

CONTENTS

CHAMPION VIGNETTES
Small descriptive sketches of important skier accomplishments are sprinkled throughout the text. They are denoted by the small ski skater logo.

CHAPTER 1

History of Ski Skating

Figure 1-1 *Three-Event Gold Medal Champion in the 1924 Olympics (50 km, 18 km, and Nordic Combined), and Bronze Medal in Ski Jumping, **Torleif Haug,** NOR, a legend in Nordic ski racing history, shows strength and speed in his uphill technique as he wins the 17 km in Holmenkollen, Norway, 1924. The coordinated movements of arms and skis he shows is almost identical to the "Paddle Skate" which suddenly became the fastest uphill cross country skiing "freestyle" technique in 1986, and has remained so.*

CHAPTER 1
History of Ski Skating

CONTENTS

I. SKATING - AN OLD TECHNIQUE FOR DIRECTIONAL CHANGES

In the years before modern track-grooming machinery evolved, race courses were set and foot-packed with skis that were usually a little wider and heavier than those used by the racing athletes. To make a firmer support for the pole-plant, both sides of the ski track would also be compacted by skis.

Such a ski course would have numerous natural directional changes. The skating technique was normally used at all these turns and the rule was that these should be packed and foot-groomed for one long skate turn. The angle of the skate would vary from a few degrees up to 90° depending on the natural terrain. Thus the skier had to be a good skater to master all these variable angles efficiently. There could easily be 100 changes of direction with skate turns in an 18 km course. The most efficient skate turn incorporated a double poling stride immediately before and after the skate.

The quality of a cross country skier's technique in those days was very often judged on his efficiency and increased speed coming out of the skate turns.

Figure 1-2 *Power, technique and excellent weight-shift is shown by* ***Johan Grøttumsbråten***, *NOR, as he skates a sharp angle turn at high speed to win the 18 km World Championship in Oberhof, Germany, 1931.*

During World War II (1940-1945) international competition ceased; then afterwards it took the skiing world some years to build up training for competition again.

Hallgeir Brenden *was the first Norwegian to win an Olympic Gold Medal after World War II (1952), in the 15 km, Oslo. Repeating his performance he also won the Olympic Gold for the same distance in Cortina, Italy, 1956.*

Figure 1-3 Hallgeir Brenden, *NOR, was a strong uphill skier and sprinter; he is shown here in a skate turn.*

Figure 1-4 Sixten Jernberg, *SWE, another legend in cross country ski history, on the way to his last Olympic victory in Innsbruck, Austria, 1964. Shown as he skate steps a turn at high speed. Jernberg won four Olympic and four World Championship Golds in his long racing career.*

II. SKATING IN DOWNHILL TURNS

In the poorly compacted snow before the advent of modern track-grooming machinery, changes of direction at high speed at the bottom of a hill required concentrated, quick lifting of the skis, utilizing the "skate step turn" technique.

Grooming machines, which came on the scene in the early 1970's, were able to set continuous grooved curves for all directional changes in the courses, and the skate step turns which had been necessary were completely eliminated from race courses.

Then in 1986, the advent of new "Freestyle" or "Skating" races with their high speeds and specialized equipment for course packing tended to eliminate the grooved tracks, resulting in a return to the original skate step turn technique at the bottom of downhills in skate races.

Figure 1-5 *A Skate Step Turn in a Downhill*

III. RECENT CROSS COUNTRY SKI SKATING HISTORY

A. *ONE-SIDE SKATING*

The introduction of present skating technique into cross country ski racing is very recent. *One-side skating* with double poling for each skate kick was introduced in the Worldloppet long distance marathon races in 1980. It was given the popular name of *Marathon Skating.*

Figure 1-6 Bill Koch, *USA, Olympic Silver Medalist, 1976, and World Championship Bronze Medalist, 1982, won the World Cup in 1982 with extensive use of the Marathon Skate throughout the season.*

During the Olympic games, 1984, in Sarajevo, Yugoslavia, the Marathon Skate was used extensively on the flats and mild uphills and downhills, although the skiers were still using kickwax under the mid-section of their skis for Classic (traditional) skiing.

B.   TWO-SIDE SKATING

The really pivotal change came at the last World Cup races in 1984, the Polar Cup Series in Northern Scandinavia, when several races were won by skating with only glide wax under the full length of the ski base. Because there is considerable less friction between the ski base and the snow when only glide wax is utilized, the skiers found their performances particularly affected on the flats, transitions and downhills. At the same time, several other skate stride techniques were introduced by the world's top skiers. It then was obvious that specialized training for skating and utilization of some variation of skating with only glide wax under the skis would give higher average skiing speeds in world competition.

During the Cross Country World Championship in 1985 in Seefeld, Austria, One-Side Skating (Marathon) with no kick wax dominated all events. Several other skate techniques were also experimented with in the uphills by some racers, utilizing Two-Side Skating, such as:

1. Staggered skating with double poling.

2. Diagonal skating with single poling.

Thus, some forms of skating, although not consistently used, became common in advanced competitive traditional cross country ski racing. The World Cup authorities and FIS now became very concerned about the skating "dilemma", since the fundamental traditional techniques of the past, Diagonal and Double Poling with a kick, seemed to be becoming obsolete. Agreement was reached that World Cup competition the next season, 1985-86, should have 2 types of race classifications, which are now common in all levels of cross country skiing competition:

1. "Freestyle" technique races where any kind of cross country technique would be allowed, and

2. "Classical", also called "Traditional", technique races where *no form of skating* would be allowed.

It was also decided that there would be an even number of each of these types of races each season for both men and women; and the rules applying to World Cup competition were approved for many other international, national and local races. The 1985-86 season, being the first test of the 2 types of race classification, turned out to be very successful.

Prior to the 1985-86 season, top international skiers spent most of the off-season training for skating, and tests indicated that Two-Side Skating, primarily versions of the Paddle Skate (Ch. 8, Sec. III), utilizing staggered glide on each ski, with double poling every other skate push would be the dominating skate technique for the 1985-86 season. This turned out to be very much true, but several other combinations of skating techniques were also used, depending on type of terrain, snow condition, and quality of the packed race courses. Thus, the first "Skating Season" showed dramatic increases in the average speed of most racers.

During the World Championship in Oberstdorf, Germany, 1987, the skating technique of 1986, was refined, capitalizing primarily on small variations of the Two-Sided Paddle Skate with some form of double-poling with each skate push.

Since 1986 many varieties of techniques have been added to ski skating. Top ski skaters apply different techniques to obtain maximum (optimum) speed, depending on individual energy resources available. Chapter 10 summarizes 17 different varieties of skating techniques that are applicable depending on type of terrain, speed of skiing, and muscle energy sources available.

Figure 1-7 **Thomas Wassberg,** SWE, is shown here in a steep uphill, using the Paddle Skate technique during the Olympic 4x10 Relay, Canmore, CAN, 1988. His team won the Gold Medal. Immediately behind, barely visible, is skier **Vladimir Sakhov,** RUS, and further downhill, **Jurg Capol,** SUI. Wassberg was one of the first champions to use skating. A superb ski skater, he won Gold Medals in the World Championships of 1982, 1987 and Olympic Golds in 1980, 1984 and 1988.

C. PURSUIT RACES

The exciting race format, *Pursuit*, recently added to Nordic skiing competition, combines the times for one Classic race and one Skating event which take place over two consecutive days. The race distances are:

	Women:	Men:
First Day:	5 km Classic	10 km Classic
Second Day:	10 km Skating	15 km Skating

The Classic races on the first day are regular 30 second interval drawn starts. In the Skating events on the second day, the winner of the Classic race starts first with the other skiers starting staggered, at the exact number of seconds they placed after the winner. Thus the finish position in the skating event is automatically also the skier's placing for the two combined events; adding the times together gives the relative time differences among the racers. Normally there are separate awards for the first day races as well as for the combined final finishing positions.

To place well in a Pursuit you have to master both Classic and Skating techniques. The format has become very popular with spectators because during the skating event on the second day it is possible to directly see a favorite skier's position at all times. The finish of the Pursuit is usually very intense - many times a photo finish with two or more skiers close together - with lots of excitement. The Pursuit is now an official event in World Championships and Olympic competition, where a maximum of four qualified skiers from each country are allowed to compete. The Pursuit has now become the most popular Nordic *spectator* event in Olympic and World Championship competition. See this book's cover and Chapter 8 for photos of pursuit races.

D. WOMEN IN SKIING

Women have skied cross country right along with men throughout history - the old artist's renditions attest to that. The author recalls as a youngster, prior to World War II, that girls competed with the boys in local races across Scandinavia. But until the later part of this century women were generally considered socially and physically unsuited for competitive sports, especially endurance ones like cross country skiing.

Organized international cross country competition for women did not really begin until several years after WW II (the first international race for women was in 1948 between Sweden and Finland), and gained momentum ever so slowly. The first Winter Olympic cross country event for women, a 10 km individual competition, was in 1952 in Oslo, Norway; it then took 32 years of adding one event at a time, until the 1984 Olympics finally presented an equal number of events for women and men.

However, the advent of Olympic competition for women sparked a real breakthrough in international organized women's training and competition. It has been exciting to see the strides women's cross country competition has since made. Women have gradually shrunk the distance and time differences between them and men's competition, and now the physical conditioning of women elite competitors is definitely comparable to men. The ski skating revolution has emerged at an ideal time for women's cross country competition, when they are ready and able to fully participate in developing the sport and its techniques. Many of the elite women racers used as examples in this book have skating technique equal to that of the elite men.

The lack of available experienced and qualified coaches for women is still hampering the attainment of the same general high level of technique execution that exists among the elite men competitors but hopefully this should eventually be remedied by the increasing number of women competitors in the future.

*The Russian woman, **Ljubov Jegorova**, has scored more points and won more medals than any other skier in the world, including men. She won six Gold Medals in the Olympics and three Golds in the World Championships between 1991 and 1994! She is shown in a sequence of Double Dance, one of the most difficult skate techniques, on pages 122 and 123.*

*Figure 1-8 Women's speed records are being broken every year. In a World Cup 5 km freestyle event in 1988, **Marianne Dahlmo**, NOR, broke the magic 14 minute barrier for women, which is compared to the accomplishment of a men's 4 minute mile in running.*

IV. CHANGES IN EQUIPMENT

The Scandinavian countries, Norway, Sweden and Finland, dominated innovations in and manufacturing of cross country wooden skis up to the 1970's, when there was a revolutionary change in the construction of cross country skis. Several Austrian ski manufacturers, experienced in the making of alpine skis of fiberglass, introduced cross country skis made of fiberglass with a polyethylene base, which were superior in glide and performance.

In the mid 1970's, there also were corresponding substantial changes in the material and design of bindings, poles and clothing for cross country skiing, with a considerably larger volume and variety produced and marketed worldwide.

In addition, during the same years, sophisticated machinery was designed for packing and daily setting of cross country tracks making cross country skiing more convenient, easier and faster to learn for the public.

All these changes laid the base for the skating revolution of the 1980's, as faster, lighter equipment and well-packed, groomed, fast cross country courses stimulated skiers to try different techniques.

And to come full circle, the experimentation with different skating techniques forced changes in equipment, so now virtually every cross country ski equipment manufacturer produces special skis, boots, and poles for skating only.

At the beginning of the 1990's the so-called "short skate skis" (being approximately 170 cm. or less) came on the market. Although there are restrictions of the use of such skis in certain international competitions, the short skate skis have become very popular among tourers as well as racers.

CHAPTER 2

The Skating Environment

Figure 2-1 Skarverennet, Geilo, Norway

Photo by: Jostein Sandsmark, Geilo, Norway

Every spring more than 12,000 skiers participate in this 37 km Freestyle tour race which crosses a beautiful, scenic mountain in the high plateau area of central Norway.

CHAPTER 2
The Skating Environment

CONTENTS

INTRODUCTION

The ski skating environment, or any skiing environment for that matter, should have an inspirational effect on the skier. The experience of skiing in a peaceful setting, alone, gliding away, free from the strain of daily work, is truly a pleasure.

While classic and touring techniques can be enjoyed in non-groomed areas, ski skating, by its nature, is usually most pleasurably accomplished under circumstances where the environment is specially prepared. Occasionally, firm snow conditions allow the ski skater to roam, skating freely in natural, untouched open terrain. This is a time to be truly treasured; but most of the time the skater's need for good glide dictates that he skate on a groomed trail. Thus, it is very important that track conditions, course layouts and other facilities for skating take into account the skiers' desire and need to be inspired by the environment, as well as provide for varying skill levels of all skiers.

This chapter addresses aspects of the skating environment that can be controlled to make all ski skating a pleasure for recreational skaters and serious racers of all ages. Natural terrain in the winter wilderness offers unlimited variations - flats, downhills, uphills, undulating ground, side-slopes, turns, etc. - sometimes all these variations are found in skiing a distance of one kilometer. *A well designed and groomed trail system should offer the same variations.*

Always keep in mind that ski skating can be enjoyed even more by selecting the right choices of technique for the particular terrain skied. By learning and practicing techniques to use on diverse types of terrain, different muscle groups can be utilized, so when physically tired from skiing one type of technique, a skier can change to a different one that uses other muscles and rest the part of the body that has become tired. As confidence is gained in executing the different techniques, more and more challenging terrain can be comfortably and successfully skied.

I. MECHANICAL METHOD OF GROOMING AND TRACK SETTING

Up until 1960, tracks for cross country touring and racing courses were set by skiers themselves who used their own skis for packing the gliding track and for tramping down the area outside each groove for firm pole planting. In Europe prior to 1974, it was the duty of the army, using hundreds of soldiers on skis, to compact and prepare the race courses for the big cross country ski competitions.

During the 1960 Winter Olympics in Squaw Valley, CA, USA mechanical methods using special machinery were used for the first time to grind up icy snow and compact and groom the race courses. Since then, custom mechanical track setting equipment has greatly evolved, now resulting in high quality, mechanically compacted and grooved skiing tracks for both touring and racing.

Larger ski areas, which are usually also involved in alpine skiing, can afford to use their highly sophisticated and efficient track packing and grooming equipment to also pack wide courses for superfast dual cross country tracks for classic and freestyle skiing.

Modern, highly sophisticated track setting equipment is quite expensive, and not affordable by many of the smaller ski clubs, or remote, sparsely populated ski areas. However, inventive and talented skiers, devoted to touring/racing, can set their own tracks by use of a snowmobile and a track setting sled. The snowmobile is used to roll down and compact the course first, and then the track-sled is pulled around the course to set the grooved tracks. There are now many versions of small track setting sleds available on the market, but not all have the ability to cut through icy snow.

Figure 2-2 *Grooming Equipment used for 1994 Olympics, Lillehammer, NOR.*

II. GROUND SPACE FOR FREESTYLE SKIING

Freestyle cross country skiing allows any form of technique to be used, so such a skiing course has to always provide a *separate groomed track for classic skiing in addition to smooth space* for skating. It is the responsibility of the skater to not destroy the classic grooved portion of such a skiing course.

It should be noted that most skaters take advantage of the grooves in a *Classic track* by using them in downhills, and for Double Poling. They also have the choice of limited use of one groove (nearest the skating area) of the track for one-side skating, where this would be desirable and not destructive to the grooves, such as when using the Marathon skate technique.

A. *SINGLE COURSE (ONE-WAY)*

The combined compacted width of a course which provides for both Freestyle and Classic disciplines should be at least 3.00 m., where 1.0 m is for the classic area and the remaining 2.0 m is for the skating area. In wooded or congested areas an additional 0.5 m shoulder should be provided on each side, making the overall clearance width 4.00 m *(Fig. 2-3)*.

Figure 2-4 *Freestyle Course with One Classic Track*

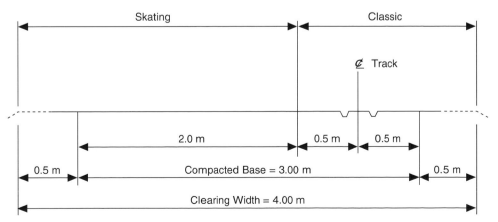

Figure 2-3 *Minimum width of One-Way Freestyle Course*

B.   DOUBLE COURSE (TWO-WAY)

A course for two-way Freestyle and Classic skiing is compacted very wide with dual classic skiing on one side and two-way skating on the other *(Fig. 2-5)*, or with one classic track on each side of a dual width skating course *(Fig. 2-6)*.

The width given in the illustrations is minimum, and is based on profiles of relatively flat undulating terrain. The right-hand rule for directional skiing should apply, with signs informing the skiers of this.

Obviously, such a freestyle skiing course requires the width of a normal roadway. It has been common for course builders to bulldoze out such roadways, sometimes destroying and eliminating the natural variations in terrain that are basic to the art of cross country skiing, thus reducing the choice of the many varieties of techniques that a good racer would apply during a race. Unfortunately, such courses commonly favor power first and technique only secondarily.

The minimum combined compacted width of the two-way course is 5.00m., where 2.0m. is for the classic area and the remaining 3.0m. is for skating.

Figure 2-6 *Minimum Width Of Two-Way Free Style Course Two-Way Freestyle **In Center** Of Course*

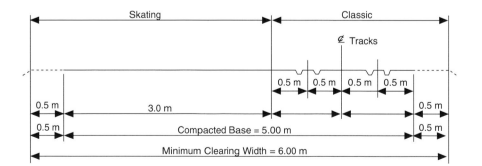

Figure 2-5 *Minimum Width Of Two-Way Freestyle Course Two-Way Freestyle Using **One Side** Of Course*

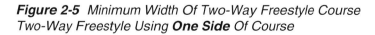

III. COURSE LAYOUT AND PROFILES

A. *GENERAL CRITERIA*

The quality of teaching and learning proper cross country skiing technique is directly related to the design of the ski course terrain, and the preparation of the courses. Designing courses for any type of cross country skiing is a complex task, and should be done by experts who have professional qualifications, experience related to cross country racing, and knowledge of the educational and economical aspects of the sport.

Every cross country *race course* should be planned to test all the physical, mental and technical skills of a competitor. A cross country *training course* should be designed with the idea of maintaining a *continuous rhythmic movement* for an *experienced skier moving at a fair tempo*. A course that has long tough uphills followed immediately by steep, sharply curved downhills in which a skier must strenuously side slip or skid through the curves, and then repeats a no-transition tough uphill *interrupts a skier's rhythm*. Training courses should have easy, but fast, adequately super elevated downhill curves and be primarily technically, not physically demanding. A course should stimulate speeding and rhythm, and have a lot of flexibility in terrain, so many techniques can be applied.

When selecting a site for a groomed track layout, the first necessity is mapping of the area. From the map a course layout is made which should follow the natural terrain, avoiding extensive grading and environmental impact. Natural terrain variations are always utilized and enhanced with proper course design. Adequate drainage should be provided to insure quality skiing with relatively little snowfall and no water pooling on the course.

A drawn profile of the course represents the longitudinal section of the course, illustrating the variations in the terrain - the flats, uphills, and downhills. The following are some basic simple international rules and criteria set for longitudinal profiles for cross country competition courses that should be followed in designing courses for *all levels* of cross country skiing.

- ◆ 1/3 of the distance to be variable flats (rolling terrain).
- ◆ 1/3 of the distance to be uphills of variable steepness.
- ◆ 1/3 of the distance to be downhills, incorporating curves to left and right.

The rules also specify a limitation on maximum vertical climbs and steepness in a race course.

1. VARIABLE FLATS (ROLLING TERRAIN)

The beginning of a course should be easy, naturally undulating terrain for physically "warming up" the skier, a necessity before entering any demanding portion of the course.

2. UPHILLS

Course planning should have in mind that shorter uphills and light, natural rolling terrain provide several physiological and technical advantages for training and racing. In such terrain the muscles develop less lactate and the potential for developing faster skiers is greater.

3. DOWNHILLS AND CURVES

Modern cross country courses have very few short straight downhill sections, but instead incorporate many smooth curves, sometimes super elevated, designed for high speed skiing. Curved sections allow for more variations of techniques and can generate increased acceleration. Acute side-slipping curves should be avoided in designing downhills since they tend to slow down the skier, and reduce recovery because of excessive muscle strain. One of the important criteria for a training/race course is that it should allow the skier to recover in the downhills. Dangerous downhills do not belong in any cross country skiing course. Safety should be of primary concern in high speed cross country downhills.

A course that starts with a long downhill and then has primarily long uphills to return to the start is wrongly designed. Recovery opportunities need to be planned throughout the course, not used up all at one time. This type of course will develop slow skiers, for both physiological and technical reasons.

Most well planned cross country course layouts should contain **several loops** with skiing in **one direction**, where the cross section in Figure 2-3 would be the minimum width clearance criteria. At least **one lighted loop** for night skiing should be planned, which is a necessity to stimulate more interest in cross country skiing, to develop better skiers, and to fully utilize the facilities, since most people only have the opportunity to ski after work in the evening.

The shortest practice course is one where the skiers ski in **both directions** *(See Fig. 2-5 and 2-6)*. Such a course demands a very wide space and should meet minimum width and clearance criteria to accommodate separate classic and skating in both directions.

Under And Over Crossing Of Courses

Courses that are confined to a small area for spectator purposes or where land area availability is limited can apply under and over crossing of the courses as shown in Figure 2-7. Such over crossing is a simple wood bridge made strong enough to support grooming equipment in addition to the snow load.

Figure 2-7 *Under and Over Crossing of Courses*

B. SAMPLE LAYOUT FOR FLEXIBLE 7.5 KM COURSE USING 3 LOOPS

A simple, but adequate, flexible and expandable course layout using the loop concept is illustrated in Figure 2-8. It consists of a 7.5 km long perimeter track that has been divided into 3 loops, A, B, and C, each 2.5 km long, all with skiing in a clockwise direction.

Loop A, designed for beginners, has mild uphills and easy downhill skiing. This loop should have graphical illustrations mounted along the course to teach basic techniques as the skier progresses through the loop. Loop B for intermediate level skiers is slightly more difficult. Loop C is designed for advanced skiers and is technically demanding with longer uphills and steeper curved downhills. Each loop is laid out with both right and left curves. All loops should be designed and groomed for safe, high speed skiing, with no excessively sharp curves. Maps and signs should be posted indicating direction of skiing and degree of difficulty.

The access to the courses is between Loops A and B, suggesting that Loop B could become the first lighted one for night skiing. The layout shows the short distances connecting the loops have two-way skiing, so skiers can practice individual loops, if desired.

The layout should be feasible for race competition distances of all age categories and level of skills. Children and beginners would use Loop A, while juniors and intermediate skiers could race Loop A and/or B. For a standard 15 km race distance, for older juniors and seniors, the 7.5 km course would be skied twice, and 4 times for a 30 km tour race.

It is the author's experience that it is far better (and more accepted by skiers) to train and race in several loops of a 7.5 km well designed and groomed course, than a single, long, inadequately groomed track .

The loop concept allows for flexibility in future expansion where the loop orientation depends on site, terrain, access, etc.

A suggested profile for the 7.5 km course is shown in Figure 2-9, indicating relative amount of level, uphills and downhills. Such a profile should be designed and graded with natural terrain variations in mind, so all techniques illustrated in this text can be practiced.

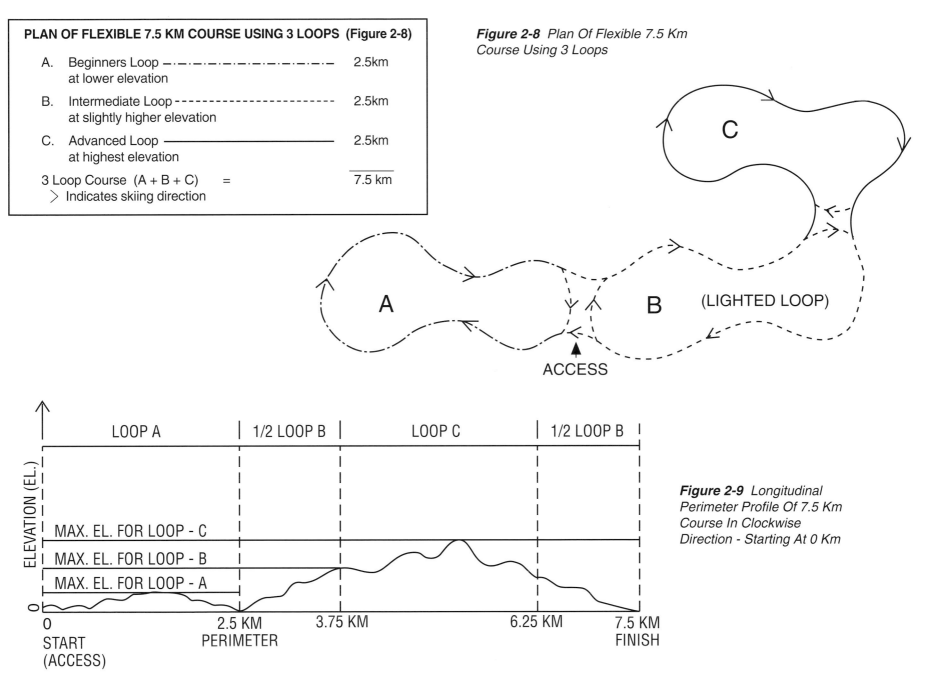

PLAN OF FLEXIBLE 7.5 KM COURSE USING 3 LOOPS (Figure 2-8)

A.   Beginners Loop —·—·—·—·—·—·— 2.5km
      at lower elevation

B.   Intermediate Loop --------------- 2.5km
      at slightly higher elevation

C.   Advanced Loop —————— 2.5km
      at highest elevation

3 Loop Course (A + B + C)   =   7.5 km
   〉 Indicates skiing direction

Figure 2-8 *Plan Of Flexible 7.5 Km Course Using 3 Loops*

C

A

B   (LIGHTED LOOP)

ACCESS

LOOP A | 1/2 LOOP B | LOOP C | 1/2 LOOP B

ELEVATION (EL.)

MAX. EL. FOR LOOP - C

MAX. EL. FOR LOOP - B

MAX. EL. FOR LOOP - A

0

0   2.5 KM   3.75 KM   6.25 KM   7.5 KM
START   PERIMETER   FINISH
(ACCESS)

Figure 2-9 *Longitudinal Perimeter Profile Of 7.5 Km Course In Clockwise Direction - Starting At 0 Km*

C. WORLD CHAMPIONSHIP COURSES: 5 AND 10 KM WORLD CHAMPIONSHIP COURSE FALUN, SWEDEN 1993

Layout of international competition course profiles in North America mistakenly strive for the *upper legal limits* on height difference, maximum climb and total climb and steepness of hills. *Training on such courses, in the author's opinion, has detrimental effects on a skier's development of speed, and produces relatively slower competitors.* Such courses also can discourage optimal performances by less elite skiers and pose serious safety problems in many cases.

In addition, designers of these extreme courses are in effect strangling the fiscal realities of the ski areas in which they are built. Such extreme courses, which offer little in terrain for an average skier and usually pose severe safety concerns, do not attract multi-use skiing and training by the public who are the ski area's main financial contributors. The ski area ends up spending it's grooming money and time on tracks that only a small fraction of skiers can use and usually ends up in an overcrowded situation on their moderate terrain. Nor is it practical for paying spectators and film crews to easily access these courses to watch and film elite race events, which would ultimately encourage and enhance the sport in North America.

Many race and training courses are also located at or above the upper limits for altitude, making the course profile situation even more important. There seems to be gross ignorance among course designers of what "recovery" means, which at high altitude needs to be longer and more frequent than at sea level.

The following illustration *(Fig. 10)* shows the basic Profile of the 5 km course used in the 1993 World Championship, Falun, SWE. This 5 km course was used for several 5 and 10 km skating events for men and women, and viewed by up to 70,000 paying spectators in a single day with hundreds of TV crews from all over the world set up along the course. This course, which was concentrated within a small area, was fast and safe, and has a much more relaxed profile than most North American courses; it also met all criteria for good training conditions. Race courses with these criteria are definitely more economically viable when they attract multi-use skiing and training in addition to races.

Figure 2-10 *Diagram And Profile Of 2 X 5km (10km) Course, Nordic World Championships 1993, Falun, Sweden.*

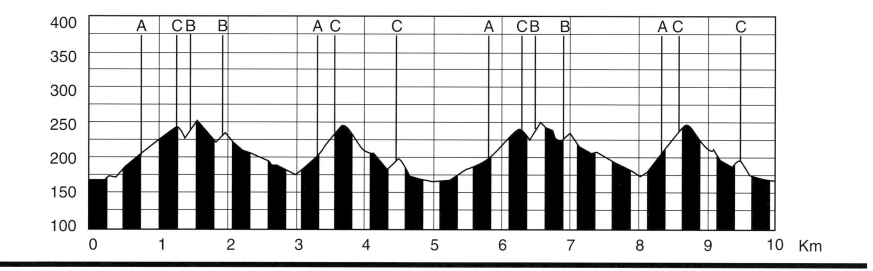

TECHNICAL SPECIFICATIONS

HD	87m	Height Difference
MM	68m	Maximum Climb
MT	312m	Total Climb

PROFILE LEGEND

A - Major uphills (>30 m height difference)

B - Shorter uphills (10-30 m height difference)

C - Steep uphills with a gradient of more than 18%

D. CROSS COUNTRY SKI GAMES AREA

A Ski Games Area promotes having fun while learning and practicing specific cross country techniques and skills for children and adults. The course layout emphasizes acquiring quickness, coordination and precision, and incorporates many technique variations. Such a layout provides for fun skiing and practice by novice skiers as well as for excellent technique training opportunities for skilled skiers.

A Ski Games Area, as designed by the author *(Fig. 2-11)*, consists of two approximately mirror-opposite clockwise and counter-clockwise course loops of approximately 0.5 km each (1.0 km total), joined to ski continuously. The course layout will be set with flexible gate poles and signs, and during the ski season the game slopes will be rolled with a snowmobile or groomer. The area should optimally be lighted for enjoyment of night skiing. It includes provisions for using the following and more diversified techniques:

1. Double poling
2. Classic techniques (diagonal and herringbone)
3. Skating uphill and curved downhills
4. Slalom and Telemark turns
5. Step turns in all terrain
6. Downhill variations
7. Alternate leg weighting and balancing (peddling)
8. Small jumps with Telemark landings
9. Passing through low arched gates
10. Variations of uphill techniques

The Ski Games area can be used for:

A) Individual, team, and group training, practice, and clinics. The game area layout is especially good for utilizing automatic video taping and display for teaching and coaching.

B) Competition

1. Intervals (1 skier doing both loops consecutively).
2. Dual (2 skiers in two parallel courses at one time.)
3. Elimination competition with 2 competing at a time.
4. Relays with many participants and many other possible competition setups.

Advantage:

The advantage of a Ski Games Area over a normal longer ski course is that it is contained in a relatively small concentrated area, which requires comparably little time and cost of grooming, while being useful for all skill levels and ages of skiers, most of all, children. If the courses are properly designed and laid out in well selected terrain, with good grooming, more technique and variable physiological exercises can be included than many competition courses 10 or 15 km long may have to offer.

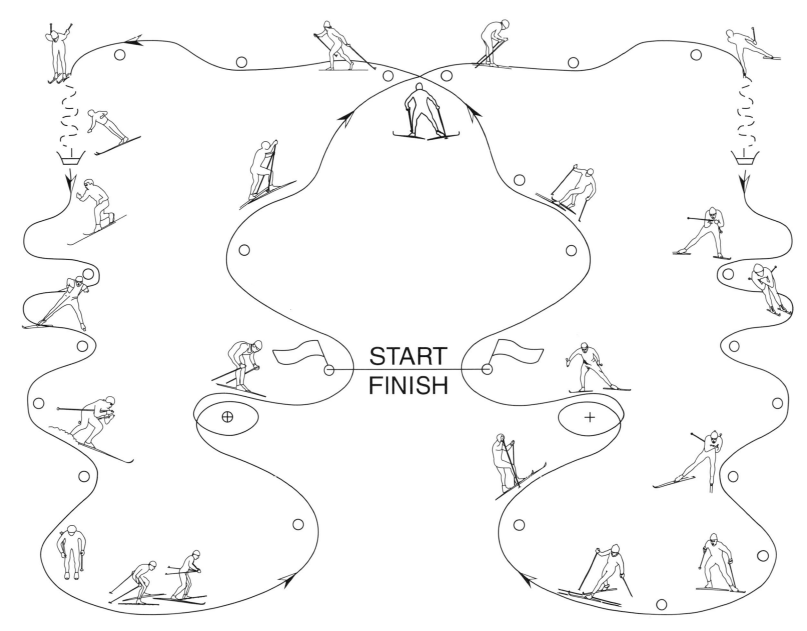

START
FINISH

Figure 2-11 *shows one of many possible layouts of a ski games area of 2 mirror-opposite courses equal to a total distance of approximately 1 km, with a mild elevation slope from top to bottom.*

In recent years winter weather in the Northern Hemisphere has been unusual. Many Nordic ski areas have had little or no snow, partly due to warm weather and partly due to little precipitation during cold weather days. For many ski areas Nordic skiing represents a long term financial investment with preparation for the ski season starting earlier in the summer; a snowless season can be a commercial financial disaster. It also adversely effects the public and the many skiers who are preparing and anticipating Nordic skiing as their winter sport and recreation.

During the last 10 years much research has been done to produce artificial snow for Nordic skiing as already done for Alpine areas. The process uses compressed air or high speed fans to freeze water droplets that are forced by high pressure through a cylinder or nozzle of a snow gun. Reliable, portable machinery is now available for artificial snow making on well graded cross country courses and the cost of such equipment has gone down substantially. Sponsors of top international Nordic ski events today are usually equipped with snow making machinery in case nature's white snowflakes fail to show.

Artificial snow is more consistently stable than natural snow (Appendix, Sec. I) and waxing for good glide is therefore not very complicated. Due to lack of snow prior to the World Championships in Falun, Sweden, 1993 the 5 km course, illustrated earlier in this chapter, was prepared with artificial snow and groomed up to the night before the first skiing event, then a foot of fresh snow fell overnight and covered the man-made snow. The artificial snow base served as a very good and fast base during the following days of competition.

Figure 2-12 *Artificial snow making machinery*
Photo courtesy of Areco, North America Equipment

CHAPTER 3

Criteria for Learning and Improving Cross Country Ski Skating

Four physical skills contribute the most to learning how to ski skate well and in improving an experienced ski skater's technique. These skills are interdependent and cannot really be separated from each other, yet to understand successful skating, it is helpful to consider each one by itself. They are the ***Criteria for Learning and Improving Cross Country Ski Skating:***

- ◆ **Balance**
- ◆ **Coordination (Technique)**
- ◆ **Rhythm**
- ◆ **Flexibility**

CHAPTER 3

Criteria for Learning and Improving Cross Country Ski Skating

CONTENTS

I. BALANCE

A. BALANCE - A PROCESS OF LEARNING

Proper balance is fundamental in developing good cross country skating technique. When learning to walk as a child, the fundamental problem was to retain balance. When learning to ski, the same situation is faced all over again. Everyone feels clumsy when they are on skis for the first time. Although the large, flat, supporting area of a pair of skis, compared to the area of the feet alone, gives greater stability (better balance), the feeling initially is just the opposite.

Balance is a sense of feeling, but is also dependent on a sense of security. To avoid falling over into the snow is a normal desire, even though the snow may be soft. Maintaining balance when gliding (dynamic balance) on a pair of skis with an even, slow speed, is not much more difficult than maintaining balance when standing still on skis (static balance).

The *"sense of balance"* is easily mastered, and can be improved considerably by using proper procedure when practicing. As better balance and a feeling of safety is achieved, skiing speed can be increased, and more of the endless variations of natural open terrain incorporated.

Balance for cross country skiing can be improved through exercises such as dancing, skating, rope skipping, jogging, walking, and use of a trampoline; and more specifically, by use of roller skis and in-line wheel skates.

In ski skating the *balanced shifting* of body weight (COG) from one ski to another is very noticeable, since the timing between movements is long. The secret of fine tuning of the technique is a smooth, rhythmic movement of COG laterally and forward to achieve the perfect balanced position.

Good balance during cross country ski skating can be achieved only through practice of the sport, incorporating varied techniques (specific patterns of movements) as illustrated later in this book. By repeating such movements over and over again the motor control of muscle fibers initiating the specific movements becomes automatic. Experience has shown that training for better balance also *improves coordination* of specific movements of body and limbs.

Skiers who do not achieve proper balance have to constantly use muscle strength to counteract the off balanced elements of their bodies and equipment, wasting energy in their inefficient technique.

B. BALANCE AND THE NERVOUS SYSTEM

The sense of balance is maintained by a complex interaction of the following parts of the nervous system:

THE INNER EARS which monitor the directions of motion, such as turning or forward-backward, side-to-side, and up-and-down motions. The inner ear consists of three fluid-filled semicircular canals. When a person moves, the fluid in these canals also moves, very much as water moves in a glass when tilted. The motion causes pressure changes in the canals, and alerts nerves in the brain of these changes. The brain then sends messages or impulses to the various muscles of the neck, trunk and limbs (feet) that maintain the balance of the body through movements.

THE EYES which monitor where the body is in space and also directions of motion. When eyes are closed, a person tends to fall out of balance.

THE SKIN PRESSURE RECEPTORS such as in the feet, which tell what part of the body or equipment is touching the ground, and how pressure, for example, is distributed over the foot.

THE MUSCLE AND JOINT SENSORY RECEPTORS which tell what parts of the body are moving.

THE CENTRAL NERVOUS SYSTEM (the brain and spinal cord), which processes all the bits of information from the above four systems to make coordinated sense out of it all.

C. BALANCE AND GROUND CONTACTS FOR BETTER STABILITY

When ski skating, body weight is constantly moved from one ski to another in varying degrees and rhythms, depending on what type of technique is applied. In skating with any one technique, at times balance may be on one ski only, with no poling support; while at other times balance may be on both skis, and, in addition, ground contact made with both poles. When learning, it is best to ski safely with good stability, which means using the poles as an aid to regain balance.

In the following, four basic ways of attaining and aiding balance in ski skating, by varying the number of *POINTS OF CONTACT* of equipment with the snow's surface, are explained. Most techniques in skating incorporate all of them, contributing to the great variety of choices available in the sport.

In learning or teaching skating techniques, *the number* of *POINTS OF CONTACT is very important*. The beginner should always take advantage of using as many points as possible, until confidence in skiing the technique has been achieved.

♦ 4 POINTS OF CONTACT ♦

The *most stable condition during skating* is when the skier's body is firmly distributed over both skis (feet), and additionally stabilized by both poles. Beginning skiers should utilize such a "four point contact" frequently since it gives a feeling of additional security and can be used to recover one's balance.

A Four Point Contact is extensively used by experienced skiers when double poling, during the skating techniques, and to recover when thrown off balance. In a high speed difficult downhill, a skier may tap the pole baskets along the surface for a feeling of additional safety.

A typical Four Points of Contact example is *Double Poling Action*, where the skier's contacts with the ground are evenly on both feet and both poles. Double poling is the first beginner's exercise, but is also used a lot by top skiers in skating because double poling or a slight variation is incorporated in most skating techniques.

One of the most used skate techniques today, the *Single Dance* (Ch. 8) utilizes Four Points of Contact, as illustrated, where the order of application for the contact points is very similar to straight Double Poling. The initiation of the *Marathon Skate* (Ch. 7) and the *Paddle Dance* (Ch. 8) are other examples of Four Points of Contact.

Figure 3-1 *Four Point Contact Single Dance Technique Skier:* **Maurilio De Zolt, ITA**

Figure 3-2 *Four Point Contact Single Dance Technique Skier:* **Maurilio De Zolt, ITA**

Figure 3-3 *Four Point Contact Single Dance Technique Skier:* **Mika Myllylä, FIN**

♦ 3 POINTS OF CONTACT ♦

Double poling while gliding on one ski is a technique used extensively in skating. In this case the skier is making Three Points of Contact with the ground to aid his balance and his forward motion.

In general, ski skating applies **Three Points of Contact** to some degree in virtually all techniques, with uneven force applications at each contact point.

The three skiers shown below in a steep uphill, Olympics, 1994, Marco Albarello, ITA (Bib #3), Mikall Botvinov, RUS (Bib #4) and Jan Räsänen, FIN (Bib #12) are all applying Double Poling during the *step forward* in the Paddle Dance (Ch. 8, Sec. III). Bib #12 uses an opposite Hang side than the other two skiers.

Figure 3-4 Three Point Contact
Paddle Dance Skating Technique
Skier: **Marco Albarello, ITA**

Figure 3-5 Three Point Contact
Paddle Dance Skating Technique
Skier: **Mikhail Botvinov, RUS** (Bib #4)

Figure 3-6 Three Point Contact
Paddle Dance Skating Technique
Skier: **Jan Räsänen, FIN**

◆ 2 POINTS OF CONTACT ◆

The fine tuning of rhythm and coordination in several skating techniques requires a Two Point Contact not only by the skis, but sometimes also by one pole and one ski.

During the pole recovery in the **Paddle** and **Single Dances**, as the three skiers below demonstrate during the Olympics, 1994, skaters briefly make Two Points of Contact with both skis during the transfer of weight from one ski to the other (Ch. 8, Sec. I and III).

In **Diagonal Skating** (Ch 8, Sec. IV), the skier utilizes opposite pole and ski simultaneously in a Two Point Contact.

Figure 3-7 Two Point Contact
Single Dance Skating Technique
Skier: **Johann Mühlegg, GER**

Figure 3-8 Two Point Contact
Paddle Dance Skating Technique
Skier: **Alois Stadlober, AUT**

Figure 3-9 Two Point Contact
Single Dance Skating Technique
Skier: **Marja Liisa Kirvesniemi, FIN**

When skating correctly, the skier constantly shifts his body weight from one ski to the other. If the poles are not actively used during such a weight shift, the skier is in balance on one ski (foot) only, which is defined as One Point of Contact.

In skating, the One Point of Contact is very common; it applies to almost all techniques for a short period of time. This is considered the most difficult balanced skiing position as it requires very good balance to support the body efficiently on one ski at a time when gliding and steering the ski forward.

When first learning skate movements, this author suggests simple skate movements without poles to get accustomed to the one point of contact coordination (Ch. 5).

In ***Single Dance*** (Ch. 8, Sec. I) during the pole recovery, the skier is in gliding balance on one ski.

The ***Double Dance*** (Ch. 8, Sec. II) is the most difficult of the skating techniques to master; balancing on one ski for an extended time is criteria number one for effective execution.

When a skier utilizes the ***Step Turn*** technique (Ch. 9) in downhill skiing, the balance is also on One Point of Contact for a short period of time, meaning all the body weight plus impact forces have to be supported by the One Point of Contact.

Figure 3-10 *One Point Contact Paddle Dance Skating Technique* Skier: **Oddvar Brå, NOR**

Figure 3-11 *One Point Contact Double Dance Skating Technique* Skier: **Hervé Balland, FRA**

Figure 3-12 *One Point Contact Step Skating Technique* Skier: **Anfissa Retsova, RUS**

D. SELF-AWARENESS OF BALANCE

To make improvements in ski skating skiers need to develop self-awareness of their own balance. Beginners and experienced skiers should be aware that balance during movement is effected by several complex physical and neurological factors and that improvement comes from keen practice with conscious physical feeling and mental understanding of what may cause one to be off balance.

The following are significant points in evaluating and improving common balance problems during skiing.

♦♦ MOVEMENT OF THE COG ♦♦

Proper movement of the COG (Center of Gravity) of the body from one ski to the other (laterally and forward, with very little vertical movement) is most crucial for retaining good balance during skating (Ch. 11). A skier should be in perfect relaxed balance on each ski for a short period of time.

Wide Stance and COG Problems

The most common technique mistake exhibited by beginners and many experienced ski skaters is caused by two interrelated *errors* in balance. The skier:

- Has **too much bending at the hip and forward lean** with the trunk.
- Uses a **too wide stance** throughout the skate without bringing the feet together.

This **"sitting"** position produces a COG too far to the rear (behind the heels), creates unstable balance and effectively prevents use of the powerful hips. If the legs are too far apart, the lateral movement of the COG during skating causes inward bending stress on the knee which may eventually result in an injury. These combine into a very *inefficient* skate position that:

- Taps energy that otherwise could be used to improve one's average forward speed substantially, and
- Reduces one's ability to ski relaxed, one of the most important aspect of ski skating.

Narrow Stance/Body Erect

Ski skating on the level and in uphills should be done with the body nearly totally erect, very little bending at the hips, and use of the powerful hip buttock muscles for lateral and forward movement. Bringing the legs together between each skate is one of the most crucial requirements in good skating. Transferring (shifting) weight from one leg to another for good skate technique is much easier from a narrow stance with an erect body.

A skier's efforts to improve in keeping legs together in a narrow stance and body erect is greatly enhanced by making a conscious effort during practice to physically contact (touch) the inside of the boot of the opposite leg during recovery of the skate leg. It is amazing how much this practice improves balance and overall skate technique.

♦♦ DIRECTIONAL VISION (EYE FOCUS) ♦♦

The second aid in promoting good skiing balance involves focusing the eyes in the direction of the skate movement.

When skiers stand on one ski and close both eyes, they will soon lose their balance. If they make a simple gliding skate step and do not focus their vision in the skate direction, the effect is similar to closing their eyes; their balance is impeded and they may even fall over.

The practice of good **Directional Vision** is an absolute necessity in becoming a good ski skater. Particularly in racing or skiing at high speeds, skill in constant shifting of direction of vision enables a skier to observe terrain and movement and carving of each ski to deal better with technique, weight shifts and safety problems.

II. TECHNIQUE AND COORDINATION

Technique in cross country skiing subjectively means specific sets of coordinated, harmonized *movements* of arms in use of the poles, and body and leg movements that guide, control and stimulate the glide of the skis.

In this book, *proper* technique is defined, in broad terms, as the most efficient way of moving on a pair of skis in an infinite variety of terrain. Skiing *"efficiently"* means coordinating movements of equipment and the body elements in such a way that requires least physical energy.

Since there is an infinite variety of terrain in cross country skiing, there theoretically also should be an infinite variety of techniques. In *Skating or Freestyle* cross country skiing there are a number of specific techniques which are identified and discussed in this book. A skier needs to master these, and learn to combine and adjust them to infinite terrain variations.

Efficient technique in skating is directed toward *reducing* two major natural forces which consume energy: *Gravity and Friction.*

Gravity

When walking up a stairway, the weight of the body is lifted vertically; this consumes energy. (In physics, they say the weight of the body is due to gravitational forces that act downward.) When skiing, the same gravitational forces acting downward on the body and equipment have to be overcome.

Friction

The other major natural force, that requires considerable energy to overcome, is the frictional resistance between the ski and the snow. It acts when gliding on skis (see Friction in Appendix, Sec. I for more detail).

So *efficient technique*, basically means coordinated movements of the body elements and skiing equipment in a manner that generates least gravitational energy and frictional resistance.

There are also several minor forces that must be overcome by use of energy, which are discussed under more advanced analysis later in Chapter 11.

Learning Technique

As experience shows, ski skating is not a series of rigidly prescribed technical exercises and techniques, but more an instinctive fluid, harmonic blending of these that adjust to type of terrain and snow conditions experienced in nature.

When learning skating technique, it is better to learn *correct execution* right from the beginning. Working through the lengthy learning of automatic motor skills of skating movements only to find later that substantial corrections are needed has not been uncommon in cross country skiing in the past, when reliance was placed on word-of-mouth unsubstantiated methods of instruction.

III. RHYTHM AND SEQUENTIAL TIMING

Rhythm and technique are inseparable; good technique, balance, and coordination cannot exist without good rhythm.

When learning and executing the different ski techniques described in this book, the continuities of motion, rhythm and timing, are as vital as they are in music. While musical rhythm can be annotated and guided by a conductor or an instrument, so it doesn't get off beat, the rhythmical motion during cross country skiing is not so easily displayed on paper.

Why is Rhythm Important?

Rhythmic skiing movement promotes speed and efficiency in skating. Rhythm **blends** separate learned movements into fluid spontaneous whole patterns of technique.

The essence of rhythm and correct timing in ski skating is to move the body and equipment fluidly in **relaxed smooth** patterns (sequences of movements) with continuity, avoiding staccato, jerky, inefficient motion. This requires smooth, elastic give during the muscle's closing of all the body's joints and conscious emphasis of muscle action radiating from the central large muscles of the body outward to the extremities (Ch. 4, Sec. IV).

Sequential Timing Analysis

When analyzing and evaluating technique in this book, skiers' movements have been divided into three stages:

1. **Pole Action**
2. **Leg / Hip Work**
3. **Recovery**

The right sequential timing and coordination of the movements of the body elements and equipment in these three stages will result in effective harmonic, rhythmic skiing.

The Pole Action and Leg / Hip Work actively contribute to the forward motion through certain muscle action; which is normally followed by a short period of Recovery when muscles for the same body elements go through a short period of relaxation during movement that requires minor energy output. One could compare this alternate activity and rest to the beats or pulses in music.

Self Analysis Helps to Develop Timing

- Studying films of champion skiers and self-videos can help with visualization of rhythm and timing and help with self-criticism to improve skiing much faster.

- Mental imaging and practice of smooth, relaxed muscle movements that radiate outward from the body's center serve to focus the mind on the natural rhythms in each technique as adaptation is made to variations in the skiing terrain.

- Listening to music that matches the skate technique being practiced can be a great help in stimulating good rhythmic development.

IV.   FLEXIBILITY

Flexibility as related to cross country skiing means ***mobility and range of movement*** of bodily elements involved when executing different skiing techniques. In skating virtually every body element is repeatedly activated; flexibility therefore is an overall important factor in relaxed mobility. Good flexibility of the hip joints is particularly important for ski skating.

Two types of flexibility are:

Single joint motion, confined to a portion of a body element, such as takes place only at the wrist when the pole handle is moved.

Composite joint motion, where several joints are involved to execute one action, such as in poling where the whole arm with joints at the wrist, elbow and shoulder are in motion.

Flexibility is an important factor in learning to ski cross country well, and it is also an important factor in preventing injury. In order to develop relaxed greater range of motion and promote general agility, a skier should do daily basic stretching exercises, where body movement forces a muscle or muscle group into a series of elongation. To be effective each stretch should last 30 seconds. There are many books that deal specifically with this subject matter (see references in the Bibliography).

CHAPTER 4

The Secret Of Power And Speed In Ski Skating:

*Understanding
Neuromuscular Function,
Control And
Sequence Of Movement*

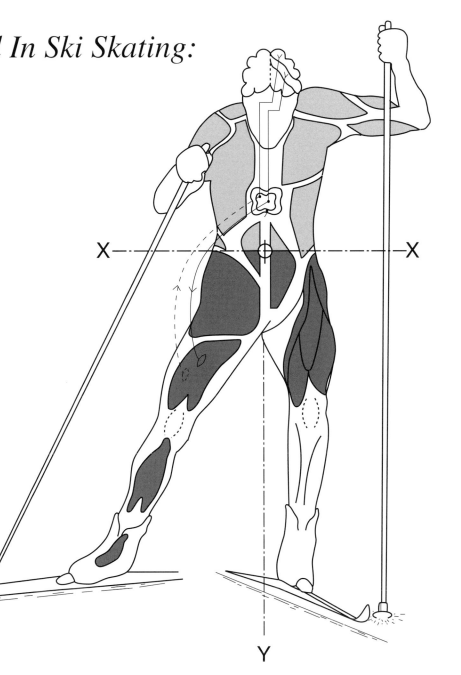

CHAPTER 4

The Secret of Power and Speed In Ski Skating:
Understanding Neuromuscular Function, Control and Sequence of Movement

CONTENTS

INTRODUCTION

The author's theory and experience is that the efficiency of all skating techniques is enhanced by ***using a sequence or progression of voluntary muscle action which correlates to the physical neuromuscular sequence.*** This produces more coordinated movements, better rhythm, and a more relaxed form for skiing. He employs this new approach extensively to analyze successfully executed skating techniques in this text.

If a skier wants to improve in cross country skating, on a modest or advanced level, an understanding of how movement is activated and executed by the body's neuromuscular system will help develop a better and more efficient ski technique faster and easier.

The correct application of muscular forces in effective skating technique depends not only on muscle strength recruited for the actions involved, but also on a number of sequential, coordinated neuromuscular functions.

The learning of correct cross country skiing techniques can be a slow process in the beginning because accurate and smooth technique movements require conscious instructions from the brain with immediate simultaneous activation and relaxation of specific muscles, or muscle groups. However, as the same pattern of skiing movement is repeated over and over, *a memory of the pattern is "imprinted" on the brain and the process is immensely speeded up* so eventually the complex, coordinated body movements are performed instantaneously and automatically.

To accomplish all movement there is integral communication between the mind and the body's muscles through the nervous system. The initiation of movement for a specific skating technique starts in the brain *("the headquarters")*. For example, a skating pattern is pictured in the mind. The brain, via sensory and motor nerves down through the spinal cord with branches out to the body's elements, instructs skeletal muscles to activate and execute the desired pattern of movements by contracting (shortening) or stretching (elongation).

The following much simplified discussions and illustrations of basic neuromuscular aspects of skiing movements attempt to bring together the separate complex elements of the:

- **Nervous system which *initiates skiing movement*, and the**

- **Muscular system which *produces skiing* movement**

while emphasizing the

- **Correct *correlated sequence of movement.***

These very complex subjects are presented here in condensed form. For more comprehensive information about the neuromuscular system, the reader should consult basic physiology and anatomy books (see references in the Bibliography).

I. NEURAL CONTROL OF SKIING MOVEMENT

The Nervous System is equipped to receive and interpret information from outside the body (*external stimuli*) and inside (*internal stimuli*) and convert it into muscular movements. The **Autonomic** part of the nervous system regulates some muscle activity without any thought upon our part: **involuntary** or **inborn** movements such as breathing, blood circulation, swallowing, the functioning of organs, and certain reflexes. Other muscle activity, called **voluntary** movements, must be **learned** with conscious effort, such as writing, typing, walking, biking, swimming and skiing. **These are the nerve/muscle activities of the *Central* and *Peripheral* nervous systems that we are concerned with in this discussion.**

A. THE CENTRAL NERVOUS SYSTEM

The Brain and the Spinal Cord compose the central *"headquarters"* which controls, directs and correlates muscular skiing movements.

1. THE BRAIN

The skating "revolution" was not an accident. It was and continues to be the result of well thought out and tested theories of efficient technique to produce faster skiing. It is no longer simply enough to train and ski with muscle power only. The brain must likewise be trained to sort out specific skate techniques for using in given circumstances and to develop tactical, smart skiing. Memory, judgment, decision making, and imagination, all higher functions of the brain, are called upon. This has made skating the interesting sport it has become and provides the intellectual motivation to improve.

Although with lots of repetition many skiing movements become nearly automatic (reflexes), real improvement begins only when skiers are **consciously aware** of their movements. That is when they concentrate on executing a technique **sequentially correctly.**

The complex Brain, an expanded bulb at the top of the spinal cord, is divided into units which have highly specialized functions in regard to regulating muscle movement. For simplicity we divide the Brain into 3 regions: *Forebrain, Midbrain and Hindbrain (Fig. 4-2).*

2. THE SPINAL CORD

The Spinal Cord is a long, thick nerve cord that extends from the Midbrain through the Brain Stem and down inside the vertebral skeletal column. The intricate design of the skeletal spinal column provides strength and freedom for lateral and twisting movement that takes place during skiing while protecting the delicate incredibly complex spinal cord inside it.

The Spinal Cord consists of outgoing (efferent) **motor nerves** that carry messages from the brain to the muscles, and incoming (afferent) **sensory nerves** with messages from the sensory organs to the brain. Figure 4-3 shows a cross-section of the spinal cord. The H shaped center called gray matter contains the nerves' cell bodies. The outer surrounding white matter contains the nerves' fibers, protected by a myelin sheath. These fibers extending out from the spinal cord to the body's muscles are part of the **Peripheral Nervous System.**

Pathways of sensory motor nerves cross over in the brain stem *(Fig. 4-5)* when entering the spinal cord and because of this crossing, the right hemisphere of the brain controls movement on the left side of the body and vice-versa. Most people are right handed because the left hemisphere dominates the right. Many skiers learning skating tend to emphasize skate action primarily to one side, probably for the reason stated above. This author had the same problem when learning skating. This situation improved, however, as he consciously decided to train both right and left sides equally and to select sides and techniques based on efficiency within terrain variations. An example: Using the Hang side in the Paddle on the uphill side when there is a lateral slope as being most efficient (Ch. 8, Sec. III).

The Message Distribution Network

The Central Headquarters which controls, directs and correlates muscular movement

In the Forebrain we store Memory of learned cross country skating techniques adaptable to terrain variations, for example:

- Single Dance on variable flat
- Double Dance in transitions
- Paddle in the Uphills
- High speed skating without poling
- Tuck in Downhill

8 PAIRS OF CERVICAL NERVES, control movements at neck, shoulder, arms and upper trunk, originate here.

12 PAIRS OF THORACIC NERVES branching out to mid-section (abdomen, lower back and sides), originate here.

5 PAIRS OF LUMBAR NERVES control movements of hips, thighs, legs and feet, originate here.

SENSORY PERCEPTION (Consciousness)(Awareness) is anything that can be recognized by the senses, such as:

1) Eyes - viewing skiing terrain, signs, obstacles, other skiers

2) Ears - spectators, coaching, music, environment, skiers

3) Touch - type of snow, smoothness of skiing, downset of ski, pole plant, friction, glide, muscle stiffness, pain

1) **Forebrain -** This largest region controls not only the "higher human functions" of reason and memory, but also movements of the skeletal muscles. It contains the *Sensory* area with the Receiving Centers for *incoming* information, and the *Motor* area which is the initiating center for *outgoing* messages (instructions) for skeletal muscle movements. The forebrain is divided into left and right hemispheres, each sphere controlling movement on the opposite side of the body.

2) **Midbrain -** This center portion, acts as a relay station between the Fore and Hind regions.

3) **Hindbrain -** Rear, lower portion controls balance, posture and coordination of movements; contains **brain stem.**

4) **Vertebral Column -** protects the spinal cord and its nerve system, and provides support, strength and flexibility for body movement.

5) **Spinal Cord** - inside the vertebral column, contains sensory and motor nerves that initiate and control skeletal muscle movement.

B. THE PERIPHERAL NERVOUS SYSTEM
(THE MESSAGE DISTRIBUTION NETWORK)

Coupled sets of sensory and motor nerve fibers extend out from the cell bodies contained in the various levels, *cervical, thoracic and lumbar,* of the Spinal Cord to control the skeletal muscles. They branch in pairs to both sides of the vertebrae, the shortest possible distances to the muscles they serve and control *(Fig. 4-2).*

1. THE SENSORY NERVES

Most activity of the nervous system originates with sensory environmental experiences: visual, auditory, taste, and touch which are received into the body (perceived) through special nerve fibers (dendrites) and their endings (sensory receptors) located in the eyes, ears, mouth, skin, and muscles. Such experience may result in an immediate reaction which initiates movement, or it may be stored as a memory in the brain, and help to determine the body's actions at a later time, from minutes to years.

The system of Sensory Nerves transmits information from the peripheral sensory receptors through the spinal cord nerves to the primary sensory areas of the Forebrain and also relays secondary signals to all parts of the nervous system.

For a cross country skier, the sensory receptors in the skin (especially numerous in feet and hands) that relay touch are particularly important. The type of **touch** and amount of **pressure** is a constant conscious factor in executing skate technique, and is a factor repeatedly emphasized in this text. Correct downset of a ski is done with *smooth contact* (touch) followed by gradual application of pressure to the ski. But in effective poling, the amount and effect of touch and pressure is the opposite - touch should have an immediate *powerful impact.*

Sensory receptors are also located in the muscles themselves, relaying sensations of movement, pressure, pain, fatigue, etc. **Awareness (perception)** of correct movement and positions of pole and ski, cooperates with muscle/joint sense in recognition of weight, friction, speed of movement, balance, etc. The sensory nerves in muscles and joints give information about how **effective** a movement pattern is, providing necessary feedback for learning correct technique.

Through sensory perception (awareness), skiing movements are performed and controlled, and through repetition, made more efficient, to help a skier become better much faster.

2. THE MOTOR NERVES

After the sensory information is received and processed by the brain, electrical signals are transmitted back down through the spinal cord by the motor nerve network into the muscles, there, triggering a chemical secretion which stimulates a release of energy that causes muscle contraction.

One single motor nerve usually supplies many individual muscle fibers within one skeletal muscle, which number varies according to the muscle mass and function of movement. For example, a single nerve cell controls the delicate movement of the eye muscles through fewer than 10 muscle fibers, while for less complex movements of the big skeletal muscles at hip and thigh, one single nerve cell may innervate 3000 muscle fibers.

The motor nerve's cell body in the Spinal Cord and it's axon (extending fiber) together with the group of muscle fibers it supplies is called the *MOTOR UNIT.* These groups of muscle fibers may be widely scattered within the muscle itself. When the nerve cell transmits messages to the muscle fibers, all the fibers in the motor unit are activated. ***The more motor units involved, the greater force can be produced by the muscle group. The muscle force may also vary depending on the rate of frequency at which the motor units operate.*** For example, if greater power is expected to be applied to the ski poles and skis, more motor units have to be activated, or some motor units have to operate at a higher frequency — all related to speed of movement.

Specific muscle strength, developed over a period of time is maintained largely by the same motor units. *An increase in the muscle force applied to specific skiing technique in order to increase speed of skiing means that 1) the same motor units must become engaged with greater frequency, and/or 2) new motor units must be recruited.*

"Reserved" motor units are thrown into action during such maximum strength effort, as in keen competition where a combined action of strength and technique play a vital role. *These "reserve units" are more easily engaged as a result of repetitious training related to specific skiing technique and speed of muscle movement.* In order to train these reserve motor units in specific movement, maximal exertion is required.

II. SKELETAL MUSCULAR SYSTEM AND MOVEMENT

All physical functions of the body involve muscle activity of which skeletal movements, contractions of the heart and blood vessels, breathing, and peristalsis in the gut are but a few. Three structurally different types of muscles (striated, cardiac, and smooth) are responsible for these activities, but all muscle actions have some common characteristics; and a similarity in the *contraction* process.

Skeletal Striated Muscles surround the bones, extending from one bone to another at a joint, attached to the bones by tendons *(Fig. 4-3)*. They provide for body movement, and are generally under voluntary, conscious control. The more than 600 skeletal muscles in the body account for 40 to 45% of the body's weight. 75% of the skeletal muscles is water, 20% is protein, and the remainder fats, carbohydrates, salts, enzymes, and pigments. These are the muscles that skiing is primarily concerned with, and to which the following discussion pertains.

A. MUSCLE FIBER (CELL) STRUCTURE

The basic unit of the muscle is the muscle fiber which consists of a *single cell.* A muscle fiber cell contains the same basic elements as other types of cells, but is unique in its *ability to contract.*

Muscle mass consists primarily of muscle fibers, some of which are several decimeters long, extending through the full length (as much as a foot) of a long muscle. Most of the skeletal muscle fibers are cylindrical, elongated cells, their thickness varying from 0.01 to 0.1 millimeter. Within each fiber (cell) there are two types of filaments (actin and myosin) which produce the actual contraction of the muscle by sliding, intermeshing movements in relation to each other when activated by action of the nervous system.

Skeletal muscles contain comparatively large numbers of fibers. Depending on the size of the muscle, the number of fibers may vary from 10,000 in a small muscle to 500,000 fibers in the outer thigh muscle in healthy younger people. With increasing age the number of muscle fibers gradually decreases, and at age of 70 may be reduced by 50%, which, accordingly, greatly reduces the muscle strength of older individuals.

B. ENERGY FOR MUSCLE MOVEMENT

The sources of energy for all neuromuscular cell functions are the food eaten and the oxygen inhaled through the lungs. Food contains nutrients: carbohydrates, fats and proteins which are the basic fuel for the energy yielding processes in the cells. Food consumed is broken down into simple chemical compounds by the digestive system and is transported to the cells where it is converted into chemical energy of ATP which is transferred into mechanical energy to move muscles.

Most of the energy needed by the muscles is produced inside the muscle cell in its "powerhouse," the *mitochondria,* through oxidation of the nutrients eaten (aerobic process). When energy demand is greater than what that process can handle, the cells can also produce energy without use of oxygen (anaerobic process).

C. HOW SKELETAL MUSCLES WORK

Movement of striated muscles is generally under voluntary, conscious control by nerve impulses transmitted from the brain through the spinal cord to the muscle which causes a muscle to contract (shorten). The muscle pulls on the bone to which it is attached, resulting in the movement of one bone in relation to the other bone about the joint. Thus, the muscle contraction produces a small lever action at each joint where bones meet (see elbow joint, *Fig. 4-3*).

1. FLEXION AND EXTENSION (FIGURE 4-3):

In order to be able to flex and then extend a limb, two principal groups of muscles work in unison. ***The Prime Movers or Flexors,*** contract (shortening and pulling) to flex a limb about a joint, bringing the ends of the muscle closer together. The Prime Movers do the bulk of the endurance strength work and require the most energy. The ***Extensors***, the opposite-acting group, cooperate by extending (elongating and relaxing). Both these actions always take place regardless of the direction of the movement that results. In the following illustration, the arm muscles during ski poling are used to demonstrate the neuromuscular principles of flexion and extension.

Other adjacent muscles, called ***Fixators***, and ***Synergists*** act to steady the bone, so the limb will move only in the intended direction.

Some other types of movements at the joints that relate to ski skating, in addition to *flexion* and *extension* are:

- *Rotation* (muscles at shoulder, hip, neck, foot, hand)
- *Abduction* (muscle on outside of hips - moves ski outward)
- *Adduction* (muscles on inner thigh - moves ski inward)

Arm Muscle Action During Ski Poling (Figure 4-3)

a. When lifting a light weight ski pole *forward and up* during poling recovery, opposite muscle action takes place. The biceps contracts and becomes the prime mover/flexor, and the triceps relaxes and is the extensor. The biceps during lifting of the pole (a relatively easy motion), is subject to very light endurance strength work.

b. When planting the pole and placing force on the pole *down and backward* (an action requiring much force and energy) the triceps (the prime mover/flexor) contracts, and the biceps (the extensor) relaxes. ***The triceps is, therefore, exposed to heavy endurance strength work during skiing, and becomes one of the primary muscles to train for effective poling and forward skiing speed.***

2. RECIPROCAL INNERVATION

The coordinated, alternating **contraction** (flexing) and **relaxation** (extending) of the muscles of the upper arm during poling is made possible and controlled neurologically by several cervical nerves in the spinal cord. One branch of nerves contracts the flexor muscle while other branches relaxes the extensor muscle; this is termed ***Reciprocal Innervation***. Understanding and correctly applying reciprocal muscle innervation during ski skating movements helps self-regulate good rhythm in skiing.

I. EXTENSION OF FOREARM DURING POLE ACTION

↓   ↓

Triceps contracts (flexes)   Biceps relaxes (extends)
to open up elbow   as elbow opens
(applying force to pole)   Muscle spindles are stretched

II. FLEXION OF FOREARM DURING POLING RECOVERY

↓   ↓

Triceps relaxes (extends)   Biceps contracts (flexes)
as elbow closes   to close elbow,
Muscle spindles are stretched   lifting pole upward

FIGURE 4-3

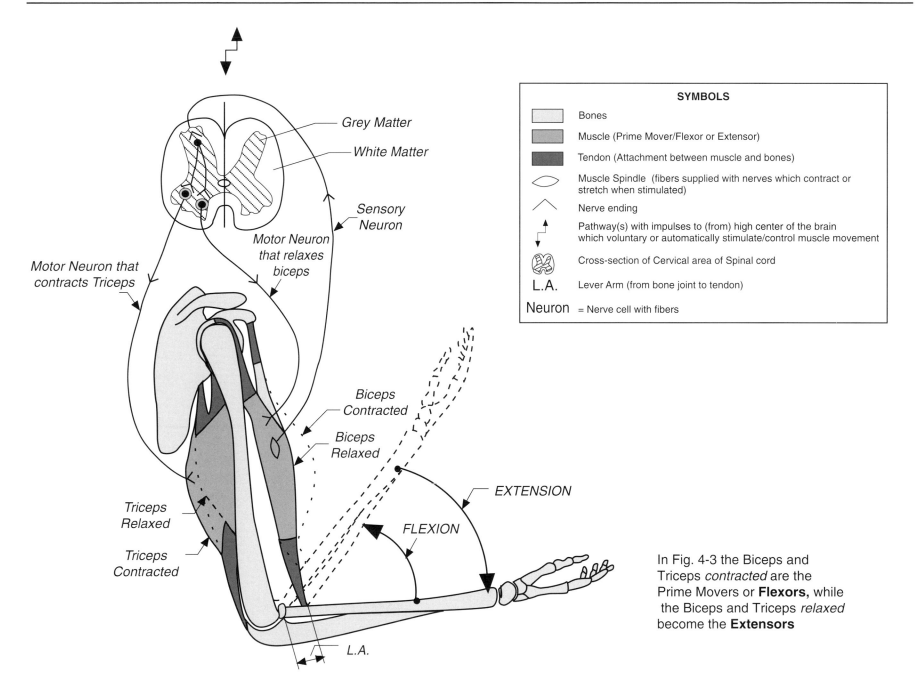

Grey Matter

White Matter

Sensory Neuron

Motor Neuron that relaxes biceps

Motor Neuron that contracts Triceps

SYMBOLS

Bones

Muscle (Prime Mover/Flexor or Extensor)

Tendon (Attachment between muscle and bones)

Muscle Spindle (fibers supplied with nerves which contract or stretch when stimulated)

Nerve ending

Pathway(s) with impulses to (from) high center of the brain which voluntary or automatically stimulate/control muscle movement

Cross-section of Cervical area of Spinal cord

L.A. Lever Arm (from bone joint to tendon)

Neuron = Nerve cell with fibers

Biceps Contracted

Biceps Relaxed

Triceps Relaxed

Triceps Contracted

EXTENSION

FLEXION

L.A.

In Fig. 4-3 the Biceps and Triceps *contracted* are the Prime Movers or **Flexors,** while the Biceps and Triceps *relaxed* become the **Extensors**

D. TYPES OF MUSCLE WORK

Muscles work:
1. Statically (isometrically) and
2. Dynamically
   a. Concentric
   b. Eccentric *(Preloading)*

During *STATIC* work a fixed non-moving position of joints is held, the length of the muscle does not change and the pressure within the muscle limits blood circulation. The muscle is thus forced to work anaerobically (without oxygen), and blood circulation and removal of lactic acid which develops in the muscle is restricted. This happens, for example, when a skier is in a tucked downhill body position for a long time (a minute or more).

During *DYNAMIC* muscle action (flexing or extending of joints), the muscle **alternates between contraction and relaxation,** which facilitates the flow of blood and oxygen and removal of lactic acid in the blood (this Chapter, Sec. II-C-1, 2).

In *Concentric* **dynamic** work the muscle contracts (shortens)

In *Eccentric* **dynamic** work a muscle is first extended before resisting a force (load), caused by gravity (body weight) or the action of antagonistic muscles. *The force and power capacity of the muscles to do work are greatest in the Eccentric mode.*

A muscle's force of contraction depends on its contracted length as compared to its length at rest. Maximum force is developed in a muscle when it is first *eccentrically* stretched 120% of its resting length. If the distance of the muscle bundle length is reduced to 50%, its force = 0 (See Wirhed reference in Bibliography).

Preloading

In effective cross country skiing, *Eccentric muscle action is used immediately prior to Concentric work to increase the force action.* In skating techniques in this text, this is also referred to as *Preloading.*

Virtually all correctly executed and well balanced technical movements in cross country skiing start with a perfect *eccentric* counter-movement where muscle *stretching* beyond 100% is immediately followed by a *contraction*. Such an *elastic recoil* enhances the maximum muscle contraction and can give the skier greater forward acceleration and speed.

Ski skating leg motion should start with a movement at COG by a relaxed forward extension of the hip followed by a flex (give) at the knee, with the knee flexors doing *eccentric* work by using the body's weight immediately prior to the sequential *concentric* muscle work of the actual skate push. Likewise, in the beginning of a poling phase, prior to opening up the elbow, *eccentric* work is done by the elbow muscles when upper body weight, with crowning of the back, is applied onto the inclined poles (Ch. 6).

III. SPEED OF SKIING: NEUROLOGICAL RESPONSE TIME, MUSCLE ENDURANCE STRENGTH AND COORDINATION

Speed of movement in cross country skiing depends greatly upon several complicated interactive neuromuscular components: neurological response time, muscle strength and endurance, and muscle coordination. Training to use these elements more effectively can produce higher speeds of movement.

A. SPEED OF SKIING AND NEUROLOGICAL RESPONSE TIME

The functioning of the neuromuscular system determines the speed of response of the muscles to conscious or unconscious stimuli and directives. The speed with which a skier can react and make specific movements is termed *Response Time.*

Response Time consists of 2 separate components:

Reaction Time + Movement Time

REACTION TIME is the short interval of time from onset of a stimulus to initiation of movement (in an experienced skier, a fraction of second). There are two neurological lags associated with Reaction Time:

1. The sensory input traveling to the brain
2. The motor impulse traveling from the brain to the muscle

The actual reaction time depends on:

- **The complexity of the stimulus -** time is required by the brain to interpret the stimulus.

- **Training -** tests have shown that repetitive practice decreases this time for a specific task by shortening the decision time and improving the movement's efficiency (precision)

- **Anticipation -** of an oncoming stimulus

- **Interfering Stimuli -** such as cold, fatigue, increased friction, and imperfect equipment may significantly increase the Reaction Time.

MOVEMENT TIME begins when reaction time ends and is defined as the interval of time from the beginning of a specific movement to completion of a skiing action. Neurologically, the speed of muscle contraction is linked to the myosin and actin fibers of the muscle (See Ch. 4, Sec. II-A), and to the stimuli, actions and substances (calcium, lactic acid, etc.) that effect their interaction. Nutrition, training, and interfering stimuli all have an effect on final speed of skiing movement along with strength and coordination.

B.   SPEED OF SKIING AND MUSCLE ENDURANCE STRENGTH

All forward movement during skiing - climbing hills, remaining stable in the downhill, turning to accelerate (increase speed) or decelerate (slow down) - is dependent on the skier's use of muscle endurance strength to overcome:

- Gravity Forces
- Change in momentum
- Friction and aerial resistances
- Effect of inertia

When muscle strength is increased specifically to help overcome the above factors, speed is normally also increased. Applying strength (effort) in a situation where there is high external resistance to movement (friction) is normally important in increasing speed. If there is little friction, increasing the motor strength has a minimal effect on speed of movement, and is a waste of energy.

Increased muscle endurance strength is a *not a product of increasing size* (volume) of muscle groups, but of *special neuromuscular training* which recruits more motor units and thus utilizes a greater percentage of one's muscle fibers (See Ch. 4, Sec. IB). During a modestly trained skier's effort to use maximal contraction of a muscle, only a portion of the motor units and muscle cells are activated simultaneously. By precise training related to the specific skiing technique and situation, more of a skier's muscle fibers can be activated and eventually, with training, close to 100% used. *Endurance strength training of muscle fibers for skiing speed is **very specific** and **must** be done by using movements that are closely related to similar skiing movements.*

C.   SPEED OF SKIING AND COORDINATION

Speed of movement can also be significantly improved by increasing muscle and muscle fiber *coordination* through *precision of movement.* Precision means performing an action with the **least number of random moves.** Economy of movement is good efficient skiing technique; i.e. skiing speed is faster with simple movements.

Proper repetitive training can improve synchronization of a muscle. This results in better coordination and simplification of a movement, thus decreasing movement time and saving of energy.

In conclusion, superior cross country athletes develop a superior complex combination of muscle endurance strength, response time, and coordination which results in more speed. Emphasis and planning of training to increase speed of movement must focus on:

1. Specific movements and neuromuscular sequence of movements
2. Specific muscles and muscle fiber types
3. Specific speed of movements
4. Specific type of strength
5. Rhythm and coordination of movements

IV. MOVEMENT SEQUENCE OF BODY ELEMENTS FOR EFFICIENT TECHNIQUE

Correct movement sequence of the body's elements is the most overlooked secret of power and speed in cross country skiing. It is a prime requirement for good technique and efficient skiing. The analysis of skating techniques in the following chapters are based upon this author's premise that all muscular actions are initiated first with activation of the larger, massive muscle groups near the body's Center of Gravity, and then radiate out to the limbs, in the identical pattern as neural messages move from the brain, through the spinal cord out to the peripheral muscles. Therefore, the skier's sequence of activating skeletal muscle movements for any technique should agree with the internal control sequences of the motor nervous system *(Fig. 4-4 and 4-5)*.

In this way muscle actions for the lower extremity are initiated at the lower abdomen, back and hips, first, then transmitted in a "chain reaction" to the thighs and hamstrings and the lower leg through the knee joint, and then lastly to the foot where the ski is controlled.

Likewise, for the upper extremity, which controls the poling movement, muscle action moves sequentially from the lower back and abdomen through the upper back, shoulder, the arm, through the elbow joint to the hand where the pole is controlled.

Muscle forces for the different body elements are therefore **superimposed** on each other in an order that produces overall greater power and efficiency onto the upper extremity's poling and the lower extremity's skate action movements *(Fig. 4-4)*.

Preloading (eccentric muscle recoil action) of the muscles in the same sequential order as described will enhance the muscle force even more, resulting in more efficient technique and faster skiing. Preloading of muscles has been included as a separate phase for all techniques in this book.

It is not unusual to see skiers do movement sequences in the opposite order; namely initiating movement of the lower arms, or doing the foot roll first. This causes delays (lags) in the internal neurological sequences because of the greater traveling distances for nerve impulses to the hands and feet, and produces uncoordinated, power-lacking technique.

Thus, if the Diagram in Figure 4-4 was shown to apply sequence in opposite order, i.e. applying the hand and foot action first, the *effective muscle power* (force **x** time) of the major muscles at the mid-section *would be much less*.

SEQUENCE AND TIMING OF MUSCLE ACTION

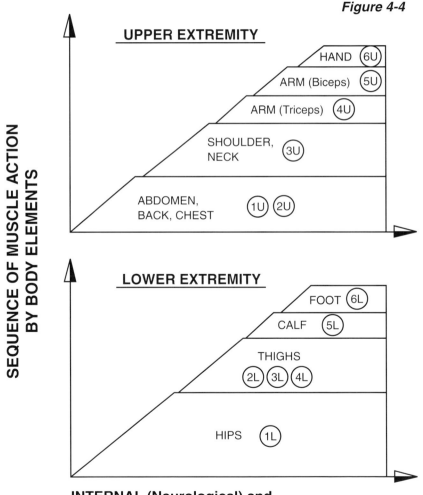

Figure 4-4

SEQUENCE OF MUSCLE ACTION BY BODY ELEMENTS

UPPER EXTREMITY

HAND (6U)
ARM (Biceps) (5U)
ARM (Triceps) (4U)
SHOULDER, NECK (3U)
ABDOMEN, BACK, CHEST (1U) (2U)

LOWER EXTREMITY

FOOT (6L)
CALF (5L)
THIGHS (2L) (3L) (4L)
HIPS (1L)

INTERNAL (Neurological) and EXTERNAL (Muscular) SEQUENTIAL TIMING

MUSCLE POWER SEQUENCE
INTERNAL NEUROLOGICAL SEQUENCE

FIGURE 4-5

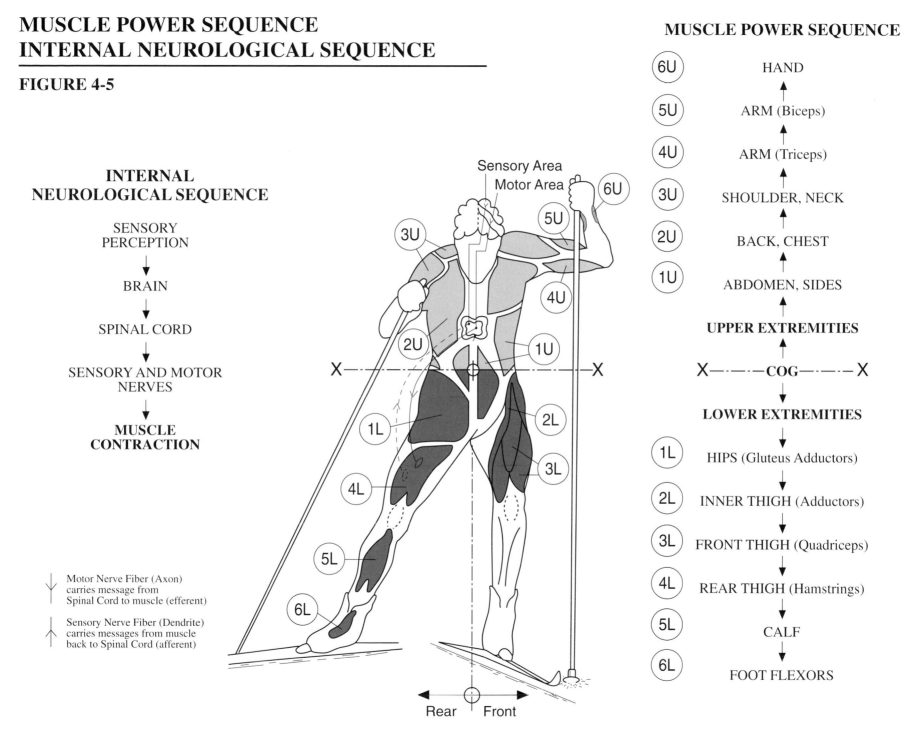

INTERNAL NEUROLOGICAL SEQUENCE

SENSORY PERCEPTION

↓

BRAIN

↓

SPINAL CORD

↓

SENSORY AND MOTOR NERVES

↓

MUSCLE CONTRACTION

Motor Nerve Fiber (Axon) carries message from Spinal Cord to muscle (efferent)

Sensory Nerve Fiber (Dendrite) carries messages from muscle back to Spinal Cord (afferent)

Sensory Area
Motor Area

Rear | Front

MUSCLE POWER SEQUENCE

6U — HAND

5U — ARM (Biceps)

4U — ARM (Triceps)

3U — SHOULDER, NECK

2U — BACK, CHEST

1U — ABDOMEN, SIDES

UPPER EXTREMITIES

X———COG———X

LOWER EXTREMITIES

1L — HIPS (Gluteus Adductors)

2L — INNER THIGH (Adductors)

3L — FRONT THIGH (Quadriceps)

4L — REAR THIGH (Hamstrings)

5L — CALF

6L — FOOT FLEXORS

Range of Movement

The neuromuscular sequence of body movement as described also coincides with the range (amount) of bodily movement taking place relative to distance from the body's COG. The range of movement and neurological time lag near COG is relatively small. As the muscular movement progresses outward from the COG, through the body and finally reaches the extreme body elements, the fingers and toes, the range of movement becomes more extensive and more time consuming.

Extreme range of movement of the body's elements should be avoided. Movement of arms and elbows during poling, and feet at the initiating of skating should be as close to the body (Y-Y) axis as possible. Extreme range of movement demands more energy and will cause uncoordinated time lags, neurologically as well as in the sequence of muscular movement, ultimately resulting in a decrease in the potential speed of skiing movements.

V. SUMMARY

This chapter has introduced a new and different approach to becoming a better skier much faster. It contains important thoughts on the significance of correlated neuromuscular functions in skiing, and for this reason at first may seem complicated. The author feels, however, that the subject matter in this chapter is extremely important as a tool to speed up the correct learning process of one of the fastest growing sports in the world - ski skating. The following four complex activities must work in unison to produce the most efficient form for cross country skiing on all levels of skill:

1. Sequence of muscular movement
2. Neurological and muscular activities
3. Speed of movement
4. Range of movement

The skier's mental concentration on the correct progression of movement (from the body's center, outward), provides, in itself, a tremendously effective *psychological focal point* that helps produce great power and speed. The skier, when practicing technique, should always visualize the correct neurologically sequential movements of the body elements. Repeating the sequence over and over again in training, then, will eventually make it an automatic reflex of correct sequential execution that ultimately will result in superb cross country skating technique.

CHAPTER 5

Learning Basic Skate Movement

Figure 5-1 *The Author*

CHAPTER 5
Learning Basic Skate Movements

CONTENTS

I. INTRODUCTION

Ski skating is not a discipline for racers only, recreational skiers can also learn and enjoy skating. Having some experience in traditional (Classic) skiing can accelerate progress in learning to skate, and practicing both classic and skating techniques will help in becoming a better overall skier. There is much more pleasure and fun in mastering both disciplines.

To learn proper skating techniques, some basics need to be mastered first. The following are the *significant criteria* for attaining good skating techniques for beginners and recreational skiers, as well as for top competitors:

1. **Correct relaxed upright body position, upper body slightly crowned, legs together at initiation**

2. **Smooth shifting of body weight completely from one ski to the other.**

3. **Coordinated control of legs, arms and poles, emphasizing harmonic rhythmic sequential movements.**

4. **Balance while gliding on the flat base of one ski at a time.**

II. SKATE MOVEMENT EXERCISES

Executing skate movements in which all the body elements, legs and arms with poling, are involved is admittedly complicated, especially since movements are lateral as well as forward. It is the author's experience that separating the components during the learning process is an easier and more beneficial approach.

Therefore, this chapter concentrates entirely on skate movement with *no pole plant action* and analyzes movements by upper and lower extremities separately. Muscles in the lower extremity, legs and hips in particular, are the main energy sources that contribute to the forward motion through the skis. Likewise, muscles for the upper extremity — back, stomach, shoulder, neck and arms — contribute to forces applied to the poling action.

The following illustrated fundamental skate movement exercises are helpful for beginners and for the skilled skier's transition to more advanced specific skating techniques. The author personally practices these exercises extensively prior to serious racing every year. The exercises are performed initially on level terrain and mild downhills to develop balance, coordination and rhythmic movement; then, as improvement is noted, continued on variable flat terrain, before going on to the more advanced specific skating techniques in this text.

Bar Charts

The BAR CHARTS below the photos divide the body into two major independent muscle action groups (also see Ch. 7, Sec. I-E):

Upper Extremity: A. Right and Left Sides

Lower Extremity: B. Right Side/Ski
C. Left Side/Ski

The author feels this concentration on major muscle group movement (action) is the *key* approach to mastering and improving ski technique.

1	2	3	4

A. UPPER BODY:	SHOULDER AND HIP AXIS PERPENDICULAR TO RIGHT SKI
B. RIGHT SKI:	DOWNSET — BALANCE AND GLIDE ON FLAT SKI
C. LEFT SKI:	WITH SKATE ACTION RECOVERY —

The photos above demonstrate an efficient method for beginners and skilled skiers to learn and practice basic leg, hip and body movement. Poles are carried across the upper back, under the elbow with arms locked in place. This position of the upper body and shoulders is similar to the initiation of poling for most skate techniques. The upper extremity is thus stabilized, preventing the skier from bending too much forward at the hips, while there is still freedom to rotate the upper extremity independently of the lower.

This exercise activates the larger muscle groups at hip, back and abdomen, which are the prime sources for developing effective leg skate action.

The ***Exercise I Bar Chart*** below the photos indicates lengths (time) of cycle of Right and Left Leg Movements (glide and skate action and recovery). The bar lines show that the Glide and Skate Action on the level is quite a bit longer than the Recovery. However, this time relationship will vary slightly with snow and glide conditions and the steepness of the slope.

a. ***Body Erect and Legs Together*** (Photo **1**). All skate maneuvers are initiated in this position. While in balance on the left flat ski with a straight leg, the skier moves the right ski from behind, inward and forward so the legs come together, while creating a small angle between the skis. Skier is in complete balance on the gliding left ski during inward movement of the right ski.

b. ***Flat Ski Base Downset and Weight Shift.*** The right ski now makes contact (downset) with the snow (**2**) by means of a forward movement of the left hip, skating off the left leg, while shifting the body weight (COG) over to the right ski. The skier at this stage should avoid too much spread of the legs, and try to position the foot ***under the body*** during the downset of the ski. Making initial contact on the ***outside*** edge of the ski, will help to ease the skier into gliding balance on a flat ski.

| 5 | 6 | 7 | 8 |

SHOULDER   AND   HIP   AXIS   PERPENDICULAR   TO   LEFT   SKI

WITH   SKATE   ACTION ▶ ◀ RECOVERY — LEGS TOGETHER ▶

LEGS TOGETHER ▶ ◀ DOWNSET — BALANCE AND GLIDE ON FLAT SKI (CONTINUE)

c. ***Skate Action by the Left Ski*** continues (**3**) with extended glide on the right straight leg while visually aligning the Nose-Knee-Ankle, with the body in a slight forward lean. The ***primary source*** of skate action for the left leg should be from muscle forces ***generated at the hips***, and not so much by the leg itself.

d. ***Upright Body Position of the Upper Extremity.*** With a slight forward lean, shoulders and poles are kept parallel with the hips. Keeping these perpendicular at all times to the gliding right ski will improve balance.

e. ***Final Skate Push-Off*** by the left leg while continuing gliding in proper balance on the flat base of the right ski (**4**).

f. While in a ***One Point of Contact*** balanced position on the right ski, the airborne left ski is brought inward and forward under the body to become nearly parallel with the right ski (**5**).

g. The ***same procedure*** as (**1** through **5**) above is now repeated for the opposite side, namely gliding on the left ski while skating on the right (**6** through **8**).

It should be noted that most skating techniques involve balanced movements similar to the exercise described. The parallel movement of upper and lower extremities is characteristic of the "Paddle Dance" (Ch. 8), the principal technique used in mastering uphill skating. Drilling in this exercise therefore will greatly benefit specific technique development.

1	2	3	4

A. ARMSWING:	LEFT ARM SWING FORWARD — RIGHT ARM SWING BACKWARD
B. RIGHT SKI:	DOWNSET — BALANCE AND GLIDE ON FLAT SKI
C. LEFT SKI:	WITH SKATE ACTION RECOVERY —

This exercise, which should be practiced in level or mild downhill terrain, is an expansion and continuation of Exercise I. It eliminates the restriction of the arms, adding their relaxed swing in diagonal (opposite) coordination with the movement of the lower extremities. A relaxed forward arm swing is one of the prime requirements of good skating technique.

The photos and **Bar Chart** show that movement of the lower extremity is much the same as for Exercise I, and the upper extremity similarly rotates diagonally in the opposite direction of the lower. To this is added the arm swing forward, in the same direction as the balanced glide on the opposite ski.

The movement pattern is symmetrical, about a vertical axis (Y-Y) through the body (Ch. 11, Sec. I); the arm swing and leg action on one side of the body is equal to the other side.

An analysis of the above photos, taken of the full sequence of skier's actions with skates and arm swings to both sides, is on the next page.

| 5 | 6 | 7 | 8 |

RIGHT ARMSWING FORWARD — LEFT ARMSWING BACKWARD

WITH SKATE ACTION · RECOVERY — LEGS TOGETHER

LEGS TOGETHER · DOWNSET BALANCE AND GLIDE ON FLAT SKI (CONTINUE)

UPPER EXTREMITY

a. Body erect with a slight upper crowning (**1**) - Initiation of arm swing starts - both arms hanging down, relaxed (**1**)

b. Arm swings begin, elbows close to body, left arm forward, right arm backward (**2**)

c. Full extension backward of right arm, left arm flexed 90° at elbow in front of chest (**3**)

d. Forward swing of right arm; backward swing of left arm starts (**4**)

e. Both arms hang down, relaxed (**5**)

REPEAT ARM SWING MOVEMENT "**a**" THROUGH "**e**" FOR THE OPPOSITE SIDE, (PHOTOS **5**, **6**, **7**, **8**).

LOWER EXTREMITY

f. Legs come together - balanced gliding on one (left) flat ski, the other (right) ski is brought inward and forward (boots almost touching each other) (**1**)

g. Downset of gliding (right) ski - skate action on left ski starts (**2**)

h. Continue gliding on flat (right) ski with final skate push-off on left ski (**3**)

i. Continue gliding on flat (right) ski while recovery of aerial (left) ski (**4**)

REPEAT MOVEMENT OF LEGS AND SKIS "**f**" THROUGH "**i**" FOR THE OPPOSITE SIDE, (PHOTOS **5**, **6**, **7**, **8**).

1	2	3	4
A. POLE ARM:	LEFT ARM SWING FORWARD – RIGHT ARM SWING BACKWARD		
B. RIGHT SKI:	DOWNSET, BALANCE AND GLIDE ON FLAT SKI		
C. LEFT SKI:	WITH SKATE ACTION		RECOVERY —

This exercise, as noted from the photos, has movements similar to Exercise II, except that the skier, for the first time, has poles in hand. A skier needs to get adjusted to using poles; their weight and leverage effects the coordinated movement of arms as well as the balance on skis. The forward momentum of pole and arm also contributes to improving a skier's speed (Appendix, Sec. II).

> Learning to control effective movement of the poles is important to all ski skating techniques, and is one of the primary objectives of this exercise. Excessive movement of the poles is one of the most common observable flaws among skiers on all levels of skill.

The poles should be held and moved (steered) in a relaxed manner, parallel to the ground. Avoid flipping the pole basket up and down. Poles should at all times point backward, with forward movement parallel and in the same direction as the glide of the opposite ski.

Do not tightly grasp the poles with cramped fingers. As the pole is moved forward (Photo **3**), the index (pointer) finger is relaxed so the handle can move freely inside the palm. Movement direction of the poles is controlled by the elbow and shoulder, not the wrist. ***Avoid twisting or flexing the wrist*** to control the poles.

Diagonal ski skating with poles in hands, as illustrated in Exercise III, is a specific technique in itself, used by world class skiers during high speed skiing on the flat and in mild downhills (Ch. 8, Sec. IV-F).

| 5 | 6 | 7 | 8 |

RIGHT   ARMSWING   FORWARD   —   LEFT   ARMSWING   BACKWARD

WITH   SKATE   ACTION | RECOVERY   —   LEGS   TOGETHER

LEGS TOGETHER | DOWNSET   BALANCE   AND   GLIDE   ON   FLAT   SKI   (CONTINUE)

UPPER EXTREMITY

a. Body erect with a slight upper crowning (**1**) - Initiation of arm swing starts - both arms hanging down, relaxed (**1**)

b. Arm swings begin, elbows close to body, left arm forward, right arm backward (**2**)

c. Full extension backward of right arm, left arm flexed 90° at elbow in front of chest (**3**)

d. Forward swing of right arm; backward swing of left arm starts (**4**)

e. Both arms hang down, relaxed (**5**)

REPEAT ARM SWING MOVEMENT "**a**" THROUGH "**e**" FOR THE OPPOSITE SIDE, (PHOTOS **5**, **6**, **7**, **8**).

LOWER EXTREMITY

f. Legs come together - balanced gliding on one (left) flat ski, the other (right) ski is brought inward and forward (boots almost touching each other) (**1**)

g. Downset of gliding (right) ski - skate action on left ski starts (**2**)

h. Continue gliding on flat (right) ski with final skate push-off on left ski (**3**)

i. Continue gliding on flat (right) ski while recovery of aerial (left) ski (**4**)

REPEAT MOVEMENT OF LEGS AND SKIS "**f**" THROUGH "**i**" FOR THE OPPOSITE SIDE, (PHOTOS **5**, **6**, **7**, **8**).

EXERCISE IV DIAGONAL SKATE MOVEMENT — WITHOUT POLING
HIP AND SHOULDER ACTION EMPHASIS

	1	2	3
A. SHOULDER AND ARM:	LEFT SHOULDER AND ARM FORWARD		
B. RIGHT LEG AND HIP:	DOWNSET — BALANCE AND GLIDE ON SKI — HIP FORWARD		
C. LEFT LEG AND HIP:	HIP FORWARD	RECOVERY OF SKI — HIP RELAXED —	

This exercise (practiced on the same terrain, a mild downhill) uses coordinated movements of the upper and lower extremities, similar to Exercise III, in a more relaxed form, by emphasizing the *secret power of the BIG HIP MUSCLES*, a prime factor in learning effective ski skating with least use of energy. A common mistake by most ski skaters is to use the legs instead of the hips as the primary source of muscle power.

This exercise is characterized by concentrating on a relaxed rotation and smooth rhythmic forward movement of the hip in the skate direction, and relaxed shoulder rotation with a shortened *aerial* arm swing with the poles. The hips should smoothly rotate, weighting forward and down in the direction of the skate ski with a slight give in the knee. When looking at the photos, notice the "walking" glide

of the legs. With correct execution, there is *no powerful leg push-off* onto the skate in this exercise. The skier makes the skis do the hard work - the real art of ski skating.

In this exercise very small skate angles are used, the skis kept as close to the surface as possible, with minimum vertical lifting, and a smooth glide laterally into a small skate angle position. A very smooth *"touch and glide"* on a flat ski base should be practiced. As a matter of fact, when the legs come together, the ski base contact can be made more on the outside edge (Photo **3**) and then rotated smoothly over to the flat base during the glide. The elite champions practice and apply this exercise a lot on the flats and mild downhills.

| 4 | 5 | 6 |

RIGHT   SHOULDER   AND   ARM   FORWARD

RECOVERY   OF   SKI   —   HIP   RELAXED   —   LEGS   TOGETHER

LEGS TOGETHER   DOWNSET   —   BALANCE   AND   GLIDE   ON   SKI   —   (CONTINUE)

Very high speed with relatively little effort can be obtained by this smooth, relaxed and rhythmic use of the powerful hip muscles and application of diagonal body rotation. The momentum (body mass times velocity) developed from the diagonal movement of elements of the upper and lower extremities contributes substantially to the skier's forward speed (see Appendix, Sec.II).

The upper body is crowned, stomach in, with little or no bending at the hips and the momentum of the body applied in the direction of each skate, by moving the hip and opposite shoulder forward in a relaxed rhythmic, harmonic fashion with a slight give in the knee. The significance of smoothness in this exercise cannot be emphasized enough.

This exercise really teaches what ski skating is all about — skating long, fast strides with little use of energy. It should be practiced at every opportunity to be able to always apply it when there is the right terrain and opportunity. It is an excellent form for recovery after high intensity training or racing.

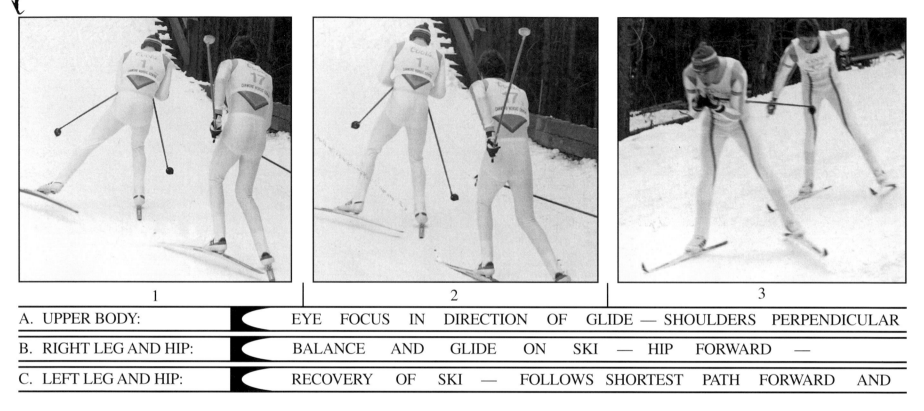

1	2	3

A. UPPER BODY:	EYE FOCUS IN DIRECTION OF GLIDE — SHOULDERS PERPENDICULAR
B. RIGHT LEG AND HIP:	BALANCE AND GLIDE ON SKI — HIP FORWARD —
C. LEFT LEG AND HIP:	RECOVERY OF SKI — FOLLOWS SHORTEST PATH FORWARD AND

The above front and rear view photos show 2 skiers:

Gunde Svan (Bib #1) is in a high tuck (Ch. 9) with poles under arms. The other skier (Bib #17) is using the diagonal pole arm swing technique similar to Exercise IV.

The **Bar Charts** refer to movement by Gunde Svan during glide and skate on the right side only, *i.e. One-Half Cycle* (See Ch. 6, Sec. V for a detailed explanation of a Cycle and Ch. 7, Sec. I-D for a Skate Cycle).

Developing Correct Skating Rhythm
For LOWER EXTREMITY Without Use Of Poles.

Two movements of the COG are combined (vertical and forward) to develop correct skating rhythm. A little vertical movement of the COG is created by a slight flex in the knee joint and an added forward movement in the skiing direction is created by the rotation of the hips. By rhythmically combining these two vertical and forward movements of the COG very smoothly and relaxed (non-staccato), speed and glide length can be increased on the skate ski. Many skaters wrongly move their midsection COG excessively vertical, and also have little or no rotation of the hip axis (See Ch. 3, Sec. I-D).

| 4 | 5 | 6 |

TO   GLIDING   ON   FLAT   SKI   —   CROWNED   UPPER   BACK   —   IN   TUCK   TO   MINIMIZE   AIR   RESISTANCE

SLIGHT   FLEX   (GIVE)   IN   KNEE   —   SKATE   PUSH-OFF ▶ | RECOVERY ▶

INWARD   —   HIP   RELAXED ▶ | SMOOTH   DOWNSET   AND   GLIDE   ON   SKI ▶

Rhythmic Movement of UPPER EXTREMITY
Without Use of Poles

Adding upper extremity rotation in a diagonal rhythmic fashion with little or no forward flexing at the hips will further increase speed and glide distance on the skate ski. Momentum from the movement of hips, arms and poles is in the same direction as the skate ski.

Practicing smooth movement of upper and lower extremities, as illustrated above, is one of the basics for developing good skating rhythm in all techniques. It will increase gliding speed with relatively little use of energy - skiing will be more efficient and harmonic rhythmic movement will be developed, one of the secrets of world class champions.

Note:

- Gunde's eye focus in the direction of the gliding ski.
- Legs together during initiation
- Perfect balance with COG over a flat ski
- Shoulder alignment perpendicular to gliding ski
- Lateral movement with very little vertical fluctuation of COG

Gunde Svan, SWE, was the dominating cross country skier in the 1980's, winning two Gold Medals in the 1984 Olympics, two Golds in the 1985 World Championships, two Golds in the 1988 Olympics, three Golds in the 1989 World Championships, and one Gold Medal in the 1991 World Championships.

CHAPTER 6

Double Poling

Figure 6-1 Intense, high frequency Double Poling takes place at the start of relays. A relay team has four skiers, the first two legs use Classic techniques and the last two legs skating techniques. Shown here is the Men's 4 x 10 km World Championship relay start at Falun, Sweden, 1993 where teams from 21 countries participated.

CHAPTER 6
Double Poling

CONTENTS

I. INTRODUCTION TO DOUBLE POLING

Double Poling is fundamental to all skating techniques and is used in most of them, sometimes with a slight variation in timing of each pole plant. It is a very important aspect of skating in mild downhills, on the level, and in uphills. The powerful double poling action by the upper extremity aided by the slightly longer poles used for skating is of great significance in achieving high skating speeds. Efficient skating is also very much controlled by the precise planting of poles and use of the upper body as in double poling. For these reasons, a discussion of skating techniques needs to start with basic Straight Double Poling.

Straight Double Poling, without use of the lower extremity, is the simplest and easiest cross country technique stride to learn, but an efficient, perfect execution is not simple. It is characterized by the use of both poles simultaneously to pull and push yourself forward, with your legs remaining substantially parallel. As in any other cross country technique, a smooth rhythmical movement with relaxed recovery is essential.

Straight Double Poling is used primarily on level ground, but also in mild downhills, mild uphills during fast conditions, or in areas having a variety of such terrain. It has become increasingly utilized because skis have become lighter and faster, and cross country courses and trails are packed firmly by mechanical equipment, giving much better pole support. Double Poling is one of the skiing techniques requiring least energy when executed efficiently and therefore is of significant use when you are getting tired.

In Straight Double Poling, there is no twisting, rotation, or lateral movement of the body. The skier's movement takes place in one plane, in the direction of skiing (DOS), the Z-Z axis, as shown in this Chapter, Sec. IV. The forward motion of Double Poling is almost exclusively caused by forces applied to the poles, created by muscle power from the (1) back, (2) abdomen, (3) shoulders, (4) arms, and (5) hands. Applying these muscles efficiently in this sequential order is the key to gaining high speed during Double Poling. However, the shifting of your body weight (COG), or segments of your body in the traveling direction also is important.

The procedure of Double Poling used in skating is similar to that applied in Classic techniques, except that ski skaters use slightly longer poles. Please note that many of the photos shown in the following discussions of Double Poling are of skiers using short Classic poles. With longer poles, there is less forward bending of the upper body.

II. DEFINITION OF DOUBLE POLING

Straight Double Poling is initiated as the skier in erect position with a slight forward body lean is preparing for the pole plant.

At the time of the pole plant, muscles for the upper extremity have been preloaded by crowning of upper back. The upper body is weighted forward onto the poles as muscle power is superimposed onto the poles by adding the arms' pulling and pushing action.

During the poling, the upper body goes through crowning and forward bending of approximately 45° (maximum of 60°); then complete recovery to an erect body position during which preparation for another pole plant takes place.

Except for a slight knee roll (flex), the lower extremity is substantially inactive, with little bending of the knees.

III. MOVEMENT SEQUENCE OF BODY

Double Poling primarily involves movements of the upper extremity; the lower extremity is substantially inactive. Muscles close to the COG, the lower back and stomach, are activated first, with a slight backward movement of the midsection, in sequential order:

1. The back and abdomen
   ⬇
2. The shoulder
   ⬇
3. The arm
   ⬇
4. And lastly, muscles controlling the hand motion.

Preloading Prior to Actual Muscle Action

During Double Poling, only the poling forces contribute to the skier's forward motion. To maximize the impact of the poles, muscle preloading immediately prior to the actual pole plant is imperative. The preloading is characterized by *crowning of the back*, and then forward rotation of the shoulders. The *recoil* effect of crowning the upper back is an important factor in maximizing power on the poles. The crowning maintained throughout the poling activates greater poling forces than an arched or straight back.

IV. BODY AXES AND ALIGNMENT

A. *3 AXES REFERENCE SYSTEM FOR DOUBLE POLING*

With reference to a skier in motion, an axes system having the following fixed established reference lines is used.

♦ **Z-Z axis**, longitudinal axis (the direction in which the skier is traveling).

♦ **X-X axis,** lateral axis (skier seen from front or rear view).

♦ **Y-Y axis,** vertical axis (skier seen from any side, front, or rear view).

The intersection of the 3 axes locates the COG of the skier's body during movement.

During Straight Double Poling the COG moves *only vertically* (Y-Y) (in skating the COG also moves significantly laterally), and continually in the Z-Z direction. When skiing with least use of energy, it is important to understand and evaluate skiers' Double Poling technique with reference to vertical movement of COG (Ch. 11, Sec. II-A-2).

During the effective poling pull and push action *(Fig. 6-2 and 6-3)*, the midsection is on one side of the vertical Y-Y axis, while the upper body and lower legs are on the opposite side of the axis.

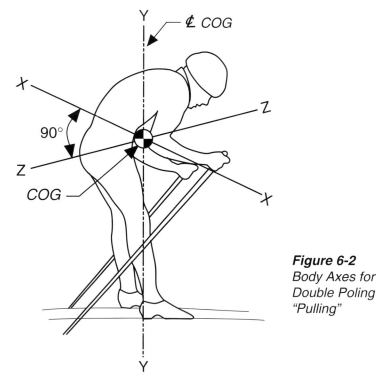

Figure 6-2
Body Axes for Double Poling "Pulling"

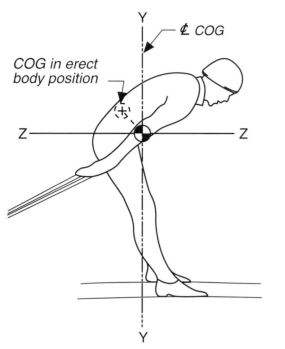

Figure 6-3 *Body Axes for Double Poling "Pushing"*

B. BODY REFERENCE ALIGNMENTS

In addition to the axes defined, three reference lines called **alignments** are used *(Fig. 6-4)*. While body axes are fixed lines, the alignments refer to segments of the body that constantly are changing with the body position and the techniques used.

Hip, Shoulder And Trunk Alignments

These alignments refer to the orientation of the three principal parts composing the greater mass of the body, namely:

1. **Hip (H-H) Alignment.** A line drawn through the center of the pelvis' hip ball joints.

2. **Shoulder (S-S) Alignment.** A line drawn through the center of the shoulder ball joints. The H-H and S-S lines will vary with movement of the hips and shoulders horizontally and vertically, individually, or both.

3. **Trunk (T-T) Alignment.** This is a symmetry line, dividing the trunk into left and right sides when viewed from the front and rear. T-T is assumed to intersect the H-H and S-S lines. T-T alignment is also a reference to the amount of forward bending of the upper extremity.

In Straight Double Poling the hip (H-H) and shoulder (S-S) lines are parallel; while during skating, the hip and shoulder alignments are usually not parallel, but function independently of each other.

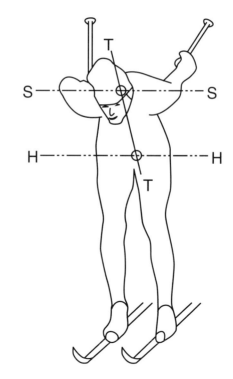

Figure 6-4 *HST Alignment in Double Poling*

ONE CYCLE OF STRAIGHT DOUBLE POLING

V. STRAIGHT DOUBLE POLING CYCLE AND FREQUENCY

THE CYCLE of the Double Poling technique can most simply be defined as the skier's motion taking place between two pole plants, or more precisely, as between two Y-Y axes drawn through the COG of the body at the beginning and end of the Double Poling.

The Double Poling Cycle involves two primary actions of the upper extremity:

♦ The Poling
♦ The Recovery

Both actions involve use of energy, although the second to a lesser degree.

During the poling action, the body's COG is lowered as muscle forces and upper body weight are applied to the poles; this takes a lot of energy. The recovery is a relaxed movement returning the upper body to a position for another pole plant. It involves, however, raising the body's COG, which also requires energy. The Double Poling cycle involves a complete movement cycle of COG, from a High COG (HCOG) to Low COG (LCOG) and back to HCOG (Ch. 11, Sec. II-B-6).

FREQUENCY is the number of consecutive Double Poling Cycles taking place per unit of time (i.e. per minute). Speed obtained is very much related to the frequency, which may vary greatly, depending on the strength and skill of the skier, skiing conditions and equipment.

The frequency achieved in Double Poling can be the highest of all techniques because movement of only the upper extremity is involved. In the finish of a race some top skiers, to produce maximum speed, have double poled efficiently at a frequency of 60 or more cycles per minute!

5   6   7   8

₵
|
(FROM ONE POLE PLANT TO ANOTHER)   COG

A comparatively less forward bending of the upper body at the hips, 45° to 60° max., permits higher poling frequency. This slightly shortens the effective length of the poling, but less energy is expended, since the skier's COG goes through less vertical movement (Ch. 11, Sec. II-A-2).

Some skiers bend forward 90° or more at the hips, while others activate more upper back and stomach muscles with considerable less flexing at the hips. A 90° forward flex involves a *longer frequency,* giving longer arm action on the poles, but this also *takes more energy.* Flexing at the hips does not give additional power onto the poles. However, the weighting forward and down of the upper body does, but also requires considerably more energy.

CYCLE SPEED (M/SEC) is the average speed attained when checking several consecutive cycles. Comparing Cycle Speeds of differ-

ent techniques helps to determine which one is most efficient. Double Poling usually requires less energy, but may not be the fastest, depending on the terrain and the glide.

CYCLE TIME (SECONDS) is related to the Frequency and Speed. Among tourers the time for One Cycle is much longer than for a top racer.

CYCLE DISTANCE (METERS) varies with the terrain, frequency and energy input during the poling.

Long Cycle applies to use of substantial power on the poles following a long glide on the skis.

Short Cycle is common among tourers skiing in conditions with poor glide and low frequency. Short Cycle is relative, and also applies to very fast skiing with high frequency.

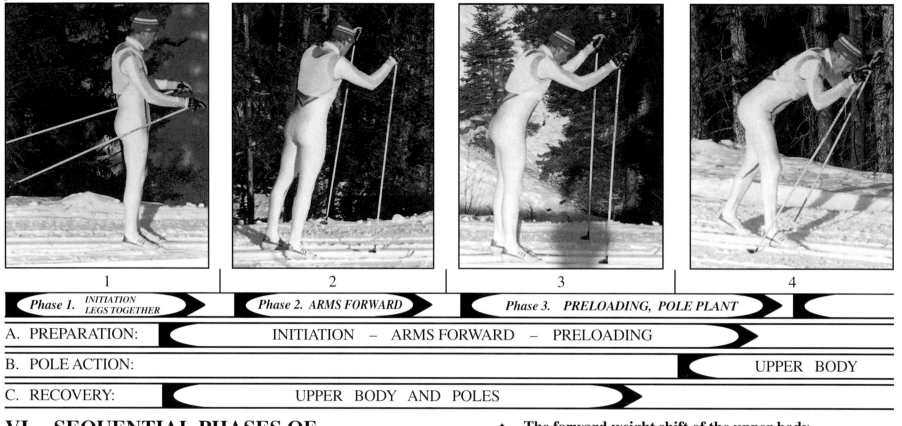

| 1 | 2 | 3 | 4 |

| *Phase 1.* INITIATION LEGS TOGETHER | *Phase 2. ARMS FORWARD* | *Phase 3. PRELOADING, POLE PLANT* | |

A. PREPARATION:	INITIATION – ARMS FORWARD – PRELOADING	
B. POLE ACTION:		UPPER BODY
C. RECOVERY:	UPPER BODY AND POLES	

VI. SEQUENTIAL PHASES OF MOVEMENT FOR DOUBLE POLING

In the descriptive illustrations that follow, the cycle has been divided into six phases, starting with the skier in an erect preparatory position before the pole plant takes place. In the correct rhythmical movements of Double Poling there is no clearly visible division between the different phases. For instructional purposes, the natural separation shown is preferred by the author to better describe and analyze the efficiency of Double Poling with more detail.

The power on the poles is caused by three sources in the following order:

♦ The forward weight shift of the upper body.

♦ Preloading of the back and shoulders.

♦ Forces are then superimposed to the poles by muscles in sequential order from the back and abdomen, shoulders, and arms.

Phase 1. Initiation - Legs Together - Body Erect

Straight Double Poling starts with the skier in erect position with the arms hanging down fully relaxed, and with the pole slanted backwards and down. Both skis are evenly weighted with the legs close together.

| 5 | 6 | 7 | 8 |

Phase 4. ARMS PULLING ▶ *Phase 5. ARMS PUSHING FORCES* ▶ *Phase 6. RECOVERY* ▶

WEIGHT SHIFT – PULLING AND PUSHING ON POLES ▶

UPPER BODY ▶

Phase 2. *Forward Arm Extension*

The skier in motion is moving the hands forward and up until the arms are fully extended with relaxed elbows. The pole baskets follow as close to the ground as possible until the baskets reach the toe of the boots. The poles are then prepared to be planted powerfully into the snow under a fairly sharp angle. The pole angle is controlled by the thumb and the top two fingers.

Phase 3. *Preloading, Pole Plant and Weight Shift*

Preloading of back and shoulder muscles with crowning of the upper back takes place immediately prior to the pole plant to gain maximum impact and power at the time of the pole plant. During forward movement of the arms, the body weight (COG) is shifted forward on the feet from the heel to the toes. As the poles are plant-ed, the weight of the upper body leans (falls) onto the poles; then the muscular forces from the back, trunk, abdomen and shoulders are sequentially superimposed onto the poles.

Phase 4. *Arms' Pulling Forces*

The pulling forces of the arms start at the pole plant, and continue until the elbows reach the side of the legs, making very sharp, efficient angles of the poles with the ground (Ch. 11, Sec. II-A-3). During the pulling phase, to gain maximum forces onto the poles from the arms, abdominal and trunk muscles are activated, and a 90° angle of the elbow is created and maintained with rotation about the shoulder. At the same time the upper body continues crowning with forward bending of approximately 45° at the hips.

Continued next page

Phase 5. Arms' Pushing Forces

During the arm movement, the pushing phase physically starts where the forces by the arms change from a "pull" to a "push" on the poles. This takes place as the elbows reach the side of the hips and open, and lasts until the full extension of the arm and the pole release.

The gradual extension (opening) of the 90° elbow and the arm characterizes the Double Poling pushing phase. The full extension of the arms backward with the poles, arms in line with the upper body, and a flick of the hands about the wrist as a final additional force marks the completion of the pole push.

The hands are completely relaxed during the poling phases, and are hanging in the pole strap upon completion of the push. During the final part of the push, the skis and feet are shifted slightly forward, moving the body weight (COG) slightly back to the heel.

The distance of the Pole Push is quite a bit shorter visually than the Pulling Phase, and the ***Arm Pulling Phase, therefore, contributes more to the forward motion.***

Phase 6. Recovery

A typical recovery phase lasts from the pole release to the next pole plant. Immediately upon the release of the poles from the snow, the arms are quickly relaxed. The forward arm swing of the poles takes place while the upper body reaches an erect, relaxed, resting position, with flexing primarily taking place at the hips. A slight knee flex makes the recovery relaxed and smooth.

The arms are dropped and fully relaxed during the forward swing of the poles. It is a very common mistake of skiers to flip the pole baskets up into the air at the beginning of the recovery. This, however, is an unnecessary expenditure of energy and waste of time by the skier. It is very important to relax the arm and hand immediately upon the pole release to prevent the pole swing-up (flip). This also reduces recovery time, and the poling frequency, and, accordingly, the speed of the skier. The inertia from the forward arm swing also contributes to the forward motion (see Appendix, Sec. II).

The skier's eyes are focused on the track 5 to 10 meters ahead. The poles follow a path parallel to the body in a vertical plane, with the arms close to the sides of the hips. The legs are very much straight, with a relaxed flex in the knees.

VII. GLIDE AND MOVEMENT CHARACTERISTICS FOR DOUBLE POLING

During Straight Double Poling, the skier is gliding on both skis continuously without any stopping. Both skis are fully weighted by the skier during the forward movement of the poles, with the body symmetrical between the two skis.

As the poles are planted, part of the body weight is immediately transferred onto the poles, thereby reducing (unweighting) the pressure and friction under the skis (Ch. 11, Sec. I-C). The arm "pull" on the poles accelerates the skier forward. The acceleration continues until completion of the arm "push", at which time the skier reaches the maximum cycle speed. During the recovery phase the skier is decelerating gradually. This is caused by friction between the skis and the snow, as well as aerial resistance (drag) acting against the skier, which becomes more prominent when the skier is fully erect under high speed (Ch. 11, Sec. III). The glide during Double Poling is therefore characterized by a continuous acceleration from muscle action during the poling phases, and a deceleration during the recovery phase.

The speed of the skier is very much dependent on how efficient he is in transferring muscle forces onto the poles after the pole plant. It is important during the recovery phase to get the upper body up and forward prior to the next pole plant.

The legs do not have to be locked perfectly parallel, but it is most important to keep the legs relaxed and flexible. One leg may move a little ahead of the other in a relaxed execution of Double Poling.

VIII. ENERGY AND EFFICIENCY

The most energy efficient muscle force application to the poles is by forward extension of the arms with relaxed elbows and an acute pole plant. As this pole angle becomes smaller during the poling, the efficiency becomes greater.

The legs should be fairly straight with knees relaxed, with a forward lean of the body and little flexing at the hips, since less vertical movement of the body's COG requires less energy.

The results of tests the author has done on Double Poling suggest that any skier with a well trained upper body can repetitively apply maximum muscle power onto the poles without building up excessive lactic acid in the muscles. The normal, relatively long, recovery time during efficient Double Poling will keep the pulse at a level that is not critical (also see Ch. 11, Sec. II-A).

IX. SPEED ZONES FOR DOUBLE POLING

The Double Pole Cycle can be divided into typical speed zones *(Fig. 6-7)*:

Zone I: Acceleration Phase / Poling

Zone II: Deceleration Phase / Recovery

During Double Poling, all motion is directed forward, parallel with the skiing direction. The accelerated increase of forward speed takes place during the poling (Zone I). Deceleration of the skier caused by the skis' drag (friction) and the body's increased air drag resistance takes place during the recovery (Zone II).

Zone I: The upper extremity is moved up and forward and partially weighted onto the poles (passively causing eccentric muscle action on the arms), actively involving the abdominal and trunk muscles. During the final arm poling phase the upper body's trunk line T-T is bent forward approximately 45° to give maximum force in the poling direction.

Zone II: The skier goes through this relaxation, resting, or recovery stage before preparing again for another active use of muscle power. Again note that the inertia (momentum) due to the forward swing of the arms and the forward movement of the midsection during the recovery does passively contribute to the forward motion. Likewise, the inertia of the arm swing backward retards the forward motion (Appendix, Sec. II).

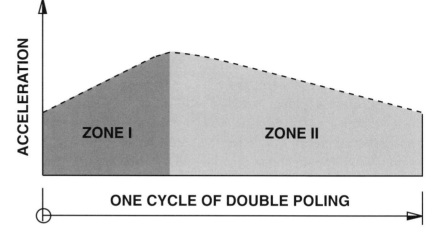

Figure 6-7 *Speed Zones For Double Poling*

X. SUMMARY OF PROCEDURE AND SEQUENCE FOR DOUBLE POLING

1. **Initiation**
   Legs together
   Body Erect
   Eye Focus 5-10 meters ahead
   Arms forward - Slight flex at elbow
   Glide on skis

2. **Preloading**
   Crowning of back
   Pole plant with acute pole angle
   Upper body weight shift forward and down onto poles.

3. **Pole action**
   Arms pulling on poles
   > Lock elbows at 90° with arm rotation about shoulder
   > Light flex (knee-roll only) at the knees
   > Upper crowned body bending forward less than 45°

   Arms pushing on pole
   > Elbows open up as they reach side of body
   > Final flip by hand.

4. **Upper body recovery**
   Extension of knees
   Trunk becomes erect

5. **Pole recovery**
   Pole release with immediate relaxation of arms
   Poles swing up to horizontal
   Forward swing of poles close to outside of the body.

1   2   3   4

Figure 6-8 *The skier above, **Silvio Fauner**, ITA, shows effective Double Poling in the Single Dance (Ch. 8, Sec. I), complying with the criteria outlined in this chapter. During high intensity skating (here, close to 10 m/sec on the level), the powerful skate leg action of the lower extremity is initiated (pre-loaded) with a slightly larger knee angle, due to angled spread of the legs. The recoil reaction released from a powerful crowning of the back has a positive effect on power transferred to poling as well as skating (also see Ch. 4, Sec. IV).*

CHAPTER 7

One-Side Skating / The Marathon Skate

Figure 7-1 *Effective Marathon Skating is characterized by a continuous glide on one ski, and a skate by the other ski. (Skier: **Bill Koch**, USA)*

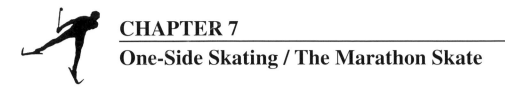

CHAPTER 7

One-Side Skating / The Marathon Skate

CONTENTS

I. ONE- SIDE SKATING / THE MARATHON SKATE

A. INTRODUCTION

The modern evolution of cross country skating started with the introduction of **One-Side Skating** into racing. The technique, which began as a supplement to the Traditional Classic techniques about 1980, was used with increasingly outstanding success in the Worldloppet's long Marathon racing distances, thus the origin of the name, **Marathon Skate**. Occasionally in Europe it was referred to as Siitonen (the name of a Finnish champion skier who earlier used the technique). For 5 years (1980-85) this was the dominating skating technique in long distance racing and touring.

It has been used primarily where there is at least one groomed ski track for the gliding steering ski, but, of course, can also be used where there is no groomed track, as in curves where the track is wiped out.

One-Side Skating (hereafter referred to as **Marathon Skating**) is executed by repetitious skating to one-side, while gliding on the opposite ski. The skier's direction is steered by the Gliding Ski, while the Skate Ski provides forward momentum by repeatedly pushing out to the side at an angle to the skiing direction. A forceful double poling pull and push is applied at the initiation of the skate. A skier usually skates less than 10 times to one side, then switches skate legs, and does a similar number of skates to the opposite side (if there is enough space on both sides of the gliding track to do so). Thus it is an excellent technique to use for recovery of certain leg muscle groups.

The photos in this chapter show top international racers employing the **Marathon Skate** technique, and some variations with and without poling. These techniques can be learned and practiced with advantage in both recreational skiing and racing.

B. DEFINITION OF ONE-SIDE SKATING / THE MARATHON SKATE

The **Marathon Skate** action starts as the skier, in erect body position with both skis parallel, initiates a double pole plant while the COG is over a continuously gliding, steering ski. The COG is then partially shifted over to the other ski which then makes a complete skate outwards. The poling and skating then go through a complete aerial recovery, where COG and the skis again are brought back to parallel for repetition of another skate.

C. MARATHON SKATE PATTERN

The Skate Pattern for One Cycle of the **Marathon Skate** is illustrated, viewed from above, as it would appear made by ski imprints in the snow.

As shown, the Marathon Skating action by the lower extremity is to one side only, with repetitive skating onto the same ski. The other ski glides continuously forward in the direction of skiing (DOS).

The upper extremity applies a typical *Straight Double Poling* technique, which starts immediately with the downset of the Skate Ski, while the legs are close together. The double poling continues as the legs spread apart, but terminates normally quite a bit earlier than the glide on the Skate Ski, depending on the speed of skiing.

The angle α is normally quite small, but varies with terrain, speed of skiing, and the frequency. The skate recovery (aerial path of boot) shows that the legs/skis come close together between each skate.

SYMBOLS FOR MARATHON SKATE PATTERN

- Pole Plant on Skate Side (Dark gray)
- Pole Plant on Continuous Glide Side (White)
- Downset of Skate Ski (Dark gray)
- Glide on Ski (White)
- Direction of skiing (DOS)
- α   Angle between skate and DOS
- Boot position during Downset of ski
- Boot position during Release of ski
- Aerial path of boot during recovery

Figure 7-2: 5 Sequential photos of Pierre Harvey, CAN, winner of several World Cup Races.

The photos correspond to the skate pattern illustrated for One Cycle of the Marathon Dance.

(1) Continuous glide and steering on one weighted flat ski, (right).

(2) Initiation, legs come together, double pole plant, downset of Skate Ski.

(3) Double pole pull and push action, weight transfer from Glide Ski onto Skate Ski.

(4) Final push off Skate Ski with weight shifted back to Glide Ski. Recovery of poling begins with forward swing of both arms and poles.

(5) Continuous glide on one weighted ski, skate leg recovery with inward movement toward the Glide Ski, preloading and preparation for double poling.

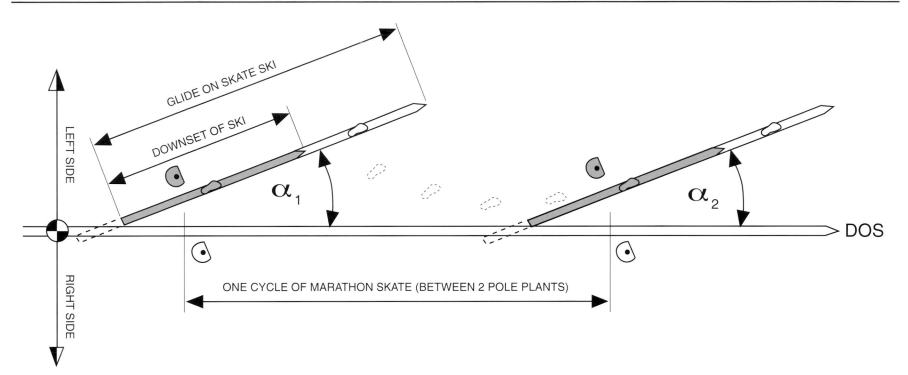

1   2   3   4

¢
COG   ONE CYCLE OF THE MARATHON SKATE (FROM ONE POLE PLANT TO ANOTHER)   ¢
COG

D. THE MARATHON SKATE CYCLE

The **Marathon Skate Cycle** is the sequence of movements a skier goes through between two consecutive double pole plants. In photo (**1**), the skier is planting his poles. His upper extremity then goes through the poling action and recovery before the poles are planted again. During the same period the skier's lower extremity goes through the skating action and recovery.

THE FREQUENCY (NUMBER)

is the number of skate cycles per time unit (a minute or less).

THE CYCLE TIME (SECONDS)

in the Marathon Skate is relatively long and is controlled by the arm's poling movements. The skate action is rather quick and short because the skate leg movement is restricted by the spread between the two legs. The continuously Gliding Ski is the direction of skiing (DOS).

THE CYCLE DISTANCE (METERS)

is measured between the exact locations of the body's COG at the time of the pole plants. It is characterized by a continuous, uninterrupted glide and steering by one (left) ski, with the other ski doing a skate push to the side. The cycle distance varies with the terrain, snow condition, skier's technique, and strength and energy resources.

1   2   3   4

¢/COG   ONE CYCLE OF THE MARATHON SKATE (FROM ONE POLE PLANT TO ANOTHER)   ¢/COG

THE CYCLE SPEED (M/SEC)

is related to a combination of the Cycle Distance and Time. When skating a curve or uphill, the frequency is usually higher with a shorter cycle distance, and the speed is less. On the flats and mild downhills under fast skiing conditions, the cycle speed is higher, the frequency is less, and the cycle distance is longer. In competition the skier is interested in optimum speed. By analyzing the skier's cycle movement, using qualified constructive criticism, the efficiency and cycle speed can be improved.

Many times during a race finish in competition with other skiers, Marathon Skating in a fast track at a high frequency has been the winning edge.

The photo sequences in Figure 7-3 and 7-4 show two skiers with different approaches to the Marathon Skate. Bill Koch has a distinctive initial Low COG, with explosive momentum forward during the skate off.

Harri Kirvesniemi of Finland, shown here Marathon skating in Holmenkollen, Oslo, NOR, 1982, has been a top elite racer for many years. He won a Gold Medal in 1989 in the World Championships.

	1			2			3	

A. UPPER BODY:	PRELOADING – POLE PLANT – POLE PULLING AND PUSHING
B. RIGHT SKI:	STEERING AND CONTINUOUS GLIDE ON FLAT SKI –
C. LEFT SKI:	DOWNSET OF SKI – WEIGHT TRANSFER, SKATE ACTION

E. SEQUENTIAL PHASES OF MOVEMENT FOR THE MARATHON SKATE

In describing the phases of movement that the body, arms, and legs go through during the Marathon Skate, we treat the **Continuous Glide on One Ski, Poling by the Upper Extremity,** and the **Skating by the Lower Extremity** separately. These actions and recoveries are interrelated within the Marathon Skate Cycle.

Body movements and equipment are described in relation to the skier's COG. The **Upper Extremity** includes the body above the horizontal X-X axis through COG. The **Lower Extremity** refers to the body below the X-X axis (Ch. 11, Sec. I-A).

Continuous Glide on One Ski

Poling by Upper Extremity	*Skating by Lower Extremity*
◆ Poling Action Phase	◆ Skating Action Phase
◆ Poling Recovery Phase	◆ Skating Recovery Phase

Pål Gunnar Mikkelplass, shown above, has been one of Norway's popular top skiers for more than a decade. He was on their Gold Medal relay teams in the 1982 and 1985 World Championships.

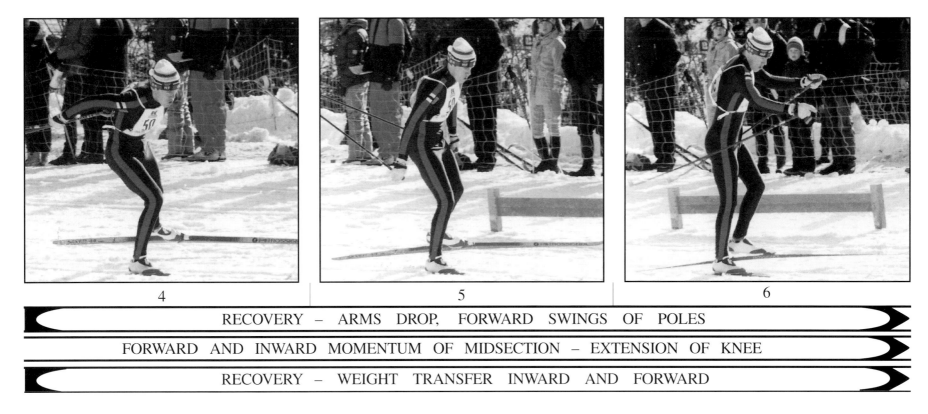

| 4 | 5 | 6 |

RECOVERY – ARMS DROP, FORWARD SWINGS OF POLES

FORWARD AND INWARD MOMENTUM OF MIDSECTION – EXTENSION OF KNEE

RECOVERY – WEIGHT TRANSFER INWARD AND FORWARD

◆ *Continuous Glide On One Ski*

During the Marathon Skate one ski (right) glides continuously without stopping. This ski steers the skier in the Direction of Skiing (DOS). During the glide the whole foot is kept in firm contact with the ski below, with body balanced through the ankle joint. The amount of weight on the Gliding Ski varies considerably during the Marathon Skate.

During preparation for the double pole plant, the legs are together, and the skier is in full balance with total body weight on the Gliding Ski (right) (**1, 6**). At the time of the pole plant, the Skate Ski is moved forward from the rear, smoothly set down, and the Gliding Ski is gradually unweighted (**1**). As the skate progresses

(**2, 3**), the Gliding Ski (right) is more and more unweighted, until the final skate push. At this moment the Gliding Ski should be barely weighted enough to perform the steering function (**3, 4**) with most of the body's weight on the Skate Ski (left).

During the skate recovery (**4, 5**), the COG of the skier in an erect position is moved forward onto the Gliding Ski with a **slight** extension of the knee. The forward momentum of the midsection further increases the speed and glide distance.

(Sequential Phases of Movement continued on next 2 pages)

◆ *The Poling Action Phase*

The initiation of the Double Poling begins with **Muscle Preloading** of the upper body as the Skate (left) Ski moves aerially inward and forward to become almost parallel with the Gliding (right) Ski (**1**). Immediately prior to the pole plant, preload and crown the back and shoulder muscles, weighting the upper extremity forward onto the poles (**1**). The downward motion of the upper body during the poling creates **Eccentric Muscle Action (EMA)** onto the arms (Ch. 4, Sec. II-D).

The skier is very much in an erect position, with a slight forward lean, legs together in complete balance on the Gliding (right) Ski. The double pole plant takes place as the Skate (left) Ski, with a slight crossing over the tail of the Gliding Ski, starts the glide and skate outward (**1**). To achieve maximum force and efficient power on the poles, the pole plant must be as close as possible to the outside of the skis, at the toe binding for the Gliding Ski and immediately prior to the downset of the Skate Ski. The arms are relaxed, but fully extended forward, and the poles are angled slightly backwards.

Maximum arm forces are now superimposed onto the poles. The elbows are kept at a 90° angle with rotation about the shoulder, until the elbows reach the body. At this time the elbows open up, the *pulling* force action on the arms then changes into a *pushing* force. Keeping the shoulders down, the hands and elbows follow a path as close to the side of the body as possible. The Double Poling direction is forward, in the direction of the Gliding Ski. Eye focus is slightly ahead of ski tips - first on the gliding ski, then on the skating ski (**2, 3**).

In order to use the least amount of energy and increase the average speed, the angle of forward bending of the skier's upper body should be less than 45° during the end of the pole push. At this time, approximately 3/4 of the body weight is shifted over to the Skate Ski (**2**).

◆ *The Poling Recovery Phase*

Immediately upon completion of the poling push (**3**) the arms, now in the recovery stage, are dropped, and swung forward (**4**) with the hands and poles following a low path, close to the body while the skier is in full balance on the gliding right ski (**4, 5**).

As the Skate Ski is brought inward towards the Gliding Ski, the arms and poles are pendulated forward and up for another pole plant (**5, 6**). The pole baskets should follow a natural low path as close to the ground as possible. During the poling recovery it is important to control the forward momentum of the pole swing, so the pole incline is less than 90° when poles are planted at the toe binding (Ch. 11, Sec. II-A). The pole swing can be controlled by the index finger, or several fingers. If the pole baskets pendulate too far forward, additional time to move the poles back to this incline prior to the pole plant means reduced efficiency of the poling and alters the rhythm.

◆ *The Skating Action Phase*

The Skating Phase starts immediately with the pole plant (**1, 2**). The skier is in complete balance on the Gliding (right) Ski, with both legs parallel and close together. The Skate Ski is moved forward with the tail crossing the Gliding Ski as its outside edge makes first contact with the snow. The first portion of the powerful skate should be on a flat ski (to minimize friction) until the skier finishes the pole push.

As the spread of the legs during the skate increases (**2**), the hip is dropped down and forward onto the Skate Ski. The gradual shifting of the skier's COG and lateral forces over to the skate leg almost completely unloads the Gliding Ski, giving that leg an opportunity to recover and reducing its frictional resistance *(Fig. 7-6)*.

The final skate push out to the side is an explosive one creating a counter reaction that moves the COG in the opposite direction towards the Gliding Ski. During the skate push the heel of the foot is in firm contact with the ski, but just before the release of the Skate Ski from the surface below, the foot rolls up onto the toe (**3**).

Figure 7-6 *Erik Østlund, SWE, Marathon Skate showing weight (COG) shift onto Skate Ski with recovery of opposite leg. In the 1980's, he was one of Sweden's best relay team members, helping to win many international relay meets.*

◆ *The Skating Recovery Phase*

Immediately upon release of the Skate Ski from the surface, the body, hips, and legs are extended up, forward, and inward to bring the COG in balance over the Gliding Ski (**4, 5**). It is important to keep vision forward, viewing the next 8 to 10 meters ahead in the direction of skiing, and to be alert to any variation in the terrain that may affect the body's motion and balance position.

The Skate Ski is now brought inward toward the Gliding Ski, following a path as close to the surface as possible. Its move inward ends with the Skate foot slightly behind the foot of the Gliding Ski, crossing its tail, preparing for downset and another skate (**5, 6**).

The inertia generated by the forward swing of the leg and ski, during the skate recovery, contributes to the skier's forward speed (Appendix, Sec. II).

F. FACTORS CONTROLLING EFFICIENT MARATHON SKATING

1. Eye focus and alertness
2. Body axes and alignment
3. Lateral and vertical movement of COG
4. Skate angle
5. Movement characteristics, momentum and rhythm
6. Smooth downset of Skate Ski
7. Friction and the Glide on a flat ski

Figures 7-7 and 7-8, *The Author, Marathon Skating*
Showing forward extension of midsection to extend the glide

To **Marathon Skate** efficiently with least use of energy, it is important to keep a high center of gravity (HCOG). There should be as little bending at the hips and in the knees as possible. This is accomplished by keeping a fairly straight leg for the Gliding Ski as the body's COG is shifted laterally and forward over to the Skate Ski. The skis and poles should follow a low center of gravity (LCOG) path, with least vertical lifting of the equipment (Ch. 11, Sec. II-B-5).

To create a greater forward *impulse momentum* (Ch. 11, Sec. II-B-9) when in complete balance on the Gliding Ski, a rhythmic forward extension of the body's midsection, with a slight extension of the knee, will enhance the forward speed and cycle distance. Figure 7-7 shows initiation of the movement and Figure 7-8, the extension of movement and glide.

During all skating techniques it is important not to rigidize the joints and the back. Movements of the body's elements should be dynamic and continually flexing slightly to stimulate good blood circulation.

G. ADVANTAGES AND DISADVANTAGES OF THE MARATHON SKATE

Advantages:

High frequency Marathon Skating can effectively be used when space is narrow, as when passing *Two-Side* skaters who occupy most of the course width.

Use of alternate skate sides during the Marathon Skate provides an excellent recovery for certain muscle groups.

Marathon Skating A Curve, when executed correctly, is some times faster and more efficient than other skating techniques.

Marathon Skating In A Tuck without poling is used extensively in curved downhills by top international racers, and could be characterized as an expanded form of the downhill skate step.

Disadvantages:

Marathon Skating is primarily a technique suitable for level, transitional, or mild downhill terrain. Other techniques are more efficient in the uphills.

In freestyle skating races today, the tracks often are wiped out by *Two-Side* skaters, making the non-skating glide ski less effective than *Two-Side* skating techniques.

H. SUMMARY OF PROCEDURE AND SEQUENCE FOR BASIC MARATHON SKATE

1. **Initiation:**
   Skis parallel
   Legs together
   Body erect with slight forward lean
   Eye focus slightly ahead of ski tips - first on the Gliding Ski, then on the right Skating Ski

2. **Upper Extremity - Pole Plant:**
   Preloading of muscles, crowning of upper back
   Upper body extremity weighted on the poles creating EMA
   Pole action starts

3. **Lower Extremity - Skate Begins:**
   Angulation
   Forward movement

4. **Body Movement:**
   COG moves laterally and slightly down
   Hip forward
   Legs spread apart

5. **Pole Pull and Final Push Action**

6. **Final Skate Action - Explosive**

7. **Continuous Glide Action On Flat Ski**
   Midsection forward movement, slight flex in knee

8. **Recovery:**
   Body and Pole Recovery: Long time and distance, continuous rhythmic movement
   Skate Recovery: Long time and distance, with ski close to surface

Repeat Above

A. *MARATHON SKATE TUCK WITHOUT POLING*

FIGURE 7-9

	1	2	3	4

UPPER BODY:	IN TUCK – WEIGHT ON GLIDING SKI	BODY WEIGHT
LEFT SKI:	STEERING AND CONTINUOUS GLIDE ON FLAT SKI	
RIGHT SKI:	LEGS TOGETHER	DOWNSET OF SKI – WEIGHT TRANSFER

When using the Marathon Skating technique with double poling, the body is in an erect position most of the time. As the speed increases in a mild downhill, say to 7 m/sec or faster, the erect body's air resistance increases (in proportion to the speed squared) and poling is not efficient.

If one goes into a tuck body position when the speed increases from 5 to 7 m/sec, the air resistance is dramatically reduced. In other words, *incorporating a tuck into the Marathon Skate increases the speed substantially* (Ch. 11, Sec. III). Excellent balance, coordination and well developed strength of the lower extremity are required to skate in a tuck position.

The skier illustrated in Photo (**1**), skiing in a prepared track, has just changed from an erect body position to a downhill tuck. His COG is shifted completely over to the Gliding (left) Ski; he then lifts the opposite ski (right) to begin the skate. The Skate Ski's tail initially crosses over the Gliding (left) Ski to maximize the length of the skate, which otherwise would be shortened in such a low position (**2**).

The COG is then gradually shifted over to the Skate Ski as the skier initiates the skate across the right track (**3**). The skier's attention (alertness) is still on what is directly immediately ahead of him while he is gradually transferring more of his weight to the Skate Ski (**4**).

With the poles pointing backwards and tucked in close to the body, the skier maintains a downhill tuck with a minimum frontal aerial resistance area (**5**).

| 5 | 6 | 7 | 8 |

PARTIALLY ONTO SKATE SKI ➤ BODY WEIGHT BACK TO GLIDING SKI ➤

PARTIALLY UNWEIGHTED DURING SKATE ➤

WITH SKATE ACTION ➤ RECOVERY – INWARD AND FORWARD MOVEMENT ➤

The skate leg is fully extended during the final portion of the powerful skate push out to the side. The extra push at the end of the skate glide brings the COG back over the Gliding (left) Ski, on which the skier regains a perfect balance (6). The Skate Ski is then brought back inward and forward toward the Gliding Ski following an angulated path close to the surface (requiring least energy) with minimal bending of the knee for the skate leg (7). Its move forward and inward ends slightly behind the foot of the Gliding Ski, crossing its tail with the skate foot.

The skier in (8) has now regained the same position as he originally started out with, repeating the same procedure as above for another skate (1) through (8). The movements from (1) to (8) represent one complete cycle of the **Marathon Skate Tuck Without**

Poling. The skier may repeat the same skate stride cycle to either side. The Marathon Skate Tuck Without Poling can also be executed without groomed tracks.

MARATHON SKATE TUCK
SIMPLIFIED PROCEDURE AND SEQUENCE

1. Continuous glide on one ski in tucked position

2. Legs together in Tuck Body Position, Poles Under Arms

3. Skate Action to One Side Starts With Lateral Body Movement

4. Skate Push Outward

5. Skate Ski Recovery

Repeat As Above

Starting at the upper right corner, photos (**1**) through (**7**) show a full cycle of skating a curve using the Marathon Skate technique with poling. Marathon skating a curve requires special skill, whether skied in grooves or on an untracked course.

Skiers using the Marathon Skate when entering a sharp curve with fairly high speed can easily be forced out of balance due to the natural forces acting on the skier. The normal gravity force (W_B) acts vertically from a skier's COG, however, in a curve, another outward force, called the centrifugal force (H_C) tends to force the skier outward, off the curve (Ch. 11, Sec. I-C-7). This force has to be counteracted by inward and forward movement of the skier's COG so the Resultant Force (R) goes through the ankle on the continuously Gliding Ski. A slight rotation inward of the upper body about the ankle for the Gliding Ski steers the skier through the curve. See Ch. 9, Sec. IV-C-2 for other examples of skating a curve.

3

4

2

1

5

6

7

CHAPTER 8

Two-Side Skating / The Skate Dances

Figure 8-1
Women's Pursuit race, World Championships, Falun, SWE, 1993
Bib #4   Jelena Välbe, RUS
Bib #5   Stefania Belmondo, ITA, Gold Medalist
Bib #7   Marjut Rolig, FIN
Bib #3   Trude Dybendahl, NOR
Bib #8   Katerina Neumannova, TCH
Bib# 9   Anita Moen, NOR

INTRODUCTION TO THE TWO-SIDE SKATE DANCES

TWO-SIDE SKATING is precisely defined by the author as skating repetitiously, alternately using left and right skis. The term, *Skate Dancing*, is also used here because this type of skiing is just plain fun. At its height of relaxed performance on easy terrain, it feels like ballet on a pair of skis. *Skate Dancing* allows one to relax thoroughly through movement and rhythm. It is an activity that can enrich one's life; a therapy on which you can wisely spend your leisure time. This skill that everyone, young and old, can learn, can be enjoyed by recreational skiers and racers alike.

Keeping the feeling of dancing alive while you practice the skate techniques included here may help you to be more relaxed and learn faster.

In **Two-Side Skate Dancing**, each ski repetitiously makes outward skate movements, combined with single or double poling. All the body's elements contribute to the forward propulsion of the skier, and greater speed can be achieved with less use of energy when doing this correctly.

In efficient *Skate Dancing*, there is a rhythmic continuation in the glide from one ski to the other with no letup. When learning ski *Skate Dancing*, this smooth transition (the transfer of weight, COG, from one leg to another) is difficult to learn, requiring good balance, flexibility, coordination and strength. A letup or delay between each skate actually requires more energy since the skier generates increased friction, and has to regain the skating momentum, which otherwise would be maintained unbroken. The result is that the skier may quickly become tired (not an unusual experience for less trained skiers.)

In the following subchapters, the four principal techniques of *Two-Side Skate Dances* commonly used are illustrated and described:

I. The Single Dance	**II. The Double Dance**
III. The Paddle Dance	**IV. The Diagonal Dance**

Skate Dance techniques involving minor variations or modifications of these four are used to a lesser degree. Chapter 10 lists all skating techniques, including variations.

In order to become a good skater, you have to master all techniques. There is no single technique that can be effectively used all the time. Certain techniques are better adapted to different types of terrain and speeds of skiing, which is further elaborated on under "Advantages and Disadvantages" in the discussion of each technique.

◆◆◆ *NOTE ON ORDER OF PRESENTATION* ◆◆◆

The author presents the *Two-Side Skate Dances* in this order because of the progression in **poling action and frequency.**

Single Dance (I) and **Double Dance (II)** utilize *Straight Double Poling,* extensively discussed in the preceding two chapters.

In the **Single Dance**, *Straight Double Poling* is applied for every **second skate**, repeatedly to one side. The Single Dance, thus allows plenty of time between each pole plant.

In the **Double Dance**, the amount of *Straight Double Poling* is **doubled;** there is poling for **every skate,** to both sides. Poling is done with a much higher frequency, and there is accordingly much less recovery time between each pole plant.

Paddle Dance (III) utilizes a slight deviation of *Straight Double Poling.*

Diagonal Dance (IV) uses *Single Poling,* not double poling. It is a natural progression of one the oldest techniques in skiing, the Classic Herringbone.

The Degree Of Difficulty in learning and executing these Skate Dance techniques does not coincide with this progression. The ease in performing the different skate dance techniques is directly determined by the factors of balance and coordination which the author discusses in detail under each technique. His new approach explains how the number of Points Of Ground Contact (Ch. 3, Sec. II) and their duration relate to this.

CHAPTER 8
I. THE SINGLE DANCE

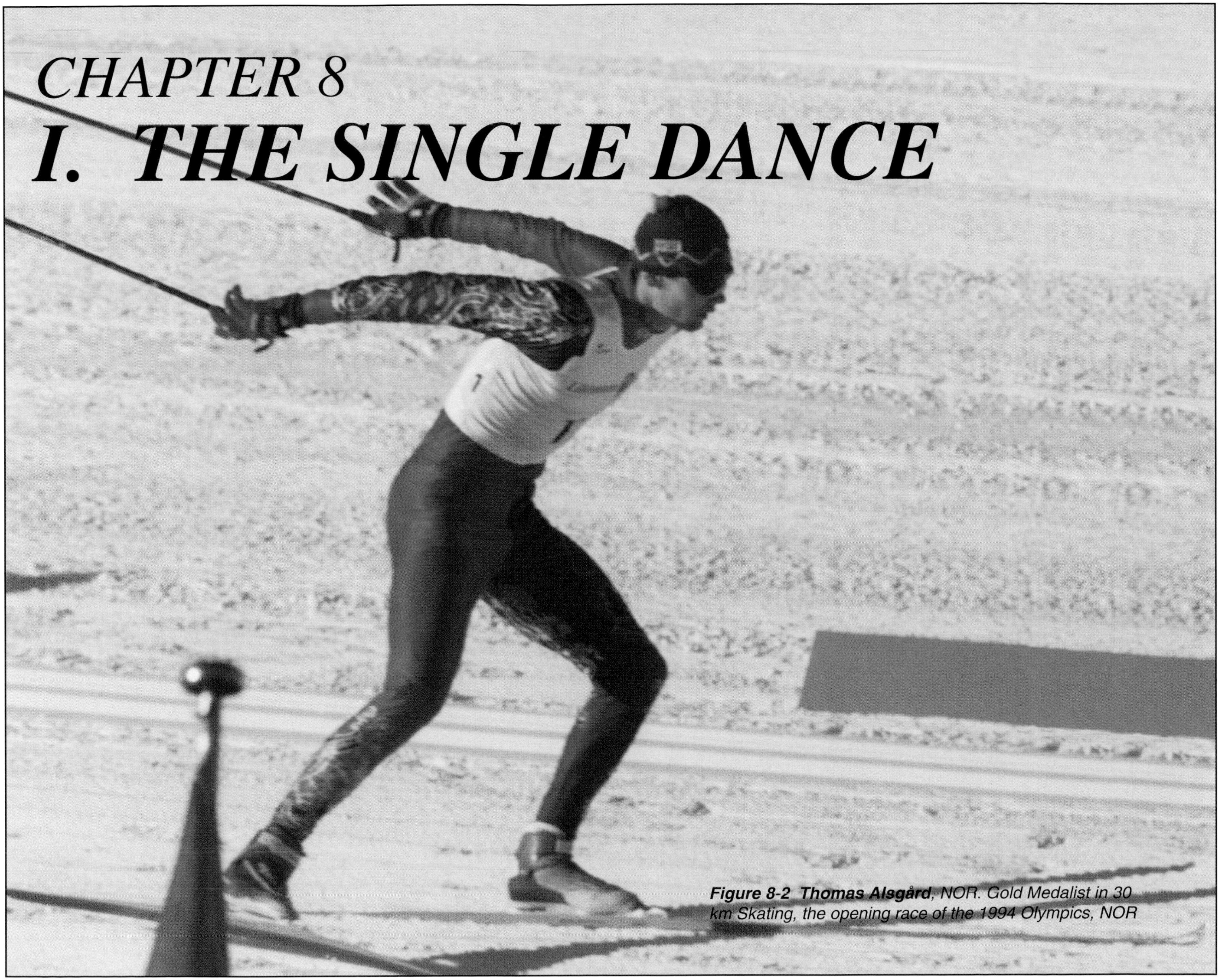

Figure 8-2 Thomas Alsgård, NOR. Gold Medalist in 30 km Skating, the opening race of the 1994 Olympics, NOR

CHAPTER 8   TWO-SIDE SKATING, *"The Skate Dances"*

I.   THE SINGLE DANCE

CONTENTS

I. THE SINGLE DANCE

A. INTRODUCTION

Single Dance utilizes one classic Straight Double Poling with two or more skates in an enjoyable, rhythmic movement. The poling takes place at the beginning of the first skate with recovery during the second skate. The technique is characterized by aggressive powerful skating, with quick, effective poling during each cycle.

In the following, the photos, illustrations and descriptions refer to Single Dance where there are two single skates (one to each side) incorporating one *Straight Double Poling.* The name Single Dance also refers to a skiing situation (a cycle) where the skier may use more than two single skates for each double poling. However, the use of two per cycle is the most common. The first skate, combined with Double Poling is very similar to the Marathon Skate, a One-Side skating technique (Ch. 7).

A skier may do several cycles of Single Dance using the left side as the Poling Side and then switch and do a similar number of cycles where the right side is the Poling Side.

Most skilled skaters use the Single Dance on variable flat terrain since very high speed can be gained when applying this technique efficiently. It is used a lot in skate racing and is becoming very popular among recreational skiers, who enjoy using the technique because of its rhythm and relaxed quality.

The Double Poling in Single Dance is a typical synchronized straight technique where the direction of poling forces are parallel to the skiing direction (Ch. 6).

We typically describe the Single Dance by indicating the two sides:

The Poling Side - the side where poling takes place.

The Poling-free Side - the side without poling (poling recovery).

Because of poling only on one side, the action of the Upper Extremity (the Poling) of Single Dance during a cycle is not symmetrical. The action of the lower extremity with skating to both sides is more symmetrical, although the skate onto the Poling side is more powerful and longer.

The effect of the first skate with glide on the Poling side during the cycle is quite a bit greater than the second skate for the following reasons:

1. The quick powerful poling maximizes the force on the first skate.

2. The second skate does not have poling assistance; therefore, the deceleration (slowing down) due to continuous friction and aerial resistance is greater.

B. DEFINITION OF THE SINGLE DANCE

In the **Single Dance** technique one *Straight Double Poling* is executed with the first of two or more skates (one to each side). It is initiated with a forceful poling action while the body is erect, having a slight forward lean, crowning (preloading) of upper back, with COG of the body over and in the direction of the Poling Ski.

As the Poling progresses, legs and skis come together (from the previous skate out to the side). At the termination of the poling (final push-off), the skier skates out to the side with the Poling Ski, and then transfers body weight (COG) to the opposite Poling-free Ski. During the poling recovery, which takes place while skating outward on the Poling-free Ski, the skier prepares for another pole plant and a repeat of the same actions.

C. THE SINGLE DANCE SKATE PATTERN

The Skate Pattern for **One Cycle of the Single Dance** is illustrated, viewed from above, as it would appear made by ski imprints in the snow. The imprints indicate the Double Pole plants at the beginning of the first skate on the left side, the Poling Side, with a second skate to the right, the Poling-free Side. The sequence is then repeated, starting with another double pole plant.

As the Skate Pattern shows, there are two skates between pole plants. Double Poling begins when the legs come together, and the poling direction is the same as the Poling Ski. The recovery of the poles takes place during the glide on the Poling-free Ski. As the legs come together again, the sequence is repeated.

The skate glide distance on the Poling Side is usually quite a bit longer than on the Poling-free Side, because there is poling assistance. However, the amount of difference will vary with the terrain and speed of skiing.

During the Skating Cycle the downset of the ski is a step forward, ahead of the gliding ski. The skate angles α_1 and α_2 vary with speed and the terrain, but are usually quite small in the Single Dance, which has relatively *long skates*.

Terje Langli, NOR, has been on the international racing circuit for a decade. He won Gold Medals in the 10km Classic and the 4x10 Relay in the 1991 World Championships.

SYMBOLS FOR SINGLE DANCE SKATE PATTERN

⊙	Pole Plant on Poling Side (Light gray)
⦿	Pole Plant on Poling-Free Side (Dark gray)
▷	Downset of Poling Ski (Light gray)
▶	Downset of Poling-Free Ski (Dark gray)
▷	Glide on Ski (White)
- -▶	Direction of skiing (DOS)
α	Angle between skate and DOS
⬭	Boot position during Downset of ski
⬭	Boot position during Release of ski
⌐⌐⌐	Aerial path of boot during Recovery

Figure 8-3: 5 Sequential photos of Terje Langli, of the winning Norwegian team, during the end of the third leg in the 4 x 10 km Relay, World Championships, Falun, SWE, 1993.

The photos correspond to the Skate Pattern for One Cycle of Single Dance.

(1) Glide and skate on Poling-free *(right)* side, Double Pole plant.

(2) Step forward with downset and glide on Poling Ski *(left)*, end of double poling.

(3) Continuing glide on Poling Ski, skate-off Poling-free ski with short recovery, recovery of double poling begins.

(4) Skate-off on Poling Ski with step forward and downset of Poling-free ski.

(5) Glide on Poling-free ski, recovery of other ski, legs come together, preparation for Double Pole plant.

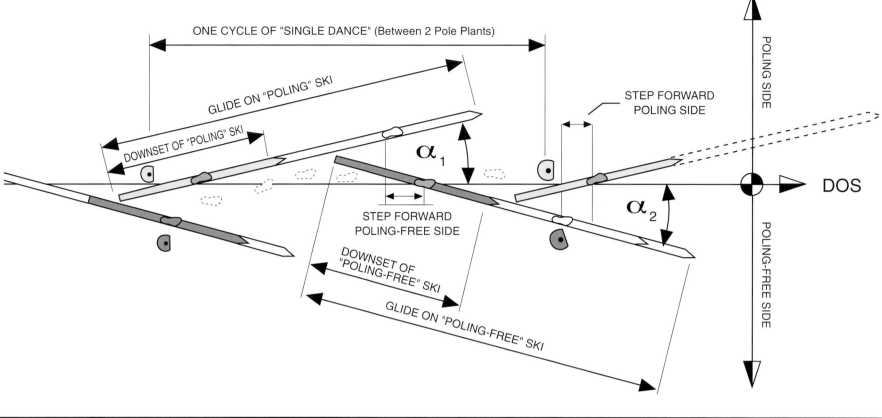

ONE CYCLE OF "SINGLE DANCE" (Between 2 Pole Plants)

GLIDE ON "POLING" SKI

DOWNSET OF "POLING" SKI

STEP FORWARD
POLING SIDE

α_1

STEP FORWARD
POLING-FREE SIDE

DOWNSET OF
"POLING-FREE" SKI

GLIDE ON "POLING-FREE" SKI

α_2

POLING SIDE

POLING-FREE SIDE

DOS

1   2   3   4   5

| 1 | 2 | 3 |

¢
COG

ONE CYCLE OF THE SINGLE DANCE

D.   THE SINGLE DANCE SKATE CYCLE

The Single Dance Cycle begins with a typical Double Pole plant, as the right ski, which has just completed the previous skate, is moved inward and forward from behind to be nearly parallel with the left ski. The downset, followed with weighting, of this ski (the Poling Ski) takes place immediately after the pole plant (Photo **1**). The poling action, which lasts a relatively short time during the Cycle, takes place during the beginning of the glide on the Poling Ski, with a skate out to the side on the (left) Poling-free ski, and terminates as the skate progresses (**2**).

During the Single Dance Cycle (from one pole plant to another) the skier rhythmically makes two skates, one to the left (**1, 2, 3**), and one to the right (**4, 5**). The skier may do the Cycle in opposite order, depending on the side slope of terrain (if any) and individual preference. On a side slope, the poling is most efficient when done on the uphill side.

Since poling takes place only for every second skate, the *skating during the Single Dance is the primary contribution to the forward motion* and poling during high speed therefore is secondary.

4   5   6

(FROM ONE POLE PLANT TO ANOTHER)

¢
COG

THE FREQUENCY (NUMBER) is the number of skate cycles per time unit (a minute or less), which varies with the Cycle Distance and the Speed.

THE CYCLE TIME (SECONDS) for the Single Dance is the *longest* of any of the skate dances. On variable flat terrain with fast skiing, the longer glide of the skate controls the cycle time, and the Double Poling effects it to a lesser degree.

THE CYCLE DISTANCE (METERS) is measured in the skiing direction (DOS) between two pole plants. This varies with the speed, the skate angles, and the glide length of each skate.

THE CYCLE SPEED (M/SEC) is related to the Cycle Frequency and Distance. Top racers apply the Single Dance on variable flat terrain to gain speed, utilizing explosive power on the poles from the crowned upper back and long aggressive skates, as demonstrated by the above Olympic and World champion skier, Torgny Mogren.

Torgny Mogren, SWE, has been one of the top ski skaters in the world during the last decade, winning two Gold Medals for the 50 km Marathon, (World Championships 1991, Val di Fiemme, ITA, and 1993, Falun, SWE) in addition to Golds in the Olympic Relay 1988, and World Championship Relays 1987, 1989.

1   2   3   4

ONE CYCLE OF THE SINGLE DANCE

¢
COG

E. BALANCE AND GROUND CONTACTS FOR THE SINGLE DANCE
(In the photos above, the *right* side is the Poling Side)

a. Initially, during the preloading phase prior to the pole plant, the skier is fully in balance on the Poling-free Ski *(left)* (ONE POINT CONTACT) Photos (**8, 1**).

b. The poles are then planted while in balance on the Poling-free Ski *(left)* (THREE POINT CONTACT) (**1**).

c. Immediately afterwards, during the pole pulling phase, the downset of the Poling Ski *(right)* takes place (FOUR POINT CONTACT) (**2**). This is an ideal time to make any adjustment with regard to balance, rhythm or coordination.

d. Upon completion of the pole push-off, the skier is briefly in partial balance on both skis, while skating out on the Poling-free ski *(left)* (TWO POINT CONTACT) (**3**).

e. The Poling-free ski and poles are now airborne, and the skier is in full balance on the Poling Ski *(right)*. (ONE POINT CONTACT) (**4, 5**).

FIGURE 8-5

SKIER: VLADIMIR SMIRNOV, KAZ

5   6   7   8

(FROM ONE POLE PLANT TO ANOTHER)

COG

f.   As the skis come together, the skier steps forward with downset of the Poling-free *(left)* ski (TWO POINT CONTACT) (**6**).

g.   The second skate is now executed on the Poling Ski *(right)* (TWO POINT CONTACT) (**7**), as the skier continues gliding on the *left* ski.

h.   As the skier recovers the *(right)* ski, he is back to the beginning, in balance on the *left* ski (ONE POINT CONTACT) (**8**, **1**).

Note:

Smirnov is skiing with a fairly erect body, with very little vertical movement of COG. His hips and midsection are well forward in the direction of the glide on a flat ski. The airborne skis are kept close to (sweeping) the surface (Ch. 11, Sec. II-B-5). This is a good example of how to ski with least energy.

Vladimir Smirnov, KAZ, has won more Silver Medals in the Olympics and World Championships than any other skier. He added a well deserved Gold in the 50 km Marathon, Olympics, 1994, NOR, in addition to winning the 1994 World Cup.

SEQUENTIAL PHASES OF MOVEMENT FOR THE SINGLE DANCE (FOR ONE CYCLE)

Silvio Fauner is using two single skates out to each side for every Straight Double Poling for One Cycle of the Single Dance.
Bar lines illustrate the ACTION and the RECOVERY during the phases of the **Single Dance** for the upper and the lower extremities.

	1	2	3	4

POLING ACTION: PRELOADING ▶ STRAIGHT DOUBLE POLING ▶

LEFT LEG ACTION: LEGS COME TOGETHER ▶ DOWNSET — STEP FORWARD — ▶

RIGHT LEG ACTION: (CONTINUE) GLIDE AND SKATE ON POLING-FREE SKI ▶

F. SEQUENTIAL PHASES OF MOVEMENT FOR THE SINGLE DANCE

1. POLING BY UPPER EXTREMITY

Note: The poling action here is executed with glide on the Poling Ski *(left)*. The poling recovery takes place while gliding on the Poling-free Ski *(right)* (also see Double Poling, Ch. 6).

♦ *Pole Action Phases (Photos 1 - 5)*

   a. Initiation of Double Poling - Preloading of upper back, abdomen and shoulder muscles. Photos (**1, 8**)

   b. Pole Plant and Pole Action (**1 - 5**)
   - Backward-inclined poles
   - Body weight on poles, crowning of back
   - Muscle action on poles
   - Sequence: Pull ⇒ Push ⇒ Release

♦ *Poling Recovery Phase (Photos 5 - 8)*

   c. The poles now swing forward, following a low profile (their own gravity), in correlation with the speed of skiing.

♦ *Repeat For Another Cycle*

FIGURE 8-6   **SKIER: SILVIO FAUNER, ITA**

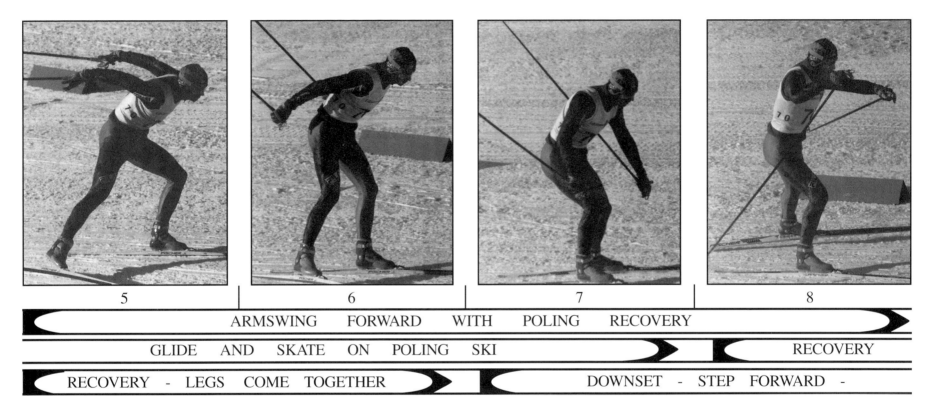

| 5 | 6 | 7 | 8 |

ARMSWING   FORWARD   WITH   POLING   RECOVERY

GLIDE   AND   SKATE   ON   POLING   SKI   RECOVERY

RECOVERY - LEGS   COME   TOGETHER   DOWNSET -   STEP   FORWARD -

2. SKATING AND GLIDE ACTION BY LOWER EXTREMITY

◆ *Skate Action Phases By Poling-Free Ski (Right) (Photos 1 - 5)*

  a. Initiation of Skate (**1, 2**) - Legs together - step forward and downset of the Poling Ski (**2, 3**).

  b. Skate begins on Poling-free ski - Weight partially on both skis (**2, 3, 4**).

  c. Termination of skate - Total body weight (COG) transferred to glide on Poling Ski (**4**).

◆ *Recovery Of Poling-Free Ski (Right) (5, 6)*

◆ *Skate Action Phases By Poling Ski (Left) (Photos 6 - 8)*

  a. Initiation of skate - Legs come together from recovery of Poling-free Ski (**5**) - Step forward and downset of ski (**6, 7**).

  b. Skate begins on Poling Ski - Weight partially on both skis (**7**).

  c. Termination of skate on Poling Ski (**7, 8**) - Total body weight transferred to gliding Poling-free Ski (**8**).

◆ *Recovery Of Poling Ski (Left) (Photos 8, 1, 2)*

◆ *Repeat Of Cycle*

	1	2	3	4
POLING ACTION:	PRELOADING		STRAIGHT DOUBLE POLING	
LEFT LEG ACTION:	(CONTINUE) GLIDE AND SKATE ON POLING — FREE SKI			
RIGHT LEG ACTION:	LEGS COME TOGETHER		DOWNSET — STEP FORWARD —	

G.   FACTORS CONTROLLING EFFECTIVE SINGLE DANCE MOVEMENT

1. BODY AXES AND ALIGNMENT

Single Dance is an asymmetric skate technique, where straight Double Poling is applied with the first skate. The body is kept fairly erect with shoulder - hip axis parallel and perpendicular to the glide direction of the Poling ski. Alignments as are discussed in Ch. 11, Sec. I-B.

2. LATERAL AND VERTICAL MOVEMENT OF COG

To maximize force action on poles and skis, and to counteract air resistance, the body has a slight forward lean from the ankle up, with crowning of back and relatively little bending at the hips at the end of the poling action. Single Dance is one of the techniques where vertical fluctuation of COG is minimal. Lateral movement varies with skate angle, speed and length of each skate, with emphasis on hip skate action (Ch. 5).

3. SKATE ANGLES

The skate angles during effective Single Dance are quite small since the skate glide distance is commonly quite long; the higher the speed, the smaller the skate angle. Most of the time the skier is on a flat ski base with edging only at the skate push-off.

5   6   7   8

ARMSWING   FORWARD   WITH   POLING   RECOVERY

RECOVERY — LEGS COME TOGETHER   DOWNSET — STEP FORWARD —

GLIDE   AND   SKATE   ON   POLING   SKI   RECOVERY —

4. MOVEMENT CHARACTERISTICS AND DANCE RHYTHM

Single Dance is a technique that has enjoyable rhythm, which when executed correctly, is perhaps more dance oriented in feeling than any other skating technique because of the rhythmic combination of two skates and one Double Pole frequency. During initiation of each skate, the legs are close together, weight and balance on one ski. The basics of skate action apply (Ch. 5). During the forward and outward movement activating the skate, the large muscles of the hips, midsection and adductors are the prime sources of power (not the knee extension) (Ch. 4).

One of the most common flaws in performing Single Dance is not coordinating the poles properly. Poles should be planted close to the skis, with elbows close to the body when legs and skis come together. Pole baskets should not flip up higher than horizontal during the recovery.

5. FRICTION AND THE GLIDE

Friction and glide are important factors as discussed in detail in the Appendix. Body weight and power is applied to poles before a smooth downset of the Poling Ski. Likewise the downset of the Poling-free ski should be soft, with legs close together. To minimize friction, the glide on both skis should be on a flat ski base, another special feature which makes Single Dance a high speed technique on variable flat terrain.

6. MOMENTUM AND INERTIA

These are factors that become important during high speed skiing, as in racing. Inertia from the Double Poling has a *positive* effect in contributing to the forward speed when arms are *moved forward* during the recovery, while the pole action inertia has a *negative effect* when arms *move against* the skiing direction.

Long, extended forward rhythmic arm swings at relative high speed will *increase the positive effect;* and effective pole action, with emphasis on 90° elbows with shoulder rotation, will *minimize the negative inertia effect* (Ch. 6. and Appendix). Forward extension of midsection with extension of knees after each skate will enhance the momentum (mv) and contribute to a longer and faster skate.

7. POWER AND SPEED

These two important factors in racing are closely related to the neuromuscular sequence (Ch. 4). *Muscle action starts at the midsection* with movement at COG and is transmitted sequentially in a *"chain reaction" as follows:*

- ♦ **Lower Extremity:** To thighs and hamstrings through the knee joint and lastly to the foot and ski.

- ♦ **Upper Extremity:** To abdomen and lower back, through upper back to shoulders, arms through elbow joint, and lastly to the hand and pole.

H. ADVANTAGES AND DISADVANTAGES OF SINGLE DANCE

Advantages:

As clearly seen from the bar chart (Ch. 8, Sec. I-F) for the Single Dance that the upper extremity is much less involved than the lower because double poling is applied only to every second skate. The work load is therefore considerably different than experienced during the *Paddle* and *Double Dance* (Sections following), where the upper extremity is more powerful and more frequently engaged. The work load distribution for Single Dance suggests that more of a skier's VO$_2$ capacity can be utilized by the lower extremity, a major advantage in certain types of light terrain and fast snow conditions.

Disadvantages:

Single Dance is primarily applicable to level and light rolling terrain. In steeper uphills, the Paddle Dance technique is more efficient in overcoming the skier's gravity forces (body weight) because the staggered Double Poling provides more poling action.

In mild downhills when speed increases, other techniques such as Diagonal Skating without poling (Ch. 8, Sec. IV-F) and Skating In A Tuck (Ch. 9, Sec. IV-C) are more efficient, less energy demanding, and usually faster.

I. SUMMARY OF PROCEDURE AND SEQUENCE FOR SINGLE DANCE

The following summary is for One Full Cycle of the Single Dance.

1. Initiation (1 Point Contact)
a. Legs together
b. Weight and glide on Poling-free Ski
c. Body erect
d. Preparation for poling - end of poling recovery
e. Preloading of upper body

2. Pole Plant (3 Point Contact)
a. Backward inclined poles
b. Upper body weight onto poles
c. Muscle action from arms "pulling" on poles
d. Skate action on Poling-free Ski

3. Step Forward And Downset Of Poling Ski (4 Point Contact)
a. Weight on both skis
b. Muscle action from crowning of back and arms, "pushing" on poles
c. Skate action on Poling-free Ski terminates

4. Release Of Poling-Free Ski And Poles (1 Point Contact)
a. Powerful push on Poling-free ski brings body weight over to Poling Ski
b. Glide on Poling Ski
c. Poling recovery begins

5. Legs Come Together (1 Point Contact)
a. Continue glide and skate on Poling Ski
b. Continue forward swing of poles and arms

6. Step Forward And Downset Of Poling-Free Ski (2 Point Contact)
a. Skate action on Poling Ski
b. Powerful push-off on Poling Ski
c. Release of Poling ski

7. This completes One Full cycle of the Single Dance

CHAPTER 8
II. THE DOUBLE DANCE

Figure 8-8 **Vegard Ulvang**, NOR, winning the Pursuit race, World Cup, Silver Star, B.C., CAN, 1991

CHAPTER 8   TWO-SIDE SKATING, *"The Skate Dances"*

II. THE DOUBLE DANCE

CONTENTS

II. THE DOUBLE DANCE

A. *INTRODUCTION*

In **Double Dance** skate technique a Straight Double Poling is rhythmically applied to every skate.

In analyzing efficiency and maximum speed in skating, it is natural to explore a technique where straight, well developed Double Poling is used with each skate stride. Theoretically this should be the fastest form for free-style skiing if efficient power in poling and skating is applied. However, such movement on skis is not so easily accomplished, since it requires excellent balance, weight shift, and good coordination and timing of the body's elements and equipment. You have to be more or less in complete balance on one ski (One Point Contact) for a fairly long time to initiate and superimpose double poling with each skate stride. The technique requires a lot of skill and training, but under special skiing terrain conditions, and when executed correctly, it is probably the fastest of all forms of skating to date.

The First Half Cycle of the Double Dance is similar to the *Marathon Skate* (Ch. 7), which also utilizes straight Double Poling and a long balanced glide on one ski. Combining these two skates during training is therefore recommended.

During fast conditions, the Double Dance requires relatively little lateral space because of the very small skate angle. The movements then closely resemble those of Straight Double Poling.

The author uses the Double Dance a lot and expects it to be used more in the future by recreational skiers and racers who enjoy the feeling of proficiency in skiing fast while still being relaxed (use of less energy). The technique is excellent for relief of any other skating stride being used for a longer period of time.

B. *DEFINITION OF THE DOUBLE DANCE*

In the Double Dance technique, one Straight Double Poling is executed with every skate. The Double Dance starts with the skier in erect body position, legs close together, in balanced glide on one *(first)* ski, while preparing for a double pole plant. The poles are planted and followed by the downset of the *second* ski, while the *first* ski executes the skate. Then a quick recovery of poles and the *first* ski takes place while the body weight is shifted completely over to the *second* ski. This completes One Skate (the *first half cycle* of the Double Dance). The Second Skate is a repeat of the same procedure, using another Straight Double Poling with a skate on the other ski/side to complete a *whole cycle*.

C. THE DOUBLE DANCE SKATE PATTERN

The Skate Pattern for one full cycle of the **Double Dance** Skate technique is illustrated, viewed from above, as it would appear made by ski imprints in the snow. The Double Dance is characterized by having double poling for *each* skate.

The Full Cycle includes a left and a right side, and left and right skates. The pole plant takes place immediately prior to the downset of the ski as the legs come together. The poling action is in the same direction as the path of the skate ski. As the photos show, the skier has to quickly shift weight (balance) from one ski to the other in order to apply a pole plant for each skate, allowing relatively little recovery time for skis and poles. There is no Poling-free side in the Double Dance.

The skate glide distance and the skate angle (α) are the same to each side in similar terrain. ***Double Dance does not have a step forward with the downset of the ski.*** During downset, the legs are very much parallel. The aerial pathway of the released ski is from behind and forward prior to the downset.

Double Dance requires relatively little lateral space, since the skate angle (α) can be quite small.

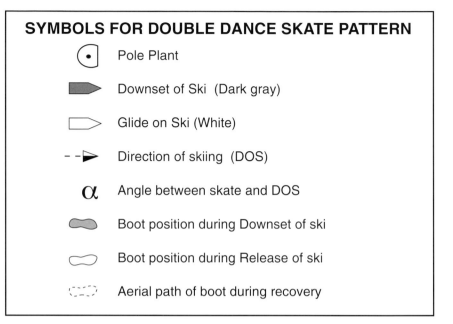

SYMBOLS FOR DOUBLE DANCE SKATE PATTERN

⊙ Pole Plant

▶ Downset of Ski (Dark gray)

▷ Glide on Ski (White)

- -▶ Direction of skiing (DOS)

α Angle between skate and DOS

⬭ Boot position during Downset of ski

⬭ Boot position during Release of ski

⬭ Aerial path of boot during recovery

Figure 8-9 5 Sequential photos of Vegard Ulvang, NOR.

The photos correspond to the Skate Pattern for **the First Half** of a Cycle of Double Dance.

(**1**) Legs are together, skier prepares for pole plants.

(**2**) Pole plants followed immediately by downset of *left* ski.

(**3**) Poling with continued glide on flat *left* ski, skate begins on *right* ski.

(**4**) Final pole push, continued glide on flat *left* ski, and skate-off on *right* ski.

(**5**) Continue glide on *left* ski, recovery of *right* ski is moved inward and forward, quick recovery of poles.

To complete the Second Half of Cycle, repeat the same sequence with the second Double Poling taking place with skate on *left* ski, and glide on *right* ski.

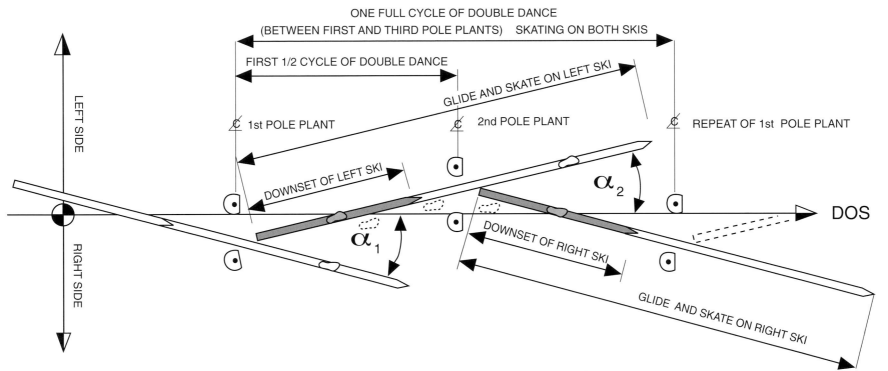

ONE FULL CYCLE OF DOUBLE DANCE
(BETWEEN FIRST AND THIRD POLE PLANTS)   SKATING ON BOTH SKIS

FIRST 1/2 CYCLE OF DOUBLE DANCE

GLIDE AND SKATE ON LEFT SKI

LEFT SIDE

RIGHT SIDE

1st POLE PLANT   2nd POLE PLANT   REPEAT OF 1st POLE PLANT

DOWNSET OF LEFT SKI

α_2

α_1

DOWNSET OF RIGHT SKI

DOS

GLIDE AND SKATE ON RIGHT SKI

FIRST 1/2 CYCLE OF DOUBLE DANCE

1   2   3   4   5

¢
COG

ONE-HALF CYCLE OF THE DOUBLE DANCE

D. THE DOUBLE DANCE SKATE CYCLE

The Photos (**1** through **6**) above illustrate *the First Half Cycle* of Double Dance. The second half cycle will be the mirror image of the one shown, namely the skier glides on the right ski, and skates on the left ski while executing a second double poling.

Double Dance is used primarily during fast skiing conditions but can also be used in variable rolling terrain by skiers with strong upper bodies. The technique begins with a quick and powerful double pole action, followed with a relatively long skate on one ski and a small skate angle.

FREQUENCY (NUMBER) refers to the number of full skate cycles per time unit (a minute or less), and varies with the speed and cycle distance.

High frequency is applied in a transition, from downhill to uphill, with short skate strides.

Low frequency is applied on the flat, in mild downhills, under fast snow conditions, with long skate strides.

CYCLE TIME (SECONDS) between three pole plants varies directly with the speed and glide distance on each skate.

4   5   6

(BETWEEN FIRST AND SECOND POLE PLANTS)

¢
COG

CYCLE DISTANCE (METERS), the distance skied between three pole plants, varies with the speed, the skate angle, and the glide length of each skate. A skier should be striving for optimum cycle distance that demands least energy and gives the highest average speed.

CYCLE SPEED (M/SEC) is simply another way of comparing speed of skiing, which, in Double Dance, depends on frequency and cycle distance. During touring, as well as racing, the skier should try to vary the cycle speed according to suitable terrain.

Vegard Ulvang, NOR, shown in the above photo sequence and in several other locations in this book is one of the recent outstanding champions in cross country skiing. He won individual Gold Medals in the 10 and 30 km Classic races in the 1992 Olympics, and three Golds in the Relays in the 1992 Olympics and World Championships 1991 and 1993.

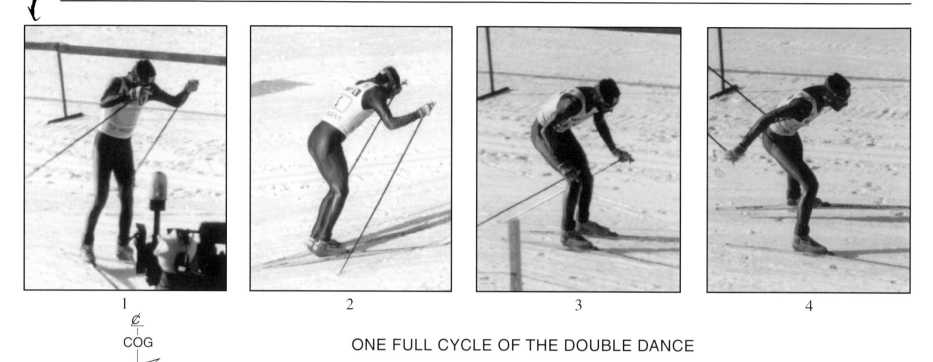

1   2   3   4

¢
|
COG   ONE FULL CYCLE OF THE DOUBLE DANCE
|
←

E.   BALANCE AND GROUND CONTACTS FOR THE DOUBLE DANCE

(In the above photos and description that follows, ***the first skate is on the left side.***)

In a Full Cycle of the Double Dance there are two Double Polings and two skates (a Double Poling for each skate). In the following, Balance and Number of Contacts for both skates (the first on the *left* ski/side and the second on the *right* ski/side) are discussed.

a.   Initially, during the preloading phases prior to the pole plant, the skier is gliding, fully in balance, on the *left* ski while the *right* ski is recovered (ONE POINT CONTACT) (Photos **8** and **1**).

b.   The poles are then planted while still in balance on the left ski

(THREE POINT CONTACT) (**1**, **2**).

c.   Immediately afterwards, during the pole pulling phase, the downset of the *right* ski takes place. (FOUR POINT CONTACT (**3**). This is an ideal time to make any adjustment with regard to balance, rhythm or coordination.

d.   The skier is briefly in partial balance on both skis immediately after the pole push-off, as the skate out on the *left* ski is finished. (TWO POINT CONTACT) (**3**, **4**).

e.   The *left* skate ski and both poles are now airborne, and the skier

FIGURE 8-11   **SKIER: GIORGIO VANZETTA, ITA**

5   6   7   8

¢
COG

(BETWEEN FIRST AND THIRD POLE PLANTS)

is in full balance on the *right* gliding ski, having completed the first skate on the *left* side (ONE POINT CONTACT) (**4**, **5**).

The skier has now completed the *First Half Cycle* of the Double Dance.

f.   As the skis come together, while in balance on the *right* gliding ski, the skier makes the second pole plant. (THREE POINT CONTACT) (**5**).

g.   Immediately afterwards, the downset and glide on the *left* ski takes place (FOUR POINT CONTACT) (**6**).

h.   The final pole push and the second skate are now executed on the *right* ski as the skier continues gliding on the *left* ski (TWO POINT CONTACT) (**7**).

i.   As the skier recovers the *right* ski, he is back to the beginning, in balance on the *left* ski (ONE POINT CONTACT) (**8**, **1**).

Note: Vanzetta is skiing at a very high speed with a fairly erect body, with very little vertical movement of COG. His hips and midsection arc well forward in the direction of the glide on a flat ski. The airborne skis are kept close to (sweeping) the surface. (Ch. 11, Sec. II-B-5). This is a good example of how to ski with least energy.

***Giorgio Vanzetta**, together with his Italian team mates, **Marco Albarello**, 43 year-old **Maurilio De Zolt** and anchor **Silvio Fauner,** won the Gold in the 1994 Olympic Relay. All four racers have been top world-class skiers for some years. At the 1987 World Championships, De Zolt won the 50 km Marathon and Albarello, the 15km Classic.*

	1	2	3	4
A. POLING ACTION:	FIRST DOUBLE POLING			RECOVERY
B. LEFT LEG ACTION:	(CONTINUE) SKATE			RECOVERY — LEGS
C. RIGHT LEG ACTION:	RECOVERY	DOWNSET OF SKI — GLIDE		

F. SEQUENTIAL PHASES OF MOVEMENTS FOR THE DOUBLE DANCE

1. POLING BY UPPER EXTREMITY

In a Full Cycle of the Double Dance there are two complete Double Polings, one for each of the two skates.

♦ *Pole Action Phase (for First Skate - on left ski) (Photos 1 - 4)*

   a. Initiation of Double Poling - Preloading of upper body muscles (Photo **1**) (Ch. 6).

   b. Pole Plant and Pole Action (**1 - 4**)
   Pole plant takes place immediately prior to downset of *right* ski.

   • Acute pole plant angle

   • Crowning of back, body weight on poles
   • Muscle action on poles
   • Sequence of action: Pull ⇒ Push ⇒ Release

♦ *Poling Recovery Phase (Photos 4, 5)*

   c. The poles now swing forward, following a path of their own gravity, simultaneously with the skate action recovery. In high frequency Double Dance, as shown, the recovery has to be very quick and precise.

♦ *Repeat above for Second Double Poling and Recovery (Photos 5 - 8)*

   The same procedure as outlined above is repeated for a Double Poling applied to the skate on the *right* ski, to make a Full Cycle of the Double Dance.

FIGURE 8-12   SKIER: LJUBOV JEGOROVA, RUS

| 5 | 6 | 7 | 8 |

> SECOND DOUBLE POLING > < RECOVERY >

TOGETHER > < DOWNSET OF SKI — GLIDE AND

AND   SKATE > < RECOVERY—LEGS TOGETHER

2. SKATING AND GLIDE ACTION BY LOWER EXTREMITY

In a Full Cycle of the Double Dance there are two skates, each starting immediately after a pole plant.

◆ *Skate Action Phase (for First Skate - on left ski) (Photos 1 - 4)*

  a. Initiation of Skate (**1**) - Legs together.
  b. Immediately after the pole plant, downset of *right* ski occurs and the skate on *left* ski begins (**2**).
  c. Glide and skate action on *left* ski (**2, 3**).
  d. Final push-off on (*left*) ski (**4**).

◆ *Skating Recovery Phase (Photos 4, 5)*

In the Double Dance recovery phase there is **no step forward** as in the other skate dances.

  e. Termination of First skate (on *left* ski) followed by recovery. Total body weight (COG) is transferred over to *right* ski (**4**).
  f. Legs come together, *left* ski is moved forward aerially and inward (see Skate Pattern Ch. 8, Sec. II-C) to become parallel with the gliding *right* ski (**5**).

◆ *Repeat Above for Second Skate and Recovery (5 - 8).*

The same Skate Action as outlined above for the first skate on the *left* ski is repeated for the second skate which is on the *right* ski, to make a Full Cycle of the Skate Action in the Double Dance.

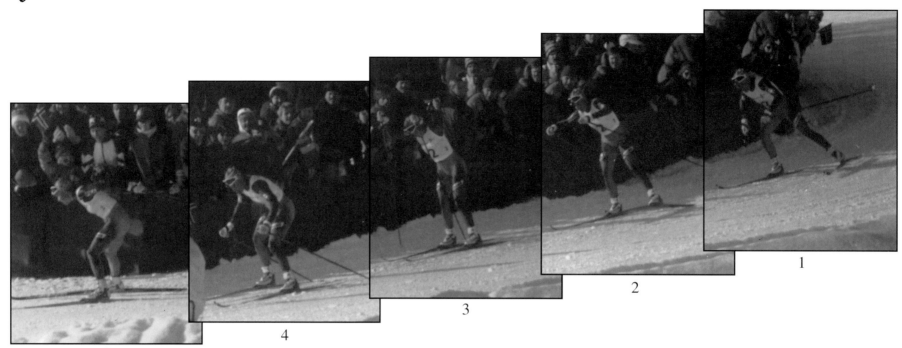

5   4   3   2   1

G. SKATING A CURVED DOWNHILL USING DOUBLE DANCE

To skate a curved, mild downhill applying the Double Dance to increase speed requires advanced technique, excellent balance, rhythm, and quick coordinated movement of poles and skis.

The photos above illustrate Manuela Di Centa rounding the curve into the Stadium in the Lillehammer Olympics, 1994, at a very high speed. She is applying the Double Dance very effectively in this difficult situation, probably one reason she won two Gold Medals in those Olympics!

The skate in the sharp turning point (**1**), where the centrifugal (outward) force is greatest, is to the outside of the curve, and then, as the curve terminates, the second skate is inward (**5**).

(See Ch. 7, Sec. II-B for an example of another technique used in skating a curve, the Marathon Skate, and Ch. 9, Fig. 9-22, for skating in low tuck without poling).

Manuela Di Centa, ITA, competed on the international circuit for more than a decade before winning her Olympic Gold Medals in 1994, in the 15 km Freestyle and 30 km Classic. She also won two Silver Medals in the 10 km Pursuit Classic and Pursuit overall, and was the 1994 Women's World Cup winner.

H. FACTORS CONTROLLING EFFECTIVE DOUBLE DANCE MOVEMENT

1. BODY AXES AND ALIGNMENT (SEE CH. 11, SEC. I-A-B)

2. LATERAL AND VERTICAL MOVEMENT OF COG

The body's COG for this technique, when correctly executed, moves little vertically, indicating a more efficient use of energy than many other skate techniques.

3. SKATE ANGLES

The Double Dance is a technique that allows for different skate frequencies, which will vary with the skate angle (as illustrated under the Skate Pattern, Ch. 8, Sec. II-C).

When skiing with fairly long skate strides, which is common when using the Double Dance on variable flat terrain, the skate angle is quite small. By increasing the frequency, the angle usually becomes larger, and the effective gliding skate force becomes greater. This suggests potentially higher speed can be achieved with the Double Dance when incorporating higher frequency with effective double poling for each skate stride.

4. MOVEMENT CHARACTERISTICS AND DANCE RHYTHM

The Double Dance technique is different than the other skate dances in timing and coordination of the body elements. The lateral, rhythmic movement of the COG has to be *fluid and smooth* when shifting weight precisely from one ski to the other, otherwise the skier will quickly be forced out of balance, interrupting the efficiency and rhythm of the technique.

Good balance is absolutely necessary for applying the Double Dance technique, since the skier is skiing with a One Point Contact, balanced on one ski, most of the time after completion of the double poling.

The pole plant provides a brief Three Point Contact balance. This takes place when the skis and legs come close together, while the skier is in an erect position, with the body's COG centered over the ankle for the Gliding Ski.

During the poling, the skier's balance is with a Four Point Contact (both skis and both poles) for an instant, while the skier transfers his COG from one ski to the other and his weight is partially on both skis. This brief Four Point Contact time period provides an excellent opportunity for the skier to readjust his body's COG, if needed, to regain a better balance before the pole push-off onto a One Point Contact skate.

During the short intervals of the Three and Four Point Contact, the skier should concentrate on efficiently applying maximum forces to the poles. In addition, while the skier is in balance on one ski (One Point Contact), the poles have to be swung forward with concentration on preloading and an efficient pole plant.

The movement of the body's COG during the first portion of the skate glide is gradually outward and forward onto the Skate ski. This skate movement creates momentum, which is another contribution to the forward speed; poling being the first one.

During the final skate push-off, the foot rolls slightly up on the ball of the foot, pushing the body's COG in the opposite direction, back to a balanced position over the ankle for the Gliding ski.

5. FRICTION AND THE GLIDE

Double Dance is an excellent example of applying body weight to poles before downset of the skis to minimize static (contact) friction. It is also a technique that can be executed mostly on a flat ski base (with very little edging of the ski). Altogether, Double Dance is probably the technique that can be executed with least frictional energy, and therefore has the potential for very high speed in suitable terrain (See Appendix, Sec. I).

I. ADVANTAGES AND DISADVANTAGES OF DOUBLE DANCE

Advantages:

The most efficient application of Double Dance is during fast conditions on flats and wide open terrain, mild long downhills and transitions from downhill to uphill, but a skier with a strong upper body can also use it with advantage in mild uphills. Double Dance is a technique that can be applied quickly and briefly in many terrain variations to relax certain muscles (such as the legs) when repeatedly using one technique (for example, the Paddle or the Single Dance).

Variable frequency of Double Poling is possible since it is applied to each skate. On flatter terrain skates can be done with smaller angles between the skis, which means the skier can actually ski an overall shorter distance from start to finish. (The actual skiing distance in direction of travel equals the length of the skate stride times cosine to the skate angle α) (Ch. 11, Sec. II-B-10). Because of the smaller angles between the skis, the Double Dance also requires less space for passing another skier or obstacle.

The technique gives more flat glide and time on each skate ski, which can generate more power and forward speed, when executed properly in certain types of terrain. The effect of the momentum (mv), in generating a long glide after termination of skate and pole forces, is another important factor (Ch. 11, Sec. II-B-9).

Many racers also have good results using the technique in mass starts of tour races and relays to gain a good start and position. To achieve this, a skier must train to develop quick rhythmic movements in the beginning with high frequency, powerful double poling and then gradually increase to longer skate glides.

Many of the recent Pursuit and Relay events in the World and Olympic Championships have shown skiers beating the competi- tion by a heart beat at the finish line because of their use and mastery of the Double Dance technique.

It should be noted that although the Double Dance is difficult to learn, being able to execute this skate efficiently helps mentally and technically with the other skate techniques. As already suggested, practicing Marathon Skating to both sides and the Double Dance together during training offers the best combination for achieving good results in ski skate dancing.

Disadvantages

The major disadvantage with the Double Dance is that it takes a lot of practice and patience to learn to execute the technique efficiently. Although it appears quite simple in definition and in viewing, it is undoubtedly the most difficult skate technique to execute correctly, that is illustrated in this text. The demand for perfect balance on one ski (One Point Contact) for a longer time, together with smooth rhythmic movement and gradual, efficient muscle force applied to the skiing equipment, is essential. To be in balance on one ski and initiate the double poling efficiently demands concentration, good coordination, strength, endurance, correct timing, and a harmonic dance rhythm.

However, a skier should not be discouraged from learning the Double Dance, for mastering it is a great accomplishment. Ultimately, the time spent on Double Dance will help a skier with other skate techniques.

Double Dance is not effective in steeper uphills when speed is slower because of the need for wider skate angles and for continuity of pole and skate action on each side to overcome uphill gravity forces (Ch. 11, Sec. II-D). In these circumstances the Paddle Dance will be the superior technique.

I. SUMMARY OF PROCEDURE AND SEQUENCE FOR DOUBLE DANCE

In the following First Half Cycle Of The Double Dance, the *left* ski is the skate ski (Fig. 8-11 and 8-12).

1. **Initiation (1 Point Contact)**
   a. Skis parallel, body weight on the gliding *left* ski
   b. Legs together
   c. Body erect

2. **Upper Extremity - Pole Plant (3 Point Contact)**
   a. Preloading of muscles
   b. Upper extremity weighting the poles
   c. Pole action starts (while gliding on *left* ski)

3. **Lower Extremity - Skate Begins (4 Point Contact)**
   a. Downset and partial weight transfer onto *right* ski
   b. Skate begins on *left* ski
   c. Slight flex in the knees

4. **Body Movement - Skate In Progress (4 Point Contact)**
   a. COG moves laterally and slightly down, toward *left* skate ski
   b Long smooth skate with little edging
   c. All movement and action is forward

5. **Pole Pull And Push Action (From 4 to 2 Points Contact)**
   a. Quick, explosive power by upper extremity
   b. Relax arms immediately with pole release

6 **Final Skate Push Action (From 2 to 1 Point Contact)**
   a. Glide on right ski, skate push off on *left* ski
   b. Leg extension
   c. Release of *left* ski

7. **Mid Section Forward Momentum (1 Point Contact)**
   a. Continue glide on *right* ski
   b. COG moved slightly up and laterally over to *right* ski, body erect

8. **Pole Recovery (1 Point of Contact)**
   a. Continue glide on *right* ski
   b. Relax upper extremity completely
   c. Quick forward swing of arms and poles

9. **Skate Recovery (1 Point Contact)**
   a. *Left* skate ski moves aerially inward and forward, close to surface
   b. Left ski becomes parallel with the *right* gliding ski
   c. Entire balance on *right* gliding ski

This completes the First Half Cycle of the Double Dance.

Repeat above items (1 through 9) for the opposite ski (right),for the Second Half Cycle.

CHAPTER 8
III. THE PADDLE DANCE

Figure 8-14 10 km Pursuit, "Mørderbakken" (Killer Hill), World Championships, Falun, SWE, 1993, which Dæhlie won by a photo finish "heartbeat"

Skiers from front to back:

Bib #4 Bjørn Dæhlie, NOR (front), Gold Medalist

  #2 Vladimir Smirnov, KAZ, Silver Medalist

  #3 Vegard Ulvang, NOR

  #1 Sture Sivertsen, NOR

III.   THE PADDLE DANCE

CONTENTS

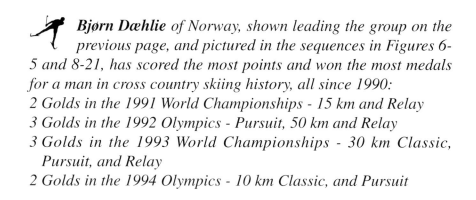

Bjørn Dæhlie *of Norway, shown leading the group on the previous page, and pictured in the sequences in Figures 6-5 and 8-21, has scored the most points and won the most medals for a man in cross country skiing history, all since 1990:*
2 Golds in the 1991 World Championships - 15 km and Relay
3 Golds in the 1992 Olympics - Pursuit, 50 km and Relay
3 Golds in the 1993 World Championships - 30 km Classic, Pursuit, and Relay
2 Golds in the 1994 Olympics - 10 km Classic, and Pursuit

III. THE PADDLE DANCE

A. INTRODUCTION

The name, **Paddle Dance** Skate, is derived from the similarity of the skier's upper body motion to that of a canoe paddler. While the Diagonal is the premier technique in Classic skiing, the Paddle Dance has been the most widely used in skating, although it is not necessarily always the most effective. It is a superior technique in steep uphills.

The Paddle Dance involves alternate skating on each leg, combined with a slightly staggered double poling for every second skate. While for most Two-Side Skating techniques the body has a line of symmetry, with balanced skating to each side, the Paddle Dance is markedly *asymmetrical.*

The rhythm may be characterized as a dance, with a relaxed lateral hip motion created by the skier's skating, first on one ski, then rhythmically in a forward step movement onto the other. This rhythmic "climbing a stairs" movement in the uphill is particularly unique to the Paddle Dance.

B. DEFINITION OF THE PADDLE DANCE

The Paddle is a two-sided asymmetrical skate technique, consisting of two action sides, a *Drive side* (with a trailing ski), and a *Hang side* (with the lead ski), legs and arms working independently.

The *Hang side* of the upper body characteristically "hangs" on the pole arm. The opposite side, the *Drive side,* executes a forceful drive onto the ski skate causing a "roll-over" of the body from the *Drive side* to the *Hang side.*

The skate cycle begins with the body erect, upper back crowned slightly forward, stomach in, hips forward, and skis in a V formation, slightly staggered. The laterally inclined pole on the Drive side, with the handle moved inward in front of the body, is planted slightly ahead of the pole on the Hang side, which is lifted higher up, to the head, and planted at a steeper angle.

During the staggered pole plants, the COG and the skating is transferred from the Drive ski to the Hang ski. At the time of the final pole push-off, the skating is shifted back to the Drive ski with a step forward. Meanwhile recovery, with a forward swing of poles and step forward on the Hang ski, takes place as the skier prepares for another staggered double pole plant.

C. DIFFERENCES BETWEEN PADDLE AND SINGLE DANCES

There are several very noticeable differences between the Paddle Dance and Single Dance as follows:

1. In the Paddle Dance, when seen from the front, the movement is asymmetrical. The body is divided into a Hang side and a Drive side, each side working independently. In the Single Dance, there is no Hang side.

2. In the Paddle Dance, uneven forces are applied to the Hang side and Drive side poles, while in Single Dance, the pole plants and forces are symmetrical.

3. The pole plants in the Paddle Dance are slightly staggered, with one taking place at the end of a skate and the other delayed, planted just before or together with the downset of the next ski. Straight Double Poling in Single Dance is a typical synchronized Classic technique, with both poles planted at the same time at the end of a skate.

4. There are distinguishable differences between the two techniques in rhythm and movement characteristics.

D. DIVISION OF BODY AND TERMINOLOGY FOR THE PADDLE DANCE

The *Body Division Axis* (T-T) divides the body into two sides (Drive side and Hang side). Also see Paddle Dance Skate Pattern (Ch. 8, Sec. III-E).

TERMINOLOGY FOR PADDLE DANCE

♦ **Drive Side** - The side of the body axis T-T where the first action (initiation) cycle of the Paddle Dance skate takes place.

1. Drive Leg - The leg on the Drive side that mobilizes the skate push on the Drive Side.

2. Drive Hip - The hip on the Drive side which initiates motion of the skate push.

3. Drive Foot - The foot of the Drive leg transferring skate push forces to the ski.

4. Drive Arm - The arm that guides the pole on the Drive side.

5. Drive Ski - The trailing ski.

6. Drive Pole - The pole planted first (laterally inclined).

7. Drive Ski Angle - The angle between Direction of Skiing (DOS) and the Drive ski.

♦ **Hang Side** - The side of the body axis (opposite the Drive side), where the second action (termination) of the Paddle Dance skate takes place.

1. Hang Leg - The leg of the Hang side mobilizing the skate push onto the Hang side.

2. Hang Hip - The hip on the Hang side.

3. Hang Foot - The foot on the Hang side transferring the leg forces to the ski.

4. Hang Arm - The arm that guides the pole on the Hang side.

5. Hang Ski - The lead ski.

6. Hang Pole - The pole plant (slightly delayed).

7. Hang Ski Angle - The angle between DOS and the Hang ski.

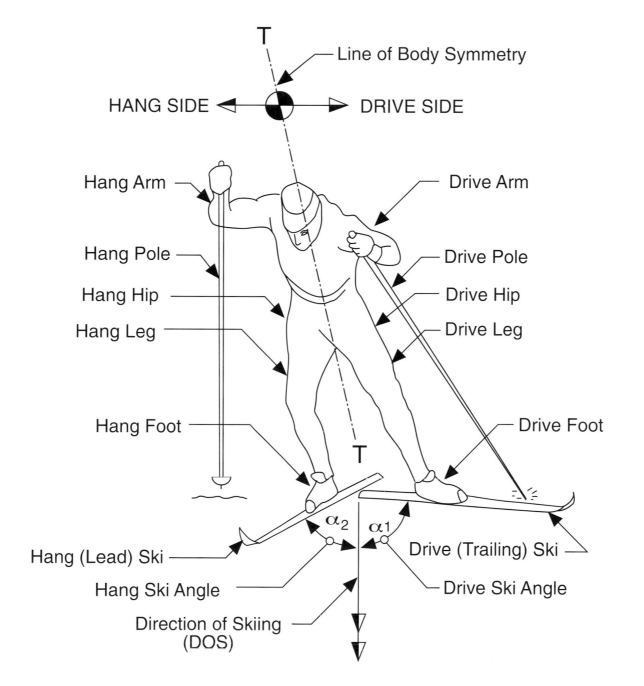

T

Line of Body Symmetry

HANG SIDE ← → DRIVE SIDE

Hang Arm

Drive Arm

Hang Pole

Drive Pole

Hang Hip

Drive Hip

Hang Leg

Drive Leg

Hang Foot

Drive Foot

T

α_2 $\alpha 1$

Hang (Lead) Ski

Drive (Trailing) Ski

Hang Ski Angle

Drive Ski Angle

Direction of Skiing
(DOS)

E. THE PADDLE DANCE SKATE PATTERN

The imprint of One Cycle of the Paddle Dance Skate in the snow would be as illustrated here. The Paddle Skates shown have a slightly longer glide on the Drive ski than on the Hang ski because of the more forceful action of the Hang side. If there is a side slope (the Hang side is normally the uphill side), the glide difference may be considerable. The Drive ski, therefore, has a smaller skate angle (α_1), to follow the Direction of skiing (DOS).

The Paddle Dance Skate Pattern is also characterized by slightly staggered pole plants. The pole on the Drive side is planted a split second before the pole on the Hang side. The pole plant on the Hang side takes place immediately prior to, or simultaneously with, the downset of the Hang ski. The pole plant on the Hang side is at the heel of the boot, and on the Drive side, at the toe.

The "Step Forward" in the Paddle is extremely important in effective "Paddling", particularly in the uphills. The step is the longest of all skating techniques.

The skate angle (α) varies, but becomes considerably larger in the steeper uphills. As the photos and illustration of the Skate Pattern show, there is little time for recovery in the Paddle Dance. Arms and legs are working independently, asymmetrically.

Anfissa Retsova, RUS, won several Gold Medals in World Championship and Olympic races from 1985 to 1992, in both biathlon and cross country.

SYMBOLS FOR PADDLE DANCE SKATE PATTERN

⊙	Pole Plant on Drive Side (Light gray)
◖	Pole Plant on Hang Side (Dark gray)
▷	Downset of Drive Ski (Light gray)
▶	Downset of Hang Ski (Dark gray)
▷	Glide on Skis (White)
--▶	Direction of skiing (DOS)
α_1	Angle between DOS and Drive ski
α_2	Angle between DOS and Hang ski
◠	Boot position during Downset of ski
◡	Boot position during Release of ski
⌣	Aerial path of boot during recovery

Figure 8-16: 4 Sequential photos of Anfissa Retsova, RUS,

The photos correspond to the Skate Pattern for One Cycle of Paddle Dance. Retsova's Hang side is her *right* side.

(1) Pole plants, sequentially, *left* side first, with skate off Drive ski -Transfer of weight from Drive to Hang ski.

(2) Pole pull, glide and skate on Hang ski - Recovery of Drive ski.

(3) Step forward and transfer of weight to glide and skate on Drive ski - Release and recovery of Hang ski and both poles.

(4) Preparation for second pole plants - step forward with weight shift to Hang ski.

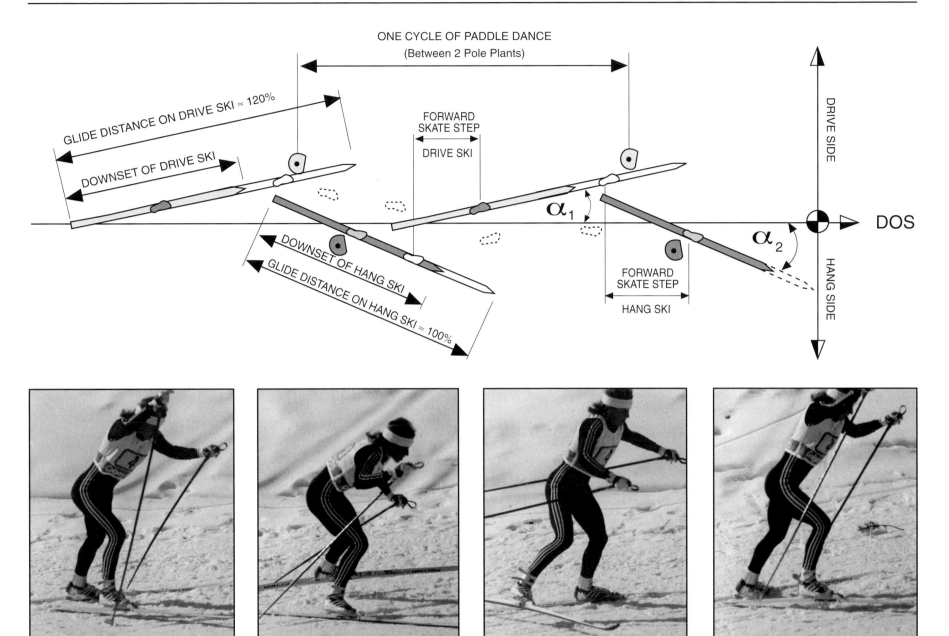

1   2   3

¢
COG

ONE CYCLE OF THE PADDLE DANCE

F.   THE PADDLE DANCE SKATE CYCLE

The Paddle Dance Cycle begins with the pole plant on the Drive side, and includes the motion the skier goes through until the same pole is planted again. The skier may change the stride pattern by doing, for example, 10 cycles with the right ski as the Hang ski and then 10 cycles where the left is the Hang ski.

In Photos (1) through (6), the Paddle Dance Cycle is illustrated by Larissa Lazutina, RUS, (Bib #1), Gold medalist in the 5 km Classic and Relay in the World Championships, Falun, SWE, 1993, and Gold in the Relay in the Lillehammer Olympics, NOR, 1994.

Lazutina is planting her *right* pole on the Drive side a fraction of a second prior to the pole plant on the Hang side *(left)*. Her upper extremity then goes through a complete double poling cycle until the Drive pole is again planted (**6**). During this cycle the skier has made one skate on each of the Drive and the Hang skis.

FREQUENCY (NUMBER) is the number of skate cycles per time unit (a minute or less). The frequency in the Paddle varies greatly with the individual skier, terrain variation and speed of skiing.

4   5   6

(BETWEEN TWO POLE PLANTS ON THE SAME SIDE)

₵
COG

CYCLE TIME (SECONDS) is controlled *by the poling* in steep uphills and on slow snow, and *the longer glide on the skis* on variable flat and fast terrain.

> The unique synchronization of staggered poling with skating enables the skier to execute more skates per Cycle Time than any other skating technique, making it the fastest and most efficient under many conditions, particularly in the uphills.

CYCLE DISTANCE (METERS) is the distance skied between two consecutive pole plants on the Drive side. It is measured between the exact locations of the body's COG at the time of the pole plants.

The glide on the Drive ski by elite skiers is normally 10 to 20% longer than on the Hang ski. The Cycle Distance varies greatly with steepness of terrain (being much shorter in the steep uphills), snow conditions, skier's individual technique, strength and energy resources.

CYCLE SPEED (M/SEC) is related to the Frequency and the Cycle Distance. In the uphills the frequency is high, and the cycle distance is short. On variable flat terrain and in fast conditions, the opposite is true. In terrain where speed becomes very fast, most top skiers switch to Single Dance with poling every second skate, a technique described earlier in this chapter in Section I.

1

2

3

G.   BALANCE AND GROUND CONTACTS FOR THE PADDLE DANCE

The Paddle Dance is distinctive in that each element (skis, poles, arms, shoulders and hips) works independently. Skiers, therefore have to have very good coordination to "paddle" effectively.

The Paddle Dance demands a strong upper body for the poling and a very high frequency of skate leg motion, with little recovery time for each skate cycle. In steep uphills, where recovery time is further reduced, it can be quickly fatiguing.

The photos and descriptions for the Paddle are very detailed. It is the most complicated technique in this book, but it is one of the techniques that offers superior stability and balance during execution, making it most attractive to the novice skater. Stability is superior because the staggered poling and skating provides several points of contact (Ch. 3) most of the time.

In the above photo sequence, Stephania Belmondo, ITA, is shown, winning a gold medal in the 10 km Pursuit in the World Championships, Falun, SWE, 1993. She efficiently uses the Paddle Dance technique in an uphill, with a side slope down to her left. Her *right* side is the Hang side.

6

5

4

a. Immediately prior to the pole plants, the Paddle has ONE POINT CONTACT when gliding on the Drive ski, Photos (**1, 6**) (see Phases of Movement, next page).

b. The Drive pole (*left*) is then planted, with a lateral incline, very briefly making a TWO POINT CONTACT on the Drive side, creating an imbalance that moves the skier's COG over to the Hang side (not shown here, see Fig. 8-19 and 8-22, Photo 2).

c. The Hang pole is then planted (THREE POINT CONTACT) followed by the downset of the Hang ski which is moved a step forward uphill and makes a full FOUR POINT CONTACT (a very stable balance position) that lasts very briefly (**2**).

d. A skate push off the Drive ski, with a continuation of double poling and skate on Hang ski reduces the balance to a THREE POINT CONTACT, which lasts a relatively long time (**3**).

e. After the final double pole push, the skier makes a step uphill, onto the Drive ski, and both skis briefly make a TWO POINT CONTACT (**4**) (also see Fig. 8-21 and 8-22, Photo 6).

f. During the pole recovery, the skier skates powerfully off the Hang ski, with a long glide on the Drive ski which brings us back to the beginning (ONE POINT CONTACT) (**5, 6**).

Stephania Belmondo, *ITA, a newcomer to racing has mastered all techniques. In a short time, she has won two Golds (the Pursuit and the 30 km Classic) in the 1993 World Championships and a Gold (the 30 km Classic) in the 1992 Olympics.*

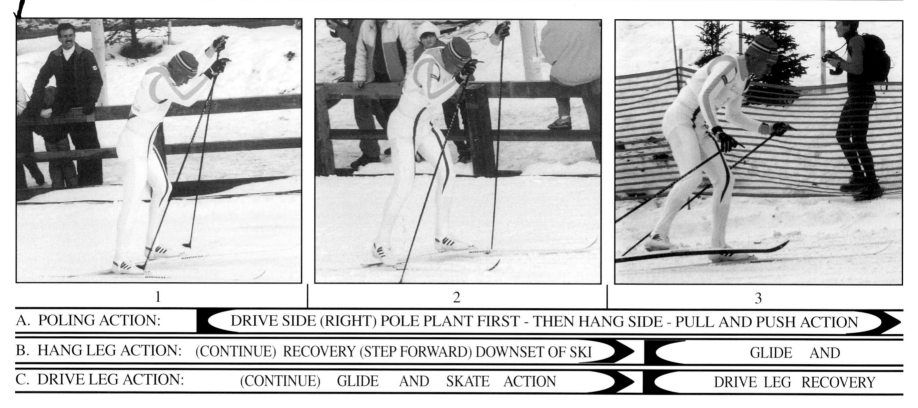

| 1 | 2 | 3 |

A. POLING ACTION:	DRIVE SIDE (RIGHT) POLE PLANT FIRST - THEN HANG SIDE - PULL AND PUSH ACTION	
B. HANG LEG ACTION:	(CONTINUE) RECOVERY (STEP FORWARD) DOWNSET OF SKI	GLIDE AND
C. DRIVE LEG ACTION:	(CONTINUE) GLIDE AND SKATE ACTION	DRIVE LEG RECOVERY

H. SEQUENTIAL PHASES OF MOVEMENT FOR THE PADDLE DANCE

The photos illustrate sequential phases of movement for one complete Paddle Dance Cycle (**Photos 1-6-1**) by the well known Olympic and World Champion, Gunde Svan, SWE, during one of his many victories.

The **Bar Charts** below the photos correspond to the beginning and end of each action by Upper and Lower Extremities.

♦ **The Upper Extremity** during the Paddle is primarily involved with:

• A powerful double poling action in the cycle's first half, and
• Recovery in the cycle's second half

Although the skis and poles are slightly staggered, the poling phase basically is a double poling sequence where the arm forces are applied to both poles simultaneously (Ch. 6).

FIGURE 8-19   **SKIER: GUNDE SVAN, SWE**

4	5	6

POLING   RECOVERY

SKATE   ACTION   HANG   LEG   RECOVERY

STEP   FORWARD   —   DOWNSET   OF   SKI   DRIVE LEG GLIDE AND SKATE ACTION

♦ **_The Lower Extremity_** has a continuity of actions, first on the Hang side (Left), then on the Drive side (right) as follows:

- Glide and skate on Hang ski (Left side)
- Glide and Skate on Drive ski (Right side)

The bar chart shows there is a recovery of each skating leg, however, the forward upward step, particular in steep uphills, demands a lot of energy.

The sequential phases of movement for **_One Cycle_** will be analyzed and described in the following order:

1. *Pole Action Phases - Upper Extremity*
2. *Leg Skate Action Phases - Lower Extremity*
3. *Paddle Recovery Phases*

The three phase actions take place almost simultaneously, but for simplicity, the descriptions are separated.

Note: The photos on these two pages and the previous two are coordinated so references to photos in the following front view (F) also refer to the same numbered photo of the side view on the previous two pages.

| 1F | 2F | 3F |

1. POLE ACTION PHASES - UPPER EXTREMITY

◆ **HANG SIDE** *(left)* **and DRIVE SIDE** *(right)*

Poling Force Action takes place primarily when the skier is in glide on the Hang ski. It is important to weight the body eccentrically onto the pole arm at the time of the pole plant to reduce contact (static) friction during downset of the ski (Appendix, Sec. I-C). Poling forces should be directed parallel to the glide direction of the Hang ski Photos (**1-4**) and (**1F-4F**). During the "Poling Recovery" the skier should prevent the pole baskets from swinging up too high, controlling the swing momentum so poles remain approximately parallel with the ground. Swinging the baskets too high changes timing, rhythm and sequence. The pole recovery takes place when the skier is shifting weight from Hang to Drive ski (**5, 6, 1**)(**4F, 5F, 6F**).

a. Preparation - higher lifting of Hang than Drive arm, preloading (crowning)of upper back and shoulder muscles, elbows down (**1, 1F**).

b. Acute and laterally inclined pole plant angle for Drive pole, which is planted slightly before Hang pole. Hang pole is planted with steeper incline, momentarily ahead of downset of Hang ski (**2**).

c. Arm **pulling** on both poles (**3, 2F**).

d. Maximum force and impulse action by upper body muscles with elbows at 90° angle.

e. Arm **pushing** forces on both poles (**3, 3F**) begin as elbows reach side of body and open up.

f. End of pole forces - release of both poles (**4, 4F**).

g. Suspension of poles (**6, 6F**), relaxation of upper body, poling recovery - forward swing (**6, 6F**).

Repeat of "**a**" through "**g**" for next Cycle.

| **4F** | **5F** | **6F** |

2. SKATE ACTION PHASES - LOWER EXTREMITY

♦ **HANG LEG (*left* Side)**

a. Step forward uphill, preparation for smooth downset of ski, advancement of Hang hip. Weighting of Hang pole immediately prior to downset of ski reduces static friction (**1, 1F**).

b. Body weight (COG) is shifted to the Hang ski (**3, 2F**), compressing (closing) all Hang side's lower limb joints (hip, knee and ankle), with slight give at the knee (eccentric muscle action) (Ch. 4, Sec. II-D).

c. Glide on flat Hang ski base (**4, 3F**).

d. Edging of Hang ski and final skate push-off (**5, 4F**).

e. Extension of leg and release of Hang ski from snow (**5F**).

f. Suspension of ski, and unweighting and relaxing (opening) of joints (hip, knee, ankle) (**6, 6F**).

g. Hang leg recovery, legs come together with inward and forward step movement of ski (**6, 1, 6F**)..

Repeat of "**a**" through "**g**" for next Cycle.

♦ **DRIVE LEG (*right* Side)**

a. Step forward uphill, preparation for downset of ski, forward advancement of Drive hip (**4, 5, 3F**).

b. Gradual, smooth contact with flat base of Drive ski (**5**).

c. The body weight (COG) is shifted to Drive ski, causing compression of all lower limb joints (hip, knee and ankle), with a slight give in the knee (**5, 4F**).

d. Glide on a flat ski base (**6, 5F**).

e. Forward movement of hips, extension of Drive leg (**6, 6F**).

f. Beginning of skate on Drive ski (**6, 1, 6F**).

g. Continue skate on Drive ski, preparation and planting of Drive pole (**1, 2, 1F, 2F**).

h. Final skate push off Drive ski and release of ski (**2, 3, 2F** and **3F**). Relaxation, lower limb joints on Drive side now open up (**3, 4,** and **3F**).

i. Drive leg suspension and recovery, legs come together with inward and forward uphill step movement of ski (**4, 5**).

Repeat of "**a**" through "**i**" for the next Cycle.

3. PADDLE RECOVERY PHASES

♦ **DRIVE SIDE (*right*) and HANG SIDE (*left*)**

The Paddle Recovery can readily be seen in the bar chart below the side view photos on the preceding two pages.

a. Drive and Hang Side Pole Recovery (**4, 5, 6**)(**4F, 5F, 6F**).

b. Hang Side Skate Recovery (**6, 1, 2**)(**5F, 6F, 1F**).

c. Drive Side Skate Recovery (**3, 4, 5**)(**2F, 3F**).

ADDITIONAL EXAMPLES OF SEQUENTIAL PHASES OF MOVEMENT FOR ONE CYCLE OF THE PADDLE DANCE (FRONT VIEW — STEEP UPHILL)

Photos of the two skiers are taken from the same spot during the 10km Pursuit in "Langbakken" (the steep, long hill). Lillehammer Olympics, NOR, 1994. Note that skiers are doing the sequence in opposite order. Bib #1 applies his right side as the Hang side while Bib #2 uses his left side as the Hang side.

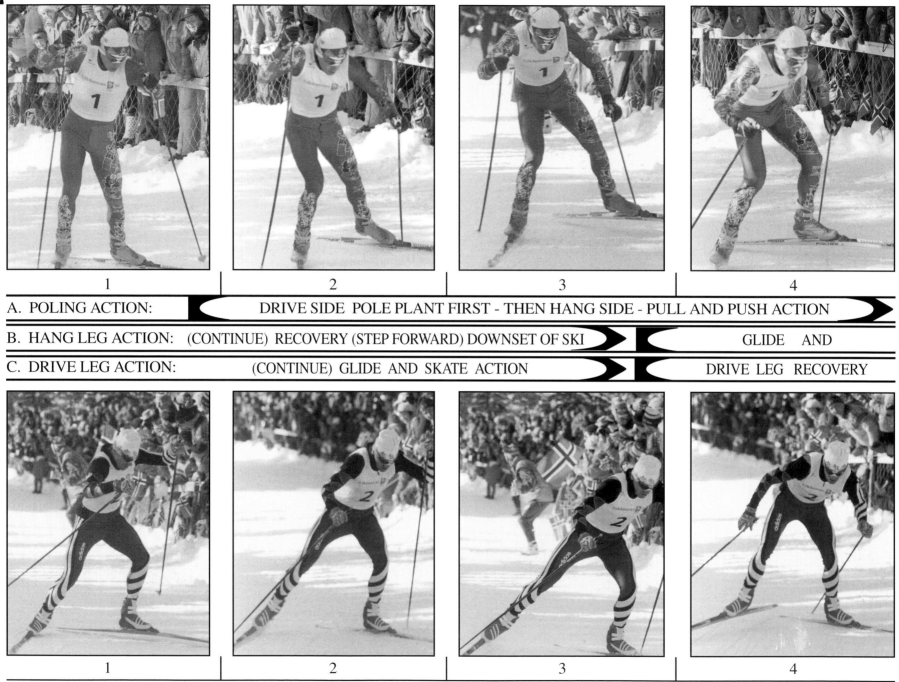

1	2	3	4

A. POLING ACTION: DRIVE SIDE POLE PLANT FIRST - THEN HANG SIDE - PULL AND PUSH ACTION

B. HANG LEG ACTION: (CONTINUE) RECOVERY (STEP FORWARD) DOWNSET OF SKI   GLIDE AND

C. DRIVE LEG ACTION: (CONTINUE) GLIDE AND SKATE ACTION   DRIVE LEG RECOVERY

1	2	3	4

POLING   RECOVERY

SKATE   ACTION   HANG LEG RECOVERY

STEP   FORWARD — DOWNSET   OF   SKI   DRIVE LEG GLIDE AND SKATE ACTION

I. *FACTORS CONTROLLING EFFECTIVE PADDLE DANCE MOVEMENT*

1. BODY AXES AND ALIGNMENT

Paddle Dance skate technique is asymmetrical in both poling and skating, and also between left and right sides during execution. This makes the technique complicated to learn correctly.

There is a marked rotation of the upper body, first in the direction of glide on the Drive ski, and then in the direction of the glide on the Hang ski (Ch. 11, Sec. I-B).

Although hip and shoulder alignments are parallel at the initiation, there is a marked difference in orientation during execution of the poling. The hip alignment, one of the most crucial concerns in learning effective "paddling", rotates noticeably, with a marked forward extension of the hip on the Drive side during the glide on that ski, then a similar extension of the Hang hip during the glide on the Hang ski. The trunk line is kept fairly straight, with a forward lean of the whole body. When in erect body position there should be very little bending at the hips.

2. LATERAL AND VERTICAL MOVEMENT OF COG

Although there is significant lateral movement of COG in the Paddle Dance, minimize this during training and *focus action more in the Direction of Skiing* (DOS) (the Z-Z axis). Even if this initially may produce less speed, eventually it will be beneficial. See Chapter 11, Sec. II-B-4 for a discussion of the factors that effect the amount of lateral movement.

During each skate cycle, particularly in the steep uphills, the body's COG moves significantly up and down. Since this is one of the important factors that use considerable energy, a skier should strive for a technique that minimizes this movement. (As outlined in Chapter 11, Sec. II-B-6, the vertical movement of COG is a function of four factors). The energy demand during vertical movement of COG may be compared to weightlifting where one's own body is the weight.

3. SKATE ANGLES

The Skate Angle is defined here as the angle between one skate ski, and the Direction of Skiing (see Skate Pattern, Ch. 8, Sec III-E). The skate angles for the Hang (lead) ski, and the Drive (trailing) ski within one skate cycle are different. Since the glide on the Drive ski normally is longer than on the Hang ski, the angle for the Hang ski is larger.

The magnitude of each skate angle will vary with:

- Steepness of slope
- Angles of side slopes
- Snow conditions
- Speed of skiing
- Efficiency of Double Poling
- Length of step forward
- Space available along skiing course
- The upper body strength and joint flexibility of the skier

a. *On Flats and Variable Terrain*

When skating at fairly high speeds on flats, transitions, or in mild uphills, the skier should use small skate angles, in order to ski a shorter total distance. As speed increases, the glide distance on each ski becomes longer and the skate angle is made smaller (see Ch. 11, Sec.II-B-10).

Often the skate angle depends on the space available along the skiing course. If the space is quite narrow, the skier has to make the skate angle smaller and the skate stride shorter and more powerful.

b. *Uphill Energy*

When skating steep uphills, the skier has to overcome gravity forces of body and equipment due to elevation differences. Gaining vertical elevation during skating uses a lot of energy, and the skier naturally increases the skate angle to reduce the vertical slope of the gliding skis and to clear the tails of his skis.

When skating uphills, the total glide distances (sum of the length of all the glide steps) are comparably much longer than using Classic Diagonal technique, depending on the skate angle and the length of the forward step.

c. Muscle Strain

The strain on the inside of the leg muscles (abductor) and the hip joints (gluteus muscles) suggest that a smaller skate angle is more energy efficient, considering other factors (such as speed) equal. However, during steep uphills, a smaller angle may demand too much energy, so the skier must use judgment gained in training and competition to select the most efficient skate angle.

4. MOVEMENT CHARACTERISTICS AND DANCE RHYTHM

a. Weight Shift

In the Paddle Dance, body weight (COG) is repetitiously shifted laterally back and forth between the two skis in a very relaxed, fluid motion. During the transfer, weight is on both skis for a short time, when the skier prepares for the double pole plant.

As noted in the photo sequences, elite skiers skate with a High Center of Gravity (HCOG), with relatively little vertical motion. During most of the cycle the body is nearly erect. A strong step forward is made when preparing for the pole plant. The powerful pole plant is initiated with a crowned back. Hips are moved up and forward, as the COG is shifted over to the Hang ski, which makes a shorter skate glide than on Drive ski.

At the final pole push-off, weight is shifted quickly over to the opposite Drive ski by a hip motion and a powerful skate push-off to the side by the Hang ski.

b. Hip, Knee And Ankle Motion

Keeping the hips loose for lateral and forward motion, and small rotations, is one of the important aspects of skating relaxed and efficiently. During the final double poling push-off, the hips are shoved forward with stomach contracted. Angling the ankle, knee and hip to the outside enables the downset of the ski to be on the *outside edge*. The knee should also be slightly forward of the ankle at all times (Ch. 11, Sec. I-B-3).

During the poling recovery, when the skier is in an erect position, just prior to the pole plants, the body weight (COG) is shifted over to the Hang ski by means of a slight forward rotation of the Hang hip.

Excessive knee flexing during the Paddle Dance is a waste of energy. However, to be able to skate-push outwards, there has to be a slight roll or flexing at the knees. A slightly flexed knee can generate a greater force during the skate action. To gain a relatively long uphill step forward, as is required in the Paddle Dance, the knee has to be projected forward.

There should be very little lateral movement of the shin and ankle during the glide. They should be primarily in line with the glide of the ski. Lateral movement of ankle and knee is one of the chief causes of skating injuries.

c. Preloading Of Leg And Hip Muscles - Eccentric Muscle Action

Sideways and forward **hip motion** is used for preloading of the outward gliding skate which increases the skate force when used properly. Otherwise, this force has to come from increased leg action which has less muscle mass and requires more energy.

Automatic leg muscle preloading is achieved by a perfect weight shift, moving the body's COG completely from one ski to the other, laterally and forward, in the direction of each skate.

To achieve an even better skate, the hip and leg muscles should be preloaded (slightly contracted). The knee is then flexed and moved forward at the initiation of the skate glide. Without preloading there will be a dead, weak skate action.

d. The Stairstep Principle - Rhythmic Stepping Uphill

The Paddle Dance uphill is a continuous rhythmic movement similar to walking up a stairway taking two steps at a time while angulating the feet outward. Attempt to make the step forward long for both legs. Using harmonic rhythmic movement will also increase forward speed. However, the step distance may vary slightly with terrain, speed, frequency and the individual skier.

5. FRICTION / GLIDE

The subject, friction, has been dealt with in the Appendix in detail. Here it is related to the Paddle Dance.

The Paddle Dance's staggered double poling push generates a strong thrust to the lead ski, but has a diminishing effect as the glide and skate continues onto the trailing ski. (Frictional resistance is first encountered under the full skate glide for the lead ski, and then additional frictional resistance is added for the skate glide on the trailing ski). Therefore, from one double pole plant to the next, the skier is decelerating, due to the continuous frictional gliding, as well as aerial resistance.

If the terrain is a side slope, the **Hang side is normally the uphill side**, and therefore, requires partially more vertical body lift than the Drive side. Reducing the time and glide distance on the Hang side, theoretically, will reduce the amount of gravitational and frictional energy demand.

The following topics can be studied under the Appendix, Sec. I:
- Stationary Friction (C-2)
- Gliding Friction (C-3)
- Gliding on Flat Ski Base (C-6)
- Gliding on Edged Ski (C-6)

6. SPEED, EFFICIENCY AND MOMENTUM

Similar to the Classic Diagonal and double poling strides, it is important to have long extended glides when skating. A study of top skaters indicates that the skier with a longer stride cycle has an **average higher speed.** The requirement for a long cycle in the Paddle Dance is that effective power is applied during the double poling, as well as an effective impulse action during the extended skate push. Impulse (the change in momentum) is defined here as the average effective skate force multiplied by the time span of the skate push force (Ch 11, Sec. II-B-9).

J. ADVANTAGES AND DISADVANTAGES OF PADDLE DANCE

Advantages:

Paddle Dance is a technique that can be applied in most terrain, depending on the skill of the skier. Among elite skiers, it is practiced primarily in the uphills, because the extended continuity of pole and skate action aids in overcoming gravity and friction forces. The movement and rhythm, similar to "climbing a stairs", makes it ideal for uphill skiing.

In skiing competition, where uphills often dominate, the skier who effectively masters the Paddle Dance and its variations places consistently at the top.

Because the staggered pole plants and several points of contact offer superior stability and balance, it is especially attractive to the novice skier.

Disadvantages:

The Paddle Dance is an asymmetric technique and more complicated in detail than most other skating techniques, and therefore can be harder to learn correctly. To develop the coordination necessary to become good in the Paddle, a lot of time has to be devoted to practicing it in the uphills.

The Paddle Dance, when used on steep hills, demands extra energy because of its high frequency of leg motion and little recovery time during its cycle. A skier needs to have a strong upper body and be in very good physical condition to effectively use it in uphills.

Some skiers seem to develop their own "personal" Paddle style, which may not necessarily be the most effective one. The technique is primarily adapted to uphill skiing as outlined, but many skiers seem to automatically and unconsciously apply the Paddle to any type of terrain. Other techniques are more efficient and are faster on variable level and mild downhill terrain.

K. VARIATIONS OF THE PADDLE DANCE

There are several individual variations of the Paddle Dance, some of which depend on the individual skier's physical characteristics, flexibility, balance, coordination, and ability to execute the technique. On the following two pages, two variations are discussed that deviate significantly from the Basic Paddle Dance:

1. Mogren's Paddle
2. Paddle Dance Hop

These photos show Torgny Mogren of Sweden in the 4x10 Olympic Relay, in Canmore, CAN, 1988, where his team won the Gold Medal. This variation is quite unique and effective and should become an important approach in the execution of **advanced** Paddle Dance in the future. The key to the success of Mogren's variation lies in that he finishes the Double Poling at an earlier stage than most other elite skiers.

While gliding on the Drive ski, Mogren plants pole on the Drive side early, and then immediately afterwards, prior to weighting the Hang ski, he plants the Hang pole (**1**). The double poling is then completed during the early phase of glide on the Hang ski (**2**). After release of the poles, he effectively applies the large hip muscles to generate a much longer and powerful skate on the Hang side (**3**). The Hang side skate thus gives a greater impulse F(t), producing an overall higher average speed of skiing. The momentum from the long powerful skate onto the Hang side has further positive effects, as it contributes to a longer glide on the Drive ski (**4**) (Ch. 11, Sec. II-9).

4

3

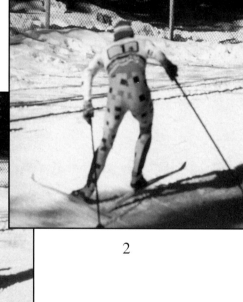

2

1

Altogether, Mogren's individual approach in execution of the Paddle Dance is different than generally practiced and taught. Through mechanical analysis, the author finds it to be very effective. Mogren's variation conforms with the author's theory on how to minimize frictional energy (Appendix I) with early weighting of the Hang Pole prior to, or simultaneously with, downset of the Hang ski. Other requirements, such as good continuity, smoothness, balance, coordination, rhythm, long forward step, and sequential timing, as outlined earlier, are a basic part of Mogren's Paddle Dance. Also, note that his body is fairly *erect with relatively little bending in the hips*. His technique allows him to use relatively small skate angles, although he is in a fairly steep uphill.

"Hop" in this context means a form of gliding jump action during the skate. This advanced technique, a special variation of the regular Paddle, used by elite skiers in steep uphills, is characterized by the skier's "cat-like" jumping action from Drive ski to Hang ski with a special *galloping rhythm.* It requires very high frequency, which may be as much as 120 single skate steps per minute.

This form of skating is very demanding and consumes a lot of energy. When the technique is executed correctly, it produces probably the fastest skating in steep uphills.

The Paddle Hop is used in a transition where a skier has had a short recovery and is entering a short steep uphill with substantial momentum.

The Paddle Hop has a slightly different rhythm and sequence than the regular Paddle; it has a powerful short glide on the Drive side with a forceful skate push/jump across to the Hang ski. Special features of the Paddle Hop are:

1. *Short, Snappy power* - on the Drive side, applying a wide skate angle with shorter glide distance (**1**).

2. Applying powerful lifting of body by poles, simultaneously with jump off the Drive foot with full roll up onto the toe (**1, 2**).

3. *Long step-hop uphill* - onto the Hang ski, with smaller skate angle and longer glide distance on the Hang ski (**3, 4**).

4

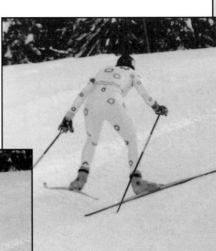

3

2

1

The Paddle Hop utilizes simultaneous muscle action by both upper and lower extremities, to generate the *"galloping, hopping"* glide action.

A quick, powerful asymmetric double pole plant has a snappy ending. To physically activate the "Hop", a powerful downset on the Drive ski produces a high static friction "braking" contact (Appendix, Sec. I-C), between ski and snow, creating an eccentric muscle contraction in the Drive leg, immediately prior to the short glide and jump action. During the poling recovery the upper extremity is moved aggressively uphill to regain an erect forward body lean.

The Paddle Hop can be practiced uphill on dryland to train the explosive action of legs and maximal pole lifting action.

Some individual skiers may find it possible to "take-off" for the Hop on the Hang foot. However, the author's opinion is that the sequence of action for this is awkward and is not in harmony with the regular Paddle Dance rhythm.

I. SUMMARY OF PROCEDURE AND SEQUENCE FOR PADDLE DANCE
(FOR ONE FULL CYCLE)

1. **Initiation (1 Point Contact)**
   a. Skis (legs) come together as Hang ski is moved inward towards the gliding Drive ski
   b. Legs together
   c. Body erect
   d. Weight shift is onto the Drive Ski

2. **Upper Extremity - Poling on Drive and Hang Sides (2 And 3 Points Contact)**
   a. Arms are moved forward and up with crowning (preloading) of upper body, elbows down
   b. Hang arm is lifting pole slightly higher uphill than the Drive pole
   c. Drive pole is brought inward toward the chest and planted downhill first with acute pole angle (2 Point Contact), which creates an imbalance that moves COG over towards the Hang side
   d. Immediately afterwards, the Hang pole is planted uphill also at an acute pole angle, but slightly steeper than the Drive pole (3 Point Contact)

3. **Lower Extremity - Body Movement - Glide and Skate on Hang Ski (4 Point Contact)**
   a. While gliding on the Drive ski, the Hang ski is moved a step uphill, and prepared for a smooth downset, simultaneously with, or immediately after planting of the Hang pole, making a very stable balanced position (4 Point Contact)
   b. Body weight (COG) is shifted over to gliding Hang ski
   c. Edging and skate off Drive ski with staggered double poling (3 Point Contact)

4. **Double Pole Pull and Push Action**
   a. Momentarily after both pole plants, arm "pulling" on both poles (4 Point Contact)
   b. Maximum force and impulse action by upper body with elbows at 90° angle
   c. Arm "pushing" forces on both poles as elbows reach side of body - elbow opens up (3 Point Contact) - while gliding on Hang ski)
   d. Final push and release of poles

5. **Lower Extremity Continued - Glide And Skate On Drive Ski**
   a. Step uphill with forward movement of Drive hip
   b. Preparation and downset on flat base of Drive ski while skating off Hang ski (2 Point Contact)
   c. Body weight is shifted over from Hang ski to Drive ski (1 Point Contact)

6. **Mid-Section Forward Momentum (1 Point Contact)**
   a. While gliding on Drive ski
   b. COG moves up and forward creating a forward momentum
   c. Skate starts on Drive ski as Hang ski is moved aerially inward and forward
   d. Legs come together

7. **Poling Recovery - While Gliding On Drive Ski (1 Point Contact)**
   a. Poles are swung forward, following a low path with elbows close to body
   b. Arms moved forward and up

This completes One Cycle of the Paddle Dance.

CHAPTER 8

IV. THE DIAGONAL DANCE

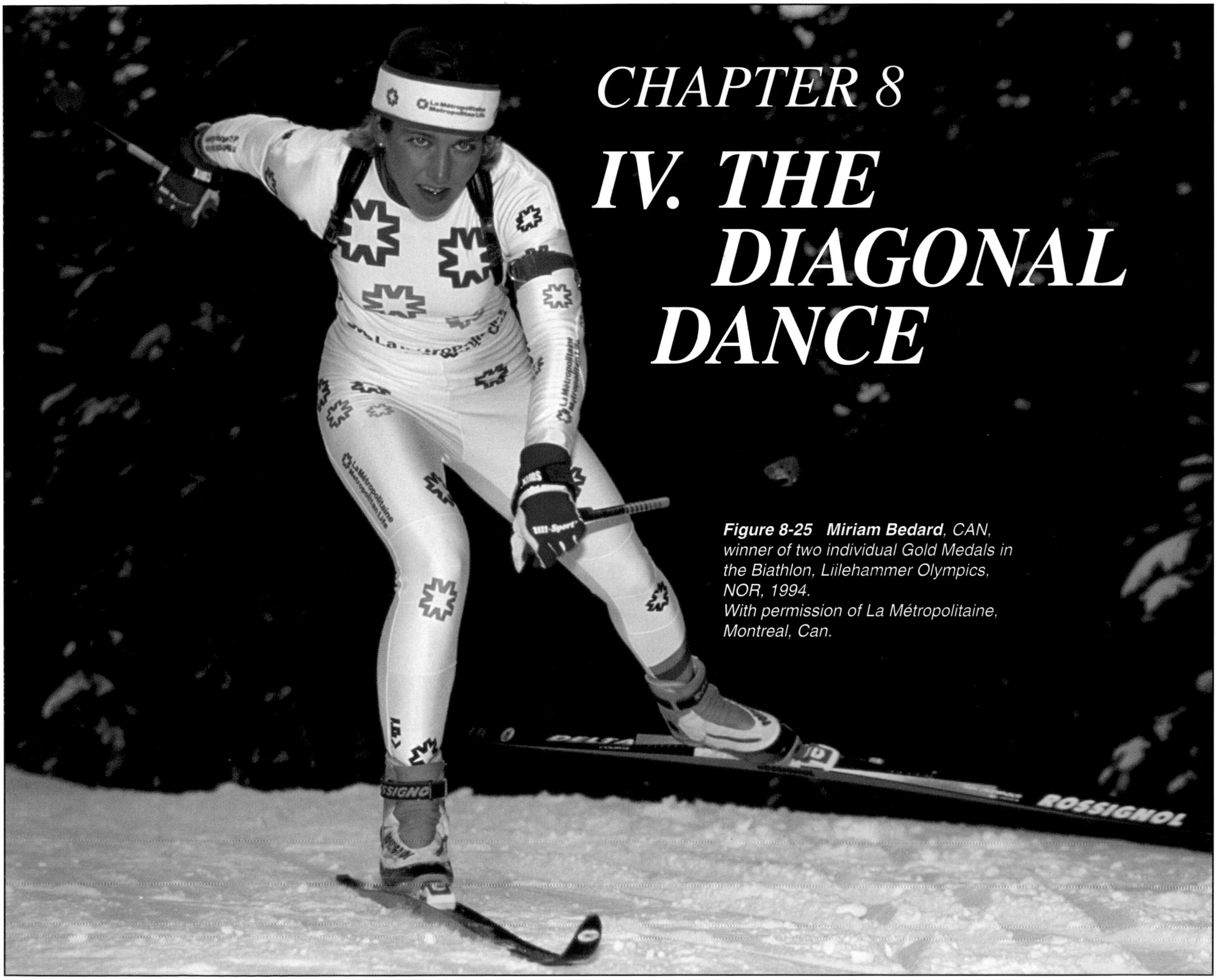

Figure 8-25 Miriam Bedard, CAN,
winner of two individual Gold Medals in
the Biathlon, Liilehammer Olympics,
NOR, 1994.
With permission of La Métropolitaine,
Montreal, Can.

CONTENTS

A. INTRODUCTION

Effective Diagonal Dance is characterized by long step distances uphill, with movements and momentum in the direction of the gliding skate ski, in harmony with single poling on the opposite side. The combined action by lower and upper extremity is coordinated with a smooth non-staccato rhythm. The uphill Diagonal Skate is particularly applicable when the steepness of a hill makes it difficult to use other techniques.

As the name suggests, there are similarities in motion to the Diagonal Stride Classic technique, but the Diagonal Skate is not as easy.

Another Classic technique, the Herringbone *(Fig. 8-26)*, is almost identical, the difference being that in the Diagonal Skate a glide is added to each of the Herringbone steps, and the rhythmic hip motion (and momentum) is more in the gliding skate direction. During the Herringbone, very little frictional energy (snow drag) is used since there is no ski gliding taking place. The energy used by the Herringbone is primarily for vertical lifting of body and equipment uphill at a high frequency.

Vertical uphill lifting also takes place during Diagonal Skate Dancing, but to that energy requirement is added the frictional resistance of the glide of the ski. If a skier tires before reaching the crest of the hill when using the Diagonal Dance, it may be smart to switch to the Herringbone Classic. There is no disqualification for selecting this option; however, Herringboning on skate skis requires a lot of skill and training to perfect the technique, because the skis are not waxed for traction.

Greater muscle forces are required over a shorter period of time in the Herringbone, while the opposite is true during the Diagonal Skate, where smaller muscle forces (impulse action) are engaged over a longer period of time during the glide and skate (Ch. 11, Sec. II-B-9).

The Diagonal Dance can be applied with and without poling, depending on speed of skiing, and can be used in combination with several other skate strides, depending on the variation of terrain, such as variable repetitious short uphills and downhills, where the switch to Diagonal Dance takes place after the transition to maintain momentum.

Diagonal Dance has, in the past, primarily been applied in the steep uphill, but in modern high speed skating, it is also frequently used on the level and in mild downhills, without poling, with aggressive diagonal arm swings similar to ice speed skating (see Ch. 8, Sec. IV-F).

As with any of the skate dances, it is good to first practice the Diagonal Dance at a slow pace on level terrain, with and without poling. The Diagonal Dance is a natural expansion of what has been discussed under Learning Basic Skate Movements (Ch. 5).

Figure 8-26 *Effective Classic Herringbone by* **Nikolai Burlakov**, *RUS. In the Diagonal Skate Dance, a glide is added to each step, making the cycle longer.*

B. DEFINITION OF THE DIAGONAL DANCE

In the Diagonal Dance the opposite arm and leg are moved forward in harmony. While **Single Poling** to one side (poling side), the skier skates forward on the opposite side's ski, and simultaneously recovers the pole on that side. The full cycle action continues with sides reversed - single poling on the other side with a skate and pole recovery on the opposite side.

It is an expansion of the traditional Herringbone, which is perhaps one of the oldest cross country skiing techniques. By adding a glide to the Herringbone, a natural diagonal skating dance rhythm is attained.

C. THE DIAGONAL DANCE SKATE PATTERN

The Diagonal Dance's Skate Pattern imprint in the snow shows actions on left and right sides that are symmetrical and equal, but alternating, with a step/glide on one side coinciding with poling on the other side - a diagonal movement. A full cycle includes actions on both sides between the pole plants on the same side. The skate angle α, equal on each side, varies directly with the steepness of the slope. The length of the glide on the ski is *inversely proportional* to the skate angle. High speed Diagonal Dance skating without poling, on the level and in mild downhills, is discussed separately at the end of this section.

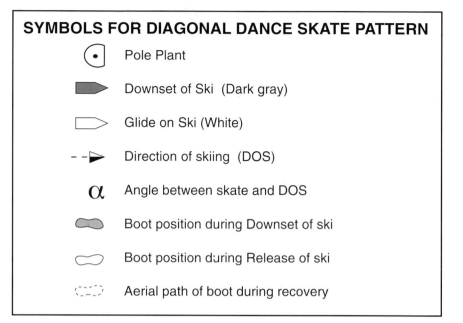

SYMBOLS FOR DIAGONAL DANCE SKATE PATTERN

- Pole Plant
- Downset of Ski (Dark gray)
- Glide on Ski (White)
- Direction of skiing (DOS)
- α Angle between skate and DOS
- Boot position during Downset of ski
- Boot position during Release of ski
- Aerial path of boot during recovery

Figure 8-27: 4 Sequential photos of Marianne Dahlmo, Nor. skating a steep uphill during the 4x5 Women's Olympic Relay, Canmore, CAN, 1988.

The photos correspond to the Skate Pattern illustrated for One Full Cycle of the Diagonal Dance.

LEFT SIDE SKATING

(**1**) The skier initiates poling with *right* arm and begins skate on *left* ski.

(**2**) Poling action with *right* arm and skating on *left* ski takes place simultaneously, while the *left* pole is recovered.

RIGHT SIDE SKATING

(**3**) Pole plant with *left* arm, and beginning of skate on *right* ski.

(**4**) Poling action with *left* arm, and skate on *right* ski, while the *right* pole is recovered.

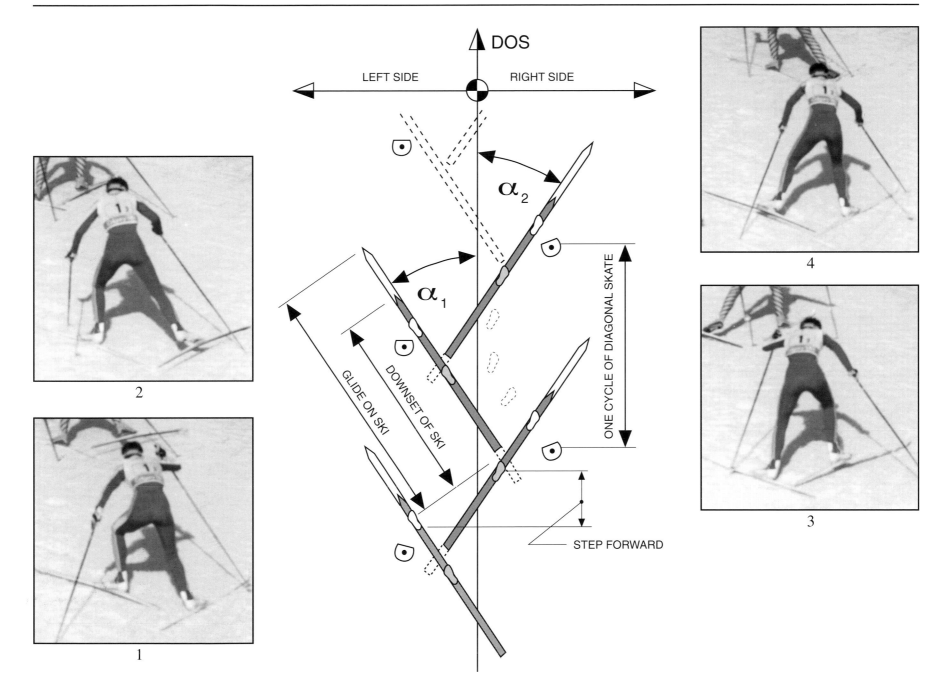

D. DIAGONAL DANCE SKATE CYCLE

The Cycle photos taken during the 4x5 km Women's Relay, Canmore, CAN, Olympics, 1988, show a good comparison of two entirely different techniques in a very steep uphill. Matikainen, Bib #3, (Bronze medal winner) is doing the Paddle Dance, while Dahlmo, Bib #1, (Silver medal winner) applies the Diagonal Dance. In this special occurrence, the Cycle Frequency, Time, Distance and Speed is the same for both techniques. Matikainen, Bib #3, in front, is probably not aware that Dahlmo, behind her, is using the Diagonal Dance technique. Since the cycle data are all the same (in the author's opinion), Dahlmo, with training and knowledge of both techniques, has selected to use the Diagonal Dance because it demands less energy. The Hang Side in the Paddle (Ch. 8, Sec III) is particularly energy demanding in steep uphills.

In the Diagonal Dance, high Frequency of poling is applied in the steep uphills and the Cycle Time and Distance are short. When skating the technique without poling, on variable flat terrain or in mild downhills during fast conditions, the opposite is true.

The photo sequence here is a Cycle of the Diagonal Dance between two pole plants on the *left* side. It begins and ends with a single pole plant on *left* side, taking place immediately prior to a smooth downset of the skate ski on the *right* side (**1, 2**).

3

1

2

₵
|
COG
|

ONE FULL CYCLE OF THE DIAGONAL DANCE

(For Skier Bib #1)

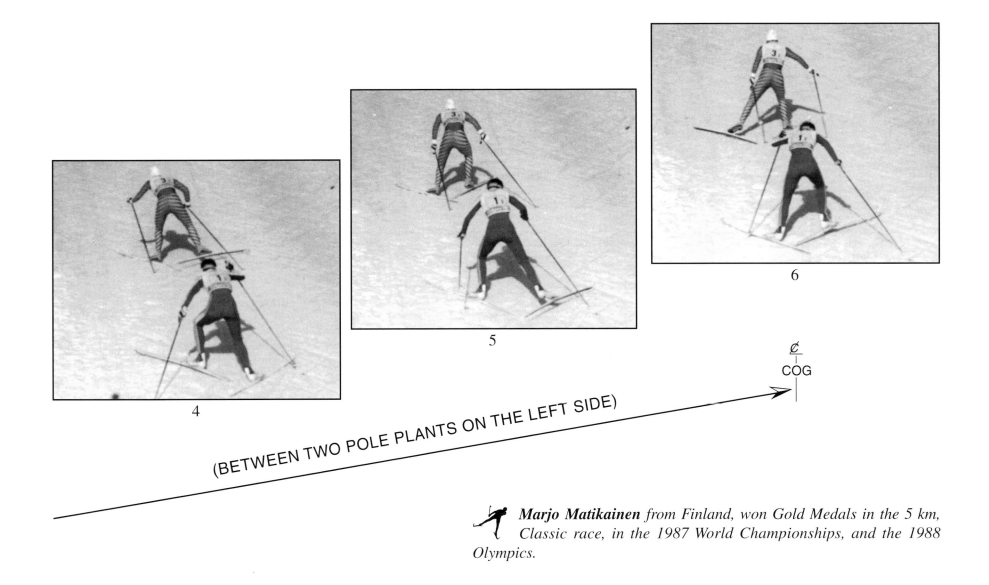

6

5

4

₵
COG

(BETWEEN TWO POLE PLANTS ON THE LEFT SIDE)

Marjo Matikainen *from Finland, won Gold Medals in the 5 km, Classic race, in the 1987 World Championships, and the 1988 Olympics.*

1	2	3	4

A. UPPER BODY: LEFT SHOULDER AND ARM FORWARD — POLE PLANT — PULL AND PUSH ACTION ➤

B. LEFT SKI: (CONTINUE) SKATE ACTION ➤ | RELEASE OF SKI (RECOVERY)

C. RIGHT SKI: AERIAL STEP FORWARD ➤ | LEGS TOGETHER , DOWNSET ; GLIDE

E. SEQUENTIAL PHASES OF MOVEMENT FOR THE DIAGONAL DANCE

1. POLING BY UPPER EXTREMITY

♦ *Pole Action Phase Between Two Pole Plants On The Left Side*

The poling phases for Diagonal Dance are distinguished by the use of *Single Poling* instead of Double Poling as is used for the other skate techniques shown in this text.

a. Initiation starts with upper extremity (*left* shoulder) rotated in direction of downset of opposite ski, with a slight crowning (preloading) of upper back, elbows at 90° (**1**).

b. Laterally inclined pole plant (*left*) is close to heel of (*left*) boot for gliding skate ski (on the same side) (**2**).

c. Muscle action on pole (**3 and 4**).

Sequence: Preloading ⇒ pull ⇒ push ⇒ release

The same pole action phases take place on the right side in Photos (**5** through **8**).

♦ *Pole Recovery Phase*

The pole (*left*) follows a low profile (its own gravity), in sequence with glide on opposite ski. The baskets should not swing up further than parallel with the ground. (Note: The poling recovery also includes the shoulder, rotating forward, relaxed, in harmony with the pole swing.)

a. **Right side:** Release of pole (**8, 1**)

Forward swing of pole (**2 - 5**)

b. **Left side:** Release of pole (**5, 6**)

Forward swing of pole (**6** continuing through **1**).

| 5 | 6 | 7 | 8 |

RIGHT SHOULDER AND ARM FORWARD — POLE PLANT — PULL AND PUSH ACTION

— AERIAL STEP FORWARD ▷ ◁ LEGS TOGETHER , DOWNSET , GLIDE AND — — — —

AND SKATE ACTION ▷ ◁ RELEASE OF SKI (RECOVERY) —

1. SKATE AND GLIDE ACTION BY LOWER EXTREMITY

♦ ***Glide and Skate on Right Ski***

    a.   Legs come together, smooth downset of *right* ski (**1** and **2**)

    b.   *Right* hip forward, glide on ski with a slight *give* by the knee (**3**)

    c.   Weight shift (COG) over to *right* ski, body erect, forward momentum of midsection (**4** and **5**)

    d.   Skate action on *right* ski
       Sequence: Hip $\Rightarrow$ thigh $\Rightarrow$ calf $\Rightarrow$ foot (**4 through 7**)

♦ ***Glide and Skate on Left Ski***

    a.   Legs come together, smooth downset of *left* ski. (**6**)

    b.   *Left* hip forward, glide and skate with slight give by the knee (**7**)

    c.   Weight shift (COG) over to *left* ski, body erect, forward momentum of mid-section (**8** and **1**)

    d.   Skate action of *left* ski

       Sequence: Hip $\Rightarrow$ thigh $\Rightarrow$ calf $\Rightarrow$ foot (**8** through **3**)

♦ ***Recovery of Lower Extremity - Right Ski***

    a.   Release of ski (**7**)

    b.   Aerial inward and forward movement, legs come together (**8** and **1**)

    c.   Step forward uphill, downset (**2**)

♦ ***Recovery of Lower Extremity - Left Ski***

    a.   Release of ski (**4**)

    b.   Aerial inward and forward movement, legs come together (**5**)

    c.   Step forward uphill, downset (**6**).

This completes One Full Cycle of Sequential Movement of the Diagonal Dance, which includes both left and right actions.

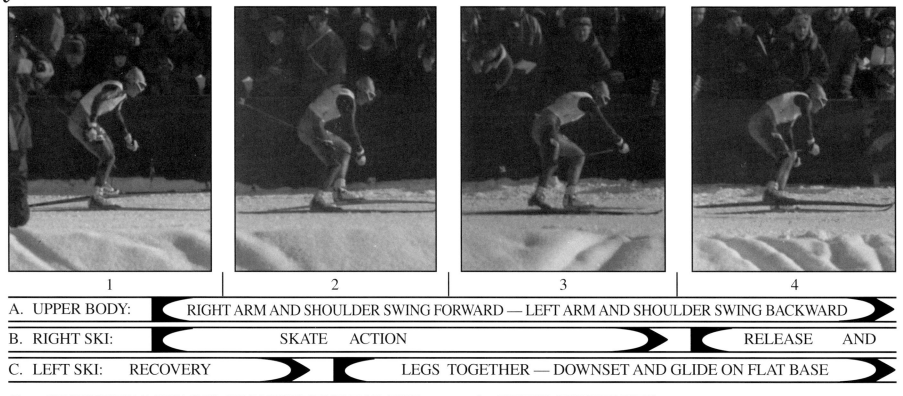

1	2	3	4

A. UPPER BODY:	RIGHT ARM AND SHOULDER SWING FORWARD — LEFT ARM AND SHOULDER SWING BACKWARD ▶
B. RIGHT SKI:	SKATE ACTION ▶ ◀ RELEASE AND
C. LEFT SKI:	RECOVERY ▶ ◀ LEGS TOGETHER — DOWNSET AND GLIDE ON FLAT BASE ▶

F. SEQUENTIAL PHASES OF MOVEMENT FOR THE DIAGONAL DANCE IN TUCK WITHOUT POLING

The Bar Chart and photos above show Manuela Di Centa, ITA, applying the Diagonal Dance without poling, on the level, in the Olympic 10 km Pursuit race, Lillehammer, NOR, 1994. She was the Silver Medalist in this race, and also won a Gold in the 15 km Freestyle. To minimize aerial resistance, she skates in a *Tuck Body Position* which produces a higher speed (Ch. 11, Sec. III).

In the Diagonal Dance, the arm swing, together with rotation of the upper body is in the same direction as glide on the opposite ski (also see Ch. 5, Exercise III). Good coordination, balance and rhythm are keys to efficiency and speed in this technique.

1. UPPER EXTREMITY

a. Upper body is inclined forward approx. 60° - both arms hanging down, relaxed (**1**).

b. *Right* arm swing forward begins, together with counter-clockwise rotation of upper body (**2**).

c. Forward extension with *right* arm and backward extension with *left* arm (**3**).

d. Both arms hang down parallel and relaxed (**4**).

Repeat arm swing action on the opposite side, execute the same movements of opposite shoulder and arm, "**a**" through "**d**".

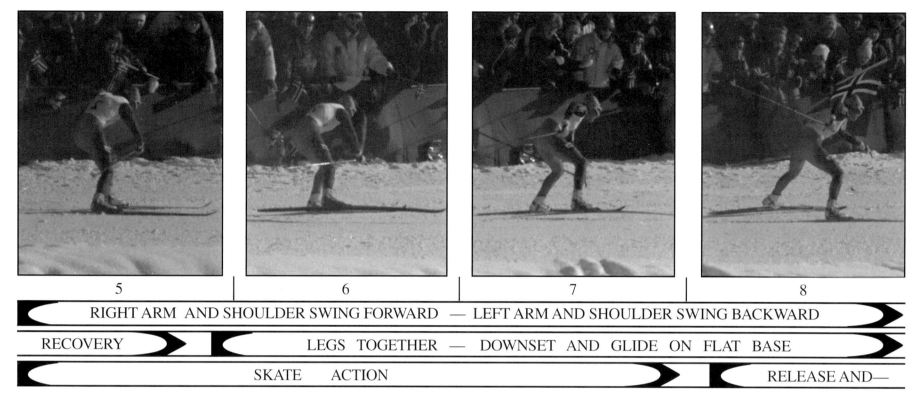

| 5 | 6 | 7 | 8 |

RIGHT ARM AND SHOULDER SWING FORWARD — LEFT ARM AND SHOULDER SWING BACKWARD

RECOVERY   LEGS TOGETHER — DOWNSET AND GLIDE ON FLAT BASE

SKATE ACTION   RELEASE AND—

2. LOWER EXTREMITY

e. Legs come together - balanced glide on one *right* flat ski base, the other ski *left* has just terminated the outward skate, and is brought inward and forward (**1**).

f. Downset of gliding *left* ski - skate action on opposite *right* ski starts (**2**).

g. Continue glide on flat *left* ski base with final skate push-off on *right* ski (**3**).

h. With aerial recovery of *right* ski the glide continues on *left* flat ski base (**4**).

For the opposite side, execute the same movements, of opposite leg and ski, "**e**" through "**h**".

G. BALANCE AND GROUND CONTACTS FOR THE DIAGONAL DANCE

While most techniques have a Four Point Contact for a short time period, Diagonal Dance is unique in that it does not have more than Three Points at any one time.

1. From Sequential Phases of Movement in Figure 8-29, immediately prior to the single pole plant, while both poles are suspended very briefly, when legs come together, the skier is in balance on one *(left)* gliding ski. (ONE POINT CONTACT) Photo (**1**).

2. As skier continues gliding on the *left* ski, a smooth downset of the *right* ski and pole plant by the opposite *(left)* arm takes place simultaneously (THREE POINT CONTACT) (**2**).

3. The skier now skates on the gliding *left* ski while pulling on the same side pole, as weight is shifted over to a balanced glide on opposite *(right)* ski (a continuation of the THREE POINT CONTACT above (**3**).

4. After the "skate-off" (release) of the *left* gliding ski, the skier is in typical Diagonal Dance position, namely in balance on one gliding *right* ski, while pushing on the pole by opposite arm (TWO POINT CONTACT) (**4**).

The released *left* ski is now moved inward and forward while gliding on the opposite *right* ski simultaneously with the final pole push release on the same side *(left)*. This is exactly the opposite position of Photo (**1**) above (ONE POINT CONTACT) (**5, 6**).

5. The skier continues gliding on the *right* ski with a smooth downset of opposite *(left)* ski. Simultaneously, the pole plant by opposite *(right)* arm takes place close to the ski behind the heel (THREE POINT CONTACT) (**6**).

6. The skate-off on the *right* gliding ski now takes place with weight shift and balance onto the opposite *(left)* ski, together with final pole push by the *right* arm (TWO POINT CONTACT) (**7, 8**).

7. With release of the *right* pole, skier is back to starting position for a complete cycle of the Diagonal Dance (ONE POINT CONTACT) (**8, 1**).

Repeat 1 through 7 for another cycle.

H. FACTORS CONTROLLING EFFECTIVE DIAGONAL DANCE MOVEMENT

Because of the unique diagonal movement this technique will have to practiced with poling in the steep uphill and without poling on the flat and in the mild downhills for a skier to improve. The diagonal movement involves more rotation of the upper extremity than any other skating technique.

In applying the Diagonal Skate there should be little vertical fluctuation of the body's COG. Energy is spent primarily in moving COG uphill, parallel with the ground, with the frictional snow drag comparatively small, making this an energy efficient technique.

An efficient Diagonal Skate requires excellent weight shift from one ski to the other, very quick relaxed motion of the hips and all body elements, and full extension of the body and leg during the skate push-off.

In steep uphills, because of the relative slow speed, a skier can maintain an almost erect body position; while skating *without poling* under very fast conditions, a skier uses a crouched body form for smaller frontage area to reduce the air drag forces.

Constant shifting of direction of vision in direction of glide on the ski enables the skier to better observe terrain variations and carving (gliding) of each ski, together with precise pole plant.

Skiing with Single poling is unique to the Diagonal Dance, and to apply *effective maximum poling* with one arm at a time seems to be a problem for many skiers who do not regularly practice the technique.

Although the Diagonal Dance may look simple to execute, efficient technique involves flexibility, good coordination, balance, rhythm and correct sequential timing.

I. ADVANTAGES AND DISADVANTAGES OF DIAGONAL DANCE

Advantages:

The Diagonal Skate Dance is an excellent technique for beginners to learn basic skate movements on the level, since the body's movements forward are similar to diagonal walking and therefore easy to adapt to (Ch. 5).

Efficient Diagonal Dance skating demands comparatively less energy, which is beneficial for skiers who have less VO_2 (oxygen) capacity, such as older masters. Because it uses different muscles, switching to Diagonal Dance for a short time gives the muscles a chance to recover when tired from using other techniques. Good blood circulation is stimulated by its rotation of the body (spine) and stretching (flexing) of the sides of the upper extremity.

Diagonal Dance with poling is often used by skilled skiers in steep uphills, since the Paddle can be very strenuous (particularly, the action on the Hang side).

Diagonal Dance *without poling* is frequently applied by skilled and elite skiers under fast conditions, since the rhythmic diagonal movements with aerial swing of arms and no pole plants on the level and particularly in the mild downhills can generate very high speeds (Appendix, Sec. II).

Like any other skating technique, to become good at it, the Diagonal Dance also requires practice and analysis for efficient execution.

Disadvantages:

The main disadvantage of using Diagonal Dance *with poling* is that speed is generally limited. Lateral movements and the skate angle in Diagonal Dance which result from the Single poling are normally greater than in Double and Single Dance, where more powerful double poling is applied. Other techniques adapted to specific terrain are therefore commonly applied.

J. SUMMARY OF PROCEDURE AND SEQUENCE FOR THE DIAGONAL DANCE *(FIGURE 8-29)*

In the following First Half Cycle, the *right* ski is the skate ski, with pole plant on the *left* side. (Photos **1-5**)

1. Initiation - Legs Together (1 Point Contact) (Photo 1)

    a. Skiing in an uphill, while gliding on the *left* ski, the *right* ski, in the recovery phase, is moved inward and forward, with the tail across the gliding ski. Both poles are airborne, the *left* one is up and forward, prepared for a pole plant

    b. Legs are close together

    c. Weight (COG) over the *left* gliding ski

    d. Body is erect

    e. *Right* hip and leg move forward, uphill, in a "step action"

2. Upper Extremity - Left Pole Plant (3 Point Contact) (Photos 2, 3)

    a. Preloading of muscles for upper back and *left* shoulder

    b. Pole plant at heel on *left* side simultaneously with or immediately prior to downset of *right* ski

    c. *Left* pole pull action starts

    d. *Left* elbow at 90° with rotation about the shoulder with maximum pulling force on the pole, inclined backward and laterally

Pole Recovery (*Right* Arm) (Photos 1 - 5)

(Pole recovery of *right* arm takes place simultaneously with the pole action of the *left* arm)

Right pole arm and relaxed shoulder follow a low profile as they swing forward and inward. Hand is toward the chest, elbow flexing to 90° prior to next pole plant

3. Lower Extremity - Weight on Both Skis (3 Point Contact) (Photo 3)

    a. Smooth downset of *right* ski with glide action

    b. Both skis are briefly weighted

    c. Skate-off action for opposite *left* ski

4. Body Movement - Weight Transfer (2 Point Contact) (Photo 4)

    a. Weight (COG) shifted over to gliding *right* ski

    b. Rotation of upper body and shoulder in forward direction of the gliding *right* ski (see Ch.11, Sec. I-B)

5. Continuing Pole Pull and Push Action (Left Arm) (Photos 4, 5)

    a. *Left* elbow opens up as hand reaches the side for final pushing on the pole

6. Final Skate Push on Left Ski (2 Point Contact) (Photo 4)

    a. Skate off *left* ski

    b. Release of *left* ski

    c. Continued glide on *right* ski - hip moves forward

    d. Legs are coming together

This completes the First Half Cycle of the Diagonal Dance.

Repeat above items (1 through 6) for a description of the actions for the opposite (*right*) ski for a Second Half Cycle, which will be the mirror image of the first. (Photos 5, 6, 7, 8, 1)

CHAPTER 9
Downhill Skating and Turning Techniques

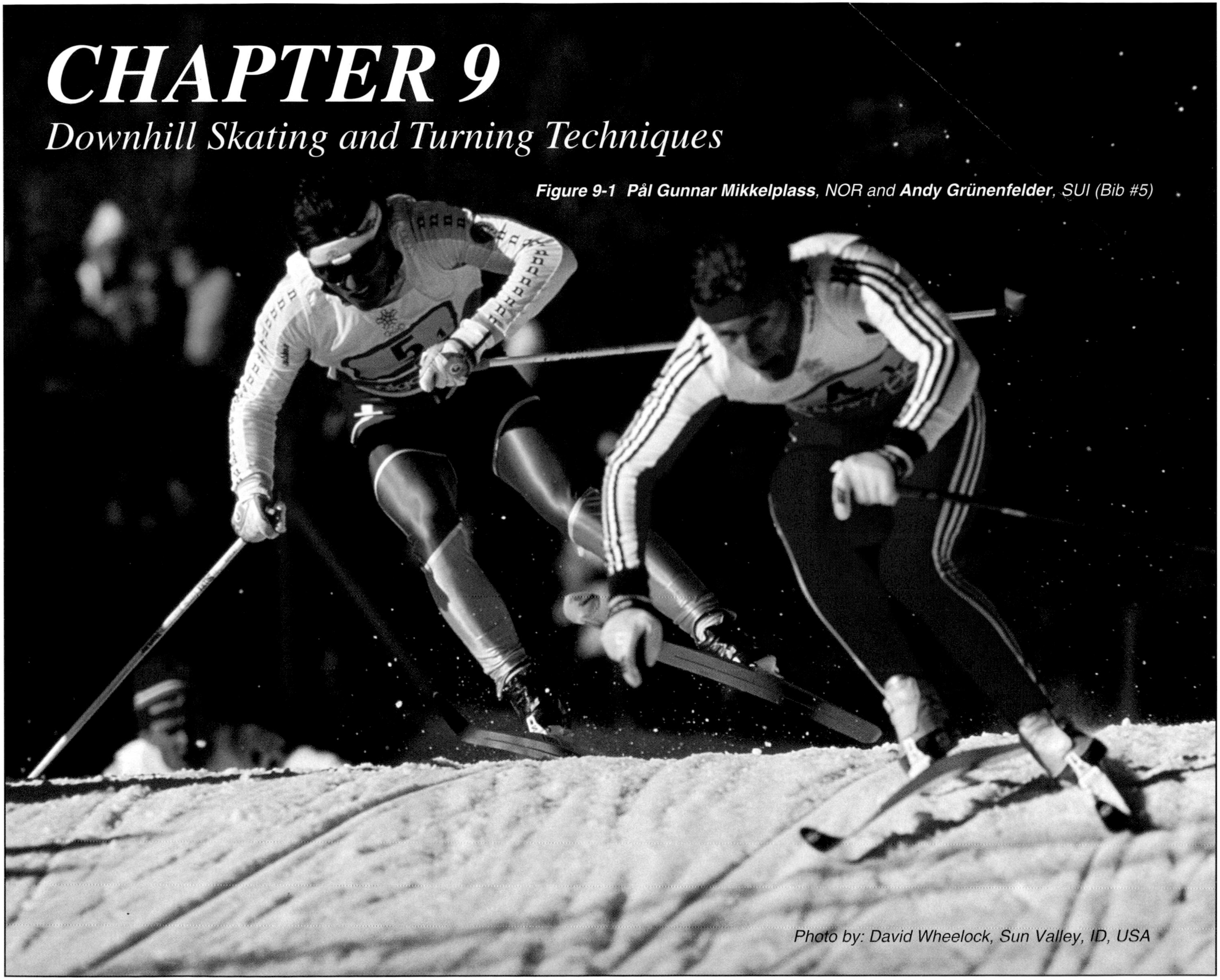

Figure 9-1 **Pål Gunnar Mikkelplass**, *NOR* and **Andy Grünenfelder**, *SUI (Bib #5)*

Photo by: David Wheelock, Sun Valley, ID, USA

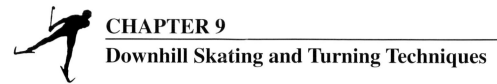

CONTENTS

I.   INTRODUCTION

One of the enjoyments of cross country skiing is to be able to ski comfortably, safely, and with confidence in the downhills. Anyone who cross country skis is faced with the challenge of skiing downhills with various degrees of difficulty. International track standards for racing call for a significant amount (1/3) of a course's distance to be downhill terrain.

There are hundreds of books written on alpine downhill skiing, but very little about cross country downhill. In this chapter, the basic downhill and turning techniques, which also apply to ski skating, are briefly discussed and illustrated. Ski Skating in downhill terrain, is a more advanced form of downhill skiing.

Ski Skaters can apply a variety of downhill techniques and turns, depending on their skill and the type of terrain involved. Skilled downhill skaters may use techniques that accelerate them downhill, while others, not feeling that confident in the downhill, may use techniques that maintain or reduce speed.

Cross country downhill skiing is often looked at as a resting phase. This is only partially true, as downhills also require energy and strength, depending on technique chosen, and how the body's position (COG) moves vertically and horizontally, relative to gravity and lateral forces that act throughout the glide and all turns.

A. STRAIGHT DOWNHILL (SKIING DOWN THE FALL-LINE)

In its simplest form, downhill skiing begins when the skier overcomes skiing friction and the skis start gliding by themselves, without use of any of the skier's body motion or energy. In this case, the skier's gravity (weight) is the only force that causes downhill movement. (Please see Downhill Dynamics, Chapter 11, Sec. II-C, for more detail).

As the hill becomes steeper, and the skier picks up more speed, aerial resistance becomes a factor in gaining speed, and the skier may crouch his body to minimize the frontal area and lower the COG. On a hill with an even slope, speed increases with the downhill distance.

Straight Downhill Skiing means skiing perpendicular to the contour lines used in the mapping of slopes. Another expression frequently used is "skiing down the fall-line", the fall-line being the path a ball would take when rolling down the slope.

In this situation both skis are evenly weighted. The skier glides downhill, in a relaxed position, even if not in a rested stage, keeping a good view of the terrain just ahead *(Fig. 9-2)*.

All skiers, by nature, feel for the most stable position. This is achieved by crowning the back and bending the upper body slightly forward at the hips, thereby lowering the body's Center of Gravity (COG) closer to the skiing surface. A good forward lean of the upper extremity should be maintained. Stability in both the lateral and skiing directions is improved by keeping one ski (foot) slightly ahead of the other *(Fig. 9-3)*.

Poles are tucked under the arms, close to the body, above the hips, and kept approximately parallel with the skis.

Straight Downhill Technique Suggestions

1. Legs (from knee to the ankle) are bent (pressured) forward. The front ski-to-leg angle should be less than 90°.

2. A line through the COG of the body and the ankle should be perpendicular to the skiing slope for good balance. Hands to be extended in front of the head, with elbows at approximately 90°.

3. This body position can be practiced first on a mild slope, where the skis are barely gliding, then, with gradually increased steepness of slope and speed.

4. As learning accelerates, a soft flex in the knee can be incorporated, slightly and smoothly moving COG up and down, imitating the feel of counteracting terrain variations normally experienced when skiing downhill.

5. As more confidence develops, variable, gently undulating terrain with slopes that change from moderately steep to level, can be tried.

Figure 9-2 *Straight downhill technique, Front View*
Skier: The Author

Figure 9-3 *Straight downhill technique, Side View*
Skier: The Author

B. TRAVERSE DOWNHILL SKIING

Skiing downhill, along the side of a slope, with the uphill ski higher than the downhill ski, is called ***traversing*** the slope. Traversing is one of the fundamental postures for all types of downhill skiing and turning (Ch. 9, Sec. III).

When traversing, body weight (COG) is laterally shifted slightly outward and is primarily on the downhill ski, while the uphill ski is kept slightly ahead and becomes the ***lead ski***. This causes the knee for the ***uphill ski*** to bend slightly more. The spread leg position gives better lateral and forward balance *(Fig. 9-4)*.

By relaxing the hips, the weight shift of COG over to the downhill trailing ski adjusts itself for ideal balance, which feels more comfortable during skiing.

When skiing untracked, steep, downhill terrain, where there is no groomed track or course, the traverse is usually used. It is therefore important to understand the traverse well and practice skiing both to the left and right across the slope.

Primary guidelines in traversing a downhill:

1. Avoid edging the skis

2. Glide as much as possible on a flat base

3. Angle the ankles slightly sideways (downhill)

During icy conditions and high speed, however, edging to prevent sideways slipping might be unavoidable when following a prescribed path or marked course.

Figure 9-4 Traverse Downhill
Skier: The Author

C. SIDE SLIPPING

This technique is simply slipping downhill sideways, by alternately edging and flattening the skis, while slowly traversing the slope. The ski tips are rotated uphill by means of weight shift and leg and hip action, thereby slowing or braking to a full stop.

It is a method primarily used to get safely downhill on steeper slopes when a skier may be fearful that the skiing conditions and terrain will cause uncontrollable speed.

Side slipping is one of the easier downhill techniques to learn. It is widely used by novice and expert skiers on hard surfaces as well as on new fresh fallen snow.

During side slipping, the slope is traversed with less speed, so traveling between two points takes considerable longer than when traversing between the two points.

Side slipping is initiated from a fairly erect resting position with the knees slightly bent and the skis parallel with the slope and legs close together. If the slope is fairly steep with icy snow conditions, it may be necessary to edge the skis to control the sideways sliding motion. Normally in cross country skiing too much edging of the skis is avoided, due to their weakness, and vibration encountered during edging.

The skier in Figure 9-5 is gradually shifting his body weight (COG) from the uphill to the downhill ski as he initiates the side slipping. In Photo (**1**) the rotation of the skis, which slows down the speed, is more powerful with a typical high snow spray at the tails. In Photo (**2**) the skier is picking up speed by traversing along the slope with less side slipping.

Basic Procedure Of Side Slipping

1. While traversing a slope, the legs are twisted to rotate the tips of the skis uphill and the tails downhill, to side slip and slow down. This is accomplished with leg and hip rotation, where the feet have full bearing onto the skis and the body weight (COG) is back on the heels.

2. To again traverse the slope, the knees are slightly flexed, adjusting the COG of the body's weight forward and twisting the tips of the skis slightly downhill. The hips are rotated against the direction of turning (counter-rotation).

3. It is possible to side slip backward by smoothly adjusting (shifting) the body's COG backward. This two-way technique is useful when doing back country skiing down a narrow, steep slope.

Figure 9-5 *Side Slipping while Traversing the Slope of a Glacier, in the summer. Skier:* **John Svensson**

D. SNOW PLOW OR WEDGE

All cross country skiers, experts or novices, have respect for downhills, particularly if the terrain is unfamiliar, visibility is limited and there are possibilities of hazards on the trail. The snow plow is one of the easiest and best techniques to slow down and control downhill skiing speed, and is frequently used to safely stop in a short distance.

Figure 9-6 *Snow Plow from Front*
Skier: The Author

Figure 9-7 *Snow Plow from Side*
Skier: The Author

Basic Procedure For Snow Plowing

1. The legs are spread apart and the tails of the skis slightly angle outward; maintain fairly straight legs, with very little flexing of the knees.

2. The upper body is crowned and bent almost 90° at the hips.

3. Body's COG is moved further back to the heels, weighting the rear portion of the skis.

4. The poles are kept close to the body, as recommended under straight downhill.

5. To slow down (brake), the inside edging of the skis is increased. To increase speed, the ski base is flattened out, reducing or eliminating edging.

In this position, downhill speed can easily be controlled. To reduce the speed, the angle between the skis is increased by bringing the ski tips closer together and increasing leg pressure on the skis. Likewise, if it is safe to allow speed to increase, the angle between the skis can be reduced by widening the distance between the ski tips *(Fig. 9-6, 9-7)*.

Body weight (COG) may have to be moved slightly back or forth when varying the Snow Plow speed, but this adjustment will come with practice.

To make a full Snow Plow stop, the angle between the skis is increased by spreading the tails of the skis further apart, and simultaneously moving COG slightly forward to adjust to the greater pressure on the legs.

If confidence and skill to Snow Plow down the fall-line of a hill is lacking, a snow plow traverse across the slope can be done. In this case, more of the body weight (COG) is transferred to the downhill ski, which is angled slightly more than the uphill ski.

III. TURNING IN A DOWNHILL

While "high-speed turning" used to be associated only with alpine skiing, well packed cross country skiing courses, groomed tracks, fast skis, and better boot/binding interfaces have made cross country downhill turning a challenge too. Well executed, high speed turns are crucial for the outcome in racing competition, and require special skill and strategy to gain optimal speed without a fall.

Turning in today's Classic technique consists of following a preset groomed track, or sliding around a curve where the groomed track is wiped out. In skating downhill, there is also the additional freedom to make quick skate steps on the compacted base around the curves, depending on the skier's ability to handle the speed and terrain variations. In today's courses, designed for constant changes of direction, relatively large radial curves permit fast skiing, and moderate to small radii need slower speeds.

A combination of skills in downhill skiing and turning is needed to ski on variable terrain during differing snow conditions that range from deep powder to icy surfaces.

One of the key criteria for balanced control during downhill turning is proper placement of the arms and poles. Arms should be stretched forward even though poles may be tucked under the arms.

A. SNOW PLOW TURN

A turn while in the Snow Plow (wedge) position *(Fig. 9-8)* is one of the easiest to learn and safest of downhill turns. It is widely used by cross country skiers of all skill levels, and is incorporated in many other more advanced turns. It is a turning technique also used for immediate braking or stopping.

- While snow plowing Photo (**1**).

- The turn is initiated by twisting the upper extremity toward the intended direction of skiing (**2**).

- With a slight flex in the outside knee (**3**), the body's COG is shifted down and laterally toward the outside leg (outside of the planned curve).

- A curve is carved, while applying pressure on the outside ski (**4**).

- While remaining relaxed with poles tucked under the arms, pressure is kept on the outside ski until beginning to move in the Snow Plow position across the slope, in the opposite direction (**5**).

- To initiate a turn in the reverse direction, the Snow Plow position is formed, then the upper extremity is rotated in the new turning direction (**6, 7, 8**), and the same procedure as above is repeated.

When practicing, the vertical and lateral body movements should be smooth, springy, and rhythmic, as the frequency (speed) of turns in both directions is increased. As learning accelerates, a smooth, relaxed rhythmic lateral hip motion is emphasized going into the curve.

Practice should be done on hills with differing steepness. For milder hill slopes, a smaller angle is kept between the skis. On steeper hills, this angle is increased for safety reasons.

1

2

3

5

4

6

7

8

B. STEP TURN

In the **Step Turn** *(Fig. 9-9)* technique of skating a curve, the skis move straight forward with no sliding or wedging. While all downhill techniques discussed so far have been Two Points of Contact (balance on two skis), the Step Turn uses **One Point of Contact**, the most difficult balance position in skiing (Ch. 3). During the Step Turn the body is supported on one ski only, for a short fraction of a second, and requires a quick weight shift from one ski to the other.

To learn the Step Turn, a hill with a mild slope should be selected, and stepping to both left and right practiced at slow speed, increasing the step frequency with improvement. Mastering the weight shift in the step turn is necessary before learning more complicated high speed skate step turns.

When speed is very fast in steeper downhills, as illustrated in the photos, the step from one ski to the other has to take place very quickly. To counteract centrifugal forces that act outward on the curve and tend to tip the skier over, the body's COG has to be leaned inward, Photos (**1**) and (**3**).

Skate Step turning should be practiced and executed with as little edging of the skis as possible.

Doing the Step Turn with perfect control, the skier in Figure 9-9 is in a tuck with poles under the arms. This position produces the highest speed and is characteristically used by confident, skilled skiers when making Step Turns in fast downhills.

Effectively applying the Step Turn technique is a crucial requirement in international ski skate racing, where most downhills have curved sections. For further discussion and expansion of this technique see this chapter, Section IV-2-C, Skate Step in Curved Downhill, with Stefania Belmondo of Italy.

Step Turn Procedure

When traversing across a slope with the skis parallel:

1. Weight is shifted over to the outside ski and the inside ski lifted, forming a small angle into the curve with the tails close together (**1**).

2. The inside ski is set down, pointed in the direction of the curve, and weight quickly transferred to this ski. As the ski tips continue to spread apart, the outside ski is released from the snow (**2, 3**).

3. While in balance on the inside ski, the outside ski is lifted aerially inward, and set down in the same direction as the inside ski is moving. Then the weight is transferred to the outside ski (**3, 4**).

The above Step Turn is repeated as many times as necessary to complete the curve.

Note: *Step Turns can be executed in either direction; it is the inside ski (i.e. inside of the planned curve), that initiates the change of direction.*

*In Figure 9-9, the skier's **right** ski is his "inside" ski.*

1

2

3

4

C. BASIC SWING TURN

The **Basic Swing Turn** *(Fig. 9-10)* incorporates what has been discussed about downhill skiing and turns so far. It combines four previously explained techniques in the order listed for one complete, nicely carved, Swing Turn.

In Figure 9-10, the skier's *left* ski is his "inside" ski.

a. **Traverse** - across the slope, Photo (**1**).

b. **Step Turn** - The uphill (outside) ski is unweighted slightly and moves to form a wedge. With experience, a sliding motion can be used (**2**).

c. **Snowplow** - Weighting the outside ski, a turn downhill is made into and across the fall line (**3, 4**).

d. **Step Turn** - Maintaining a tucked body position, the inside ski is lifted and slightly moved or slid toward the outside of the curve, to become parallel with the weighted outside ski (**5**).

e. **Side Slipping** - Knees are bent forward while incorporating a gentle side-slipping rotation with the skis parallel (**6**).

f. **Traverse** - The side-slipping is terminated as the skis are steered into the new traverse direction (**7**).

Repeat in reverse direction for continuing **Swing Turns** (**2**) through (**7**).

In the Basic Swing Turn, a continuous fluid motion should be emphasized, where the transition from one technique to the next is hardly noticeable.

Although the list of techniques above is long, the Swing Turn is not complicated, since it uses what has already been learned. Once the Basic Swing has been mastered, any ski slope and terrain can be skied, as direction across the fall line can be changed in one continuous fluid movement.

The most difficult aspect of the Swing Turn is pressing down in the Snow Plow position as the turn is made across the fall line. However, this is usually more a mental problem of fear, rather than physical, and confidence should return as the Side-Slipping is started. As experience is gained with the Swing Turn, the two Step Turns may be eliminated by using a *smooth sliding motion* outward with the outside ski, when going into the curve, and likewise with the inside ski going out of the curve.

Practice of the Swing Turn should be started on a fairly mild slope, making large curves and long traverses, then, with more experience, smaller curves and shorter traverses on steeper slopes following the same procedure. Gentle movement, incorporating rhythmic action and stable, safe balance during the execution should be emphasized. An effort should be made to keep the COG at the same, constant level above the snow.

The Basic Swing Turn is sometimes done by aid of a pole plant prior to closing the wedge, however, the author feels that *all cross country downhill turns should be learned without using pole plants,* as when executing high speed turns.

D. PARALLEL TURN

The ***Parallel Turn*** *(Fig. 9-11)* is used primarily for larger curves, and usually under high speeds, in order to ski with least aerial resistance and least friction under the skis. In a Parallel Turn, skis and legs are kept parallel throughout the curve, with firm base contact with the snow. This is one of "older" turns, where style and elegance are significant. A perfect execution of the turn characterizes a skilled skier with advanced technique. Gentle, delicate steering on flat skis, with slight outward lateral drift and little spray of snow, indicates a successful turn. The parallel turn in a tuck is very aerodynamically sound, having a small frontal area and an ideal, stable body shape.

To make parallel turns in a downhill, the same requirements for stability apply as for the side slipping techniques when skiing a downhill curve. A relaxed body position is maintained, with the least frontal area, a moderately crouched body position, hands forward, arms tight to the body, with poles along side at hip level, knees pressed forward, and skis approximately 30 cm. apart.

The turn is completely controlled by smoothly shifting weight of the body (COG) from one ski to the other, gliding on the flat base of both skis, kept close together. The upper extremity remains much in the same position, as the lower body (below the waist) initiates, guides and controls the turn.

An outward centrifugal force, acting at the COG tends to tip the skier over, outwards, and this force must be counteracted by leaning the body sufficiently inward. The higher the speed, the more important it is to balance the vertical body weight force and the centrifugal forces. The resultant of these two forces should act to the inside of the lower ski (Ch.11, Sec. II-C). Practice the turn with no edging of the ski.

The Parallel Turn is an excellent technique to apply in a curved downhill when a skier needs to recover from an exhaustive uphill, since little movement is needed to accomplish the turn.

Basic Procedure for Parallel Turn

1. The skier Photo (**1**) picks up speed, skiing straight down the fall-line with both skis equally weighted, prior to initiating the turn.

2. The turn (**2**) is initiated with the body weight gradually shifting over to one ski, which becomes the outer (downhill) ski, with a *slight twisting at the ankles and hip rotation outward (counter rotation)* throughout the curve. The inner (uphill) ski, partially unweighted, moves parallel with the outside weighted ski. This initiates the carving of a smooth curve (**4, 5, 6**). The basic principle of a Parallel Turn is that, on a slope, the weighted ski becomes the lower one (the downhill ski), and the partially unweighted one the upper (uphill ski).

3. Throughout the curve, the skier's crouched position remains the same without vertical fluctuation (except for the continuous weight shifting) (**4, 5, 6**). Less aerial resistance may be achieved by using a body position lower than shown in the illustrations, but more energy would be required to hold such a position.

1

2

3

4

5

6

IV. CROSS COUNTRY DOWNHILL RACING: TURNING SKILLS AND TACTICS

A. INTRODUCTION

The modern focus of downhill cross country ski racing is to *tactically attack all downhills, focused on the idea of maintaining speed or accelerating* throughout the course. To accomplish this in steep curved sections, the skier must be knowledgeable and skillful in downhill maneuvering techniques. This section discusses cross country downhill racing from both a practical and theoretical point of view, using photographs of several top international cross country racers. The basic fundamentals, previously discussed, also apply here.

A recent study of cross country international race courses shows that 30%, and occasionally up to 50% of their lengths, are downhill. This indicates that knowing how to maximize speed and master difficulties encountered in downhills is of equal importance as for other sections of a race course.

The techniques suggested by this author for cross country downhill racing are based on the most efficient use of energy while maintaining a body position that gives the fastest speed downhill. In most downhills, the cross country skier is in a recovery or resting stage, and *a body position that is the fastest some times may be too strenuous.* In well prepared race courses, with skate skis waxed their full length with downhill glide wax, speed is often very fast and the skier must have the technique and skill to overcome many obstacles such as change of steepness, transitions, bumps, and sharp, sometimes untracked, curves. Most top cross country racers are also good in downhill and can serve as models for teaching less skilled skiers to better master the downhills.

In the following section, the effect that the downhill position has on the speed, resting and recovery of the skier, will be analyzed and guidelines given about what may be the optimum downhill body position(s) for a skilled cross country skier. Obviously this varies for some skiers who prefer individual body positions and actions developed through experience and successes in racing.

B. BODY POSITIONS

In cross country downhill racing, **body position** is crucial in determining optimal speed. If there is concern that the speed in a downhill may exceed capability, the hill can be skied with a more erect body position, thereby creating a greater frontal aerial resistance with body and poles. The speed in a downhill is in *inverse proportion* to the projected body area perpendicular to the skis, as seen from the front of the skier. In other words, the smaller the frontal projection area of the body and the poles, the faster the potential obtainable speed (Ch. 11, Sec. II-C, and III).

The three downhill body positions are:

1. UPRIGHT OR ERECT   (Fig. 9-12: Skier at top of hill)

This is the most restful position when speed is not a consideration. The body weight acts through the ankle, and is evenly distributed, with legs fairly straight with a slight flex at the knees.

2. HIGH TUCK   (Fig. 9-12: The two lower skiers)

The most common downhill position used by experts and novice skiers is a semi-crouch, also called a high tuck. The skier strives for the most restful position, while maintaining high speed, keeping the trunk parallel with the skis and legs fairly straight with a slight flex at the knees. The elbows are above the knees.

3. LOW TUCK   (Figs. 9-13 and 9-14)

In elite racing, with keen competition, the skier frequently compresses the body more, bending the knees, sometimes with elbows below the knees, to further reduce the frontal resistance area, enabling maximum speed (The Mechanics of Downhill and effect of the tuck positions are discussed in detail under Ch.11, Sec. II-C; III).

Figure 9-12 *Upright and High Tuck positions*

Figure 9-13
*Low Tuck Position
from the front*

Figure 9-14
*Low Tuck Position from
the side*

4. VARYING POSITIONS IN TRANSITIONS

Cross country skiing terrain is commonly undulating, alternating among gradients of downhills, flats, and uphills. Due to these transitions in terrain, all skiers, especially top racers, need to utilize many body positions and frequently change techniques.

Depressions

When bumps and hollows appear, the skier needs to flex the body position when going down into such a transition in order to increase the momentum, and use a body lifting technique with upward momentum when leaving the depression, going into an uphill.

Hilltop Transitions from Upright to Tuck

As racers, using one of the skating techniques, reach a hilltop prior to a downhill, they are usually in an erect position and breathing heavily. The skier anticipates the downhill as a resting or recovery opportunity and is interested in completing the downhill in the least physically strenuous way, with the least expenditure of energy. At the same time the racer is interested in completing the downhill in the fastest possible time. The quicker the skier goes into a tuck position, the faster the downhill speed. Double poling combined with skating, immediately prior to going into the tuck position, helps increase average speed downhill.

C. CROSS COUNTRY DOWNHILL RACING TECHNIQUES

1. CURVED DOWNHILL IN GROOMED TRACK (Figures 9-15, 9-16)

One of the first goals in learning downhill cross country skiing is to be able to ski in prepared, machine groomed tracks, where the spacing between the grooves is approximately 6" apart most of the time. In such curved downhills, where the velocity is high, many skiers have difficulty staying in the tracks, due to a lack of proper balance, lateral inclination, tactics, and/or mental confidence. Factors that a skier must be aware of are: edging and frictional resistance, centrifugal forces, and frontal wind (drag) force.

Edging and Frictional Resistance

When skiing in a sharply curved, groomed downhill track, the tips and tails of the skis tend to edge against the track grooves and cause frictional resistance. To minimize such resistance, the skier uses a flat base and as little edging of the skis as possible.

Centrifugal Force

The external centrifugal force (H_C), acting outwards at the body's COG, tends to cause the skier to step out of the curve. (Ch. 11, Sec. I-C-7) The skier must anticipate this force going into the curve by counteracting it with a lean inward. In Photo (**1**) the skier initiates the inward lean before going into the curve, and increases the lean in Photo (**2**). Photo (**3**) shows the exit of the curve, with the skier still maintaining the lean, since the momentum from the outward centrifugal forces continues for a time after termination of the curve.

Frontal Air Drag Force

The frontal air drag force (D) is particularly noticeable when the skier is in a more erect body position. To counteract this, the skier has to lean forward, as well as inward (Ch. 11, Sec. II-C-4).

The amount of body incline inward and forward depends on speed and sharpness (radius) of the curve. From experience and training the skier has to anticipate this, and make body adjustments as needed, to make a smooth downhill curve with optimal speed and least use of energy.

Basic Procedure

1. *Anticipation* of the outward centrifugal force (H_C) starts with an inward lean of the body immediately prior to going into the curve, while maintaining a tucked body position with poles under arms, Photo (**1**).

2. The body also leans forward to counteract *air drag resistance* (D), resulting in a combined lean outward and forward.

3. A tucked body position is crucial since lowering the COG causes the potential overturning moment of the skier to be less. [Moment = centrifugal force (H_C) times height above binding (*h*)] A tuck with forward lean is more stable because it makes both the air drag resistance and the overturning moment smaller.

4. The ideal incline is when the resultant of the two forces (H_C and D) comes between the ankles of the skier, giving the skier the feeling of perfect balance throughout the curve.

5. The amount of lean inward and forward is directly related to the external forces (H_C and D), and the skier has to anticipate these when going into the curve, adjusting the lean according to speed and radius of the curve. As the speed increases and the radius of the curve becomes smaller, the lean has to be increased.

6. If the skier still experiences difficulty in maintaining balance and stability in a downhill, the following alternatives may be tried.

   ♦ A forward and outward movement of the arm toward the inside of the curve. Note that the skier in Photo (**3**) opens up the inside arm slightly to stabilize the body.

   ♦ If more counteraction is needed another alternative is to move the opposite (outside) arm forward with a slight rotation of the upper body forward and inward.

In extreme conditions, both alternatives may be used. However, this increases the frontal catch area and the air drag forces, which accordingly will reduce speed.

1

2

4

3

Figure 9-16 *Vladimir Smirnov,* KAZ, Bib #91, Bronze Medalist and *Igor Badamshin,* RUS, Bib #90.
30 km Classic, World Championships, Falun, SWE, 1993.

Figure 9-15 *Marjo Matikainen*, FIN
1988 Olympics, Canmore, CAN
4 x 5 km Women's Relay

2. SKATE STEP IN CURVED DOWNHILL

Straight downhill skiing has almost disappeared on international race courses. Instead, most race courses have fast, curved downhills where the skier has several options of how to make a turn. Courses for training and racing should preferably have an equal number of turns to each side, to balance the skiers' demand for muscle strength and energy, as well as to test the skier's versatility.

When going through a downhill curve, the choice of staying in the groomed (preset) track usually exists. However, if the radius of the curve is too small, a skier may have to ski outside the tracks and use the **high frequency Skate Step** turning technique. This technique can also help increase speed, particularly when finishing out the curve. It is now common among skilled skaters to maintain, or increase the speed, in curved downhills, by applying the Skate Step technique (see Ch. 11, Sec. II-B-7).

Skate Stepping sharp curves at high speed requires alertness, precision, perfect balance, and quick transfer of body weight, with aerial step movements from one ski to the other *(Fig. 9-1)*. A tumble in some of these high speed turns is not uncommon, even among top elite. If a skier is fatigued or does not have the confidence or enough experience to make a high speed turn with skate stepping, other turning techniques as illustrated in this chapter should be applied. This technique should be practiced at every opportunity, selecting terrain that is compatible with the skier's ability.

Tactics and strategy are very important when executing a high speed turn using the skate step. Anticipating how to get around the turn with optimal speed and least use of energy helps attain a successful outcome.

Figure 9-17 *Skate Step Turning in the Women's 10 km Freestyle Pursuit, World Championships, Falun, SWE, 1993.*

Skiers: **Anita Moen**, NOR, Bib #8
Marie-Helene Westin Østlund, SWE, Bib #11 (Gold Medal winner in the 20 km 1987 World Championships)

Figure 9-18 *Skate Step Turning by a Canadian skier at Silver Star, B.C., CAN, 1991*

1

Women's 10K Freestyle Pursuit
World Championships, Falun, SWE, 1993.

Bib #5: **Stefania Belmondo**, *ITA,*
Belmondo who won the Gold Medal in this race, takes the lead by Step Skating aggressively and superbly in the downhill. Following close behind are three top world class skiers from Russia.

Bib #1: **Larissa Lazutina**, *Silver Medalist*
Bib #2: **Ljubov Jegorova**, *Bronze Medalist*
Bib #4: **Jelena Välbe**

2

4

3

Jelena Välbe, *one of the great Russian women skiers, won seven Gold Medals in the World Championships and two Golds in the Olympics from 1989 to 1994.*

3. SKID TURN AT HIGH SPEED

When the speed through a sharp curve is too fast for skate stepping, or there are icy conditions, the skier may choose to skid around the curve - a familiar technique used in Alpine skiing. The skier has to counteract lateral forces and frontal drag forces, and remain stable in the skiing direction while skiing around the curve. The skid technique at high speed is strenuous on the legs, and demands a 100% complete focus to avoid a tumble.

Skid Turn Procedure

Skis are kept parallel, with the uphill ski positioned ahead of the downhill ski, with a slight spread of the feet to retain good stability. Skier must have a good lean forward and inward to the curve to counteract lateral centrifugal and frontal air drag forces. Ideally the skier's COG should act between the ankles so both skis are equally weighted, and the skier is in a comfortable, stable position.

The skid turn is executed by a twisting movement of the hips and legs, with the skis kept parallel and edged into the upper side of the curve. If the skier does not lean forward and inward enough, the fragile skinny skis may start vibrating, a common problem encountered in making a sharp skid turn at high speed. If the skier turns too sharply, and over-does the turn, body weight (COG) should be shifted smoothly backward to counteract instability. Skiers should practice the skid turn to the left and right on a well packed downhill slope.

Figure 9-20 *Skid Turn at High Speed*

4. TWO-SIDE SKATING IN LOW TUCK WITHOUT POLING

Skating efficiently in a Low Tuck body position with poles under arms requires strength, balance and coordination. It is very similar to ice speed skating with arms on the back. The technique requires maximum concentration. In Figure 9-21, the skier is alert and vision is in the direction of the skiing glide, with attention to any terrain or snow pack variation that may effect stability and efficient skiing.

The advantage of this technique in a mild downhill is that, as potential speed increases to or beyond 10 m/sec, which is not unusual, the air resistance increases substantially and the aerodynamic body form of a Low Tuck, with its smaller frontal area increases the potential speed substantially (Ch. 11, Sec. III).

It is used frequently at the end of downhills, when approaching a flat or transition to maintain the speed caused by the forward momentum (mv) (Ch. 11, Sec. II-B-9). To become an excellent high speed skier, it is imperative to master Low Tuck Skating in special terrain.

As discussed in Chapter 5, Exercise IV, efficient skating involves use of the largest muscle groups, the hips, with little bending at the knees. By keeping COG at a constant level, less energy is required than moving COG up and down. COG is moved laterally back and forth with balance and glide on a flat ski.

Thomas Alsgård, winning the Gold in the 30 km Freestyle, Lillehammer, NOR, Olympics 1994, is shown in the Figure 9-22 sequence of photos, as he combines excellent skating in a low tuck to both sides while making a sharp turn after a mild downhill. He exhibits a very relaxed body form at a speed exceeding 10 m/sec.

Analysis of Skating Sequences

The Bar Chart between the two sets of sequential photos (Front and Side Views of two skiers) on the next two pages illustrates typical sequences for Low Tuck Skating showing separate:

> Left Side Action
> Right Side Action

Low Tuck Skating with skates to both sides, straight forward, is symmetrical. The skate on one side is *equal* to the skate on the other side, and the sequence of each glide, skate and recovery on left side, is *equal* to the glide, skate and recovery on right side. Legs come close together during the Recovery.

The bar chart illustrates that the time duration of each action is different.

a. The *longest* time period is for the Glide on the ski

b. The *second longest* time is for the Skate Action

c. The *shortest* time is for the Recovery.

See low tuck skating photo sequences on next two pages ⇒

| 1 | 2 | 3 | 4 |

A. LEFT SIDE ACTION: LEGS TOGETHER , DOWNSET GLIDE ON LEFT SKI

B. RIGHT SIDE ACTION: SKATING ON RIGHT SKI | RECOVERY OF RIGHT SKI

| 1 | 2 | 3 | 4 |

FRONT VIEW: TOP ROW
SIDE VIEW: BOTTOM ROW

FIGURE 9-21
FIGURE 9-22

Skier: John Svensson, USA
Skier: Thomas Alsgård, NOR

5   6   7   8

SKATING ON LEFT SKI   RECOVERY OF LEFT SKI

LEGS TOGETHER, DOWNSET AND GLIDE ON RIGHT SKI

5   6   7   8

Figure 10-1

10 skiers applying several different techniques
1988 Olympics, Canmore, CAN, First Leg, 4x10 Relay

#4   *Pål Gunnar Mikkelplass, NOR*
#1   *Jan Ottosson, SWE, Gold Medalist*
#14 *Radim Nyc, TCH, Bronze Medalist*
#5   *Andy Grünenfelder, SUI*
#7   *Silvano Barco, ITA*
#2   *Vladimir Smirnov, KAZ, Silver Medalist*
#9   *Svetoslav Atanassov, BUL*
#6   *Walter Kuss, FRG*
#10 *Andre Blatter, AUT*
#11 *Atsushi Egawa, JAP*

CHAPTER 10
Summary and Application of
Cross Country Ski Skating Techniques

CHAPTER 10

Summary and Application of Cross Country Ski Skating Techniques

CONTENTS

INTRODUCTION

A few years ago there were limited basic technique variations of ski skating, used only in specific cases, as in sharp step turns. When a "free" choice of style in competition was allowed, the increase in the number of skate variations was explosive and nearly unlimited. It was as if every individual was trying to develop their own style of skating.

The new sport of Skating required new types of equipment, skis, poles, and boots, with special adaptations and advantages to Skating. As the new equipment was available, it promoted more experimentation and the invention and refinement of new skate technique variations.

Free-style competition quickly indicated that Skating was a very fast sport. Its average speed was impressively faster than the traditional Diagonal and Double Pole disciplines. During ski skate racing there was no time for "researching the type of technique to be used." This had to be done prior to the race. Specialized training, applying specific types of techniques suited and adapted to different terrain, became the name of the game.

The final decision to preserve the older traditional or Classic technique as a separate form for Nordic skiing, made clear the division between Classic and Skating techniques. As a Nordic sport, there are advantages and disadvantages to each of the classifications.

I. ADVANTAGES OF SKATING COMPARED TO TRADITIONAL TECHNIQUE

A. SKATING IS EASIER TO LEARN

Correct Classic cross country skiing, such as the Diagonal technique, is technically complicated, and takes many years of practice and proper instruction to master. Basic Skating is much simpler and therefore easier to learn. However, to become an expert and learn to ski all the Skating techniques well, requires a lot of practice and knowledge.

B. FASTER SKIING

The main reason cross country ski skating gained such popularity was the introduction of skating into racing, where skating techniques were shown to be faster. Races were completed in considerably less time using skate techniques than using the traditional styles, and time is the only matter of importance in ski racing.

In cross country skiing for recreational purposes, however, speed is not usually the main objective. Ski touring in a relaxed fashion, enjoying the environment, getting away from the rush of life, places less emphasis on increased speed of skiing. But greater numbers of recreational skiers are finding that the fun of increased speed, along with the other positive attributes of skating in groomed tracks, is immensely attractive.

C. LESS ENERGY USED

In ski skating, the frictional resistance between the ski base and snow is considerably less than in the traditional style where a friction kick/traction is used, because glide wax is applied under the full length of the ski base.

Cross country skiing has always been considered a fairly strenuous sport, and known to use a lot of energy, although this depends to a large degree on how fast it is performed. The reduction of the frictional resistance, which accounts for a substantial percentage of the total energy used in skiing, obviously is an area of advantage for ski skating.

The skate push is much slower than the leg kick used in the Classic diagonal stride technique, suggesting that skating requires less force expended by the lower limb muscles (Ch. 11, Sec.II-B-1 and 2). In skating the lower limb muscle forces are distributed over a longer time period. A skier does not need to stop gliding to execute the kick (static friction) as in Classic.

D. SIMPLIFIED WAXING

Waxing for ski skating is much simpler than for traditional style skiing. Skating uses only glide wax under the full length of the ski base, which is probably one of the greatest advantages over Classic. Classic skiing has always been associated with complicated waxing for a kick and glide combination. This is particularly true when wet or icy conditions require klister for the Classic kick which basically is a mess to put on and a nuisance to clean off the skis. A suitcase of color-coded wax is common baggage for Classic racers. Correct waxing in Classic requires a lot of experience and knowledge and is time consuming. For inexperienced skiers, and occasionally even for experts, the choice of wax is a gamble.

E. MORE FREEDOM OF MOVEMENT

During skating, movement is not limited to a parallel track. As long as there is space on the course there are almost unlimited ways of making headway.

F. MORE FUN

The term "Dancing" directly reflects the feeling of the rhythmic movements in the Skating techniques that stimulates further interest and enjoyment in the sport.

II. DISADVANTAGES OF SKATING

There are also disadvantages of skating when compared to traditional Classic skiing.

A. *DEEP SNOW*

Ski skating today is practiced primarily in areas with a packed or firm ski base. Skating in deep snow is almost impossible, requiring too much energy. Tourers skiing in back country, therefore, still prefer the traditional methods, and the friction grip between ski base and the snow.

B. *SKATING REQUIRES A WIDER PACKED COURSE*

Due to the outward angled movement of the skis during skating, a much wider course or skiing track is required for skating. This is probably the biggest disadvantage of skating compared to traditional parallel track skiing. The illustrations in Chapter 2 show that a Freestyle course for skating may have to be packed three times the width of a classic single track. To comfortably pass other skiers, particularly in the uphills, requires even more space.

In Freestyle skiing the course also has to be prepared with a classic groomed skiing track on at least one side, since Freestyle means the choice of any type of technique. In a course where skating only applies, downhills are usually provided with a groomed track to the side of the course, for those who prefer to ski downhill in a preset track.

C. *BIGGER, MORE EXPENSIVE PACKING MACHINERY REQUIRED*

While a snowmobile plus an inexpensive tracksled can set professional quality skiing tracks for the Classic technique, a professional ski skating course requires much more sophisticated expensive equipment than small ski clubs and many cross country ski areas can afford to buy.

D. *GRADING OF TERRAIN MAY BE REQUIRED*

While Classic skiing is associated with mobility and variety in most terrain, skating requires at least a roughly graded roadway and terrain where packing machinery can be moved comfortably. Grading (bulldozing) of terrain for cross country skating may have an impact on the environment that some parties (public or private) consider damaging, and therefore may require special governmental approval.

III. VARIATIONS AND APPLICATIONS

Cross country ski skating has many technique variations. The following summary table details a number of them. Skating may be with double poling, single poling or without use of poles - to one side, two sides or alternately. Learning the many varieties of skating techniques is interesting and will enhance skiing enjoyment. These techniques can be used in recreational skiing and practiced on specially prepared ski skate, also called freestyle, courses.

The use of so many different technique variations promotes the development of a greater number of different muscle groups. When tired from skiing one specific technique, changing to a different one gives the muscles an opportunity to relax and recover. This is one of the reasons top international skiers use a variety of skate techniques during any one race.

After studying the illustrations and discussions of variations of skating techniques in the preceding chapters, a skier may ask which of them would best apply to a particular skiing terrain. Top international cross country skiers adapt or vary their techniques depending on type of terrain, snow conditions, and their energy resources.

Skating can be used in all types of graded terrain, steep uphills as well as in mild downhills. During ski skating in the uphills, the skate glide length is shortened and the angle of the skate ski increased, using the skate technique that requires least energy to maintain the forward propulsion movement.

As the speed during skating increases, as on level or downhill terrain, poling becomes less efficient, and the legs only may be used. The skate may be done in a crouched body position (tuck) with arms and poles close to the body, or the long distance ice skater's swinging arm technique may be used while in the tuck body position.

IV. TABLE OF SKI SKATING TECHNIQUES

The Table *(Fig. 10-2)* shows a total of 17 variations of ski skating. A real difficulty in teaching and discussing ski skating technique is the past use of numerous different English language names and identifications for one and the same technique, which has been very confusing and detrimental to the sport.

The names identifying techniques in this text are similar to or a translation of those used as the official language (terminology) of the Winter Olympics, Lillehammer, Norway 1994. The term "Dance" when applied to skating emphasizes the rhythmic, enjoyable aspects of the technique.

The technique listing in the following table attempts to follow a sequence of technique developments based upon degree of difficulty.

♦ **Chapter 5 - Basic Skate Movements -** Learning balance while gliding on one flat ski, with lateral movement from one ski to the other, and coordinated harmonic rhythmic movements of legs, arms and poles - with mental focus at all times.

♦ **Chapter 6 - Double Poling Variations -** Basic for all techniques.

♦ **Chapter 7 - One-Side Skating -** The original skate.

♦ **Chapter 8 - Two-Side Skate Dances -** The many variations in skate patterns.

♦ **Chapter 9 - High Speed Downhill Skating and Turning -** Done without poling, applying different downhill tucks.

Several variations within Two-Side skating shown in the following table have not been discussed in detail, but these are highly specialized technique variations used by top international racers only. They could either be learned from skilled international coaching, or developed individually by experienced skiers. Many variations in skating are in the developmental stage, and are analyzed or discussed by the author for perhaps the first time, in this text.

TABLE OF SKI SKATING TECHNIQUES

Number	Technique Name	Chapter and Section	Type of Upper Extremity Movement	Type of Lower Extremity Movement	Correlation Between the Extremities	Typical Signs of Identification	Applications to Type of Terrain and Speed
	A	B	C	D	E	F	G
1	Diagonal Skate with Arm Swing Exercise	Chap. 5, Sec. II, Exer. IV	Diagonal arm swing, no poling	Skating on alternate legs	Diagonal movement of arms and legs, body fairly erect	Diagonal action, opposite leg and arm	Mild downhills and fast flats
2	Skating in Tuck Body Position	Chap. 5, Sec. II, Exer. V	No arm swing, poles tucked under arms	Skating on alternate legs	Body in tuck, no arm movement	Streamlined body tuck, leg movement only	Mild to steeper downhills
3	Straight Double Poling	Chap. 6	Pre-loading, both arms poling in parallel	None, except slight "give" (flex) in knees	No leg movement Upper body only	No skating, symmetrical	Variable level and mild downhills
4	Double Poling With Forward Scissors Kick	None	Pre-loading, both arms poling in parallel	Relaxed, quick forward swing of one leg, to enhance inertia	Poling and quick forward leg swing simultaneously	No skating, forward leg swing, symmetrical poling	Same as above, primarily in high speed terrain
5	Marathon Skate (One-side skating)	Chap. 7, Sec. III	Pre-loading, both arms poling in parallel	Powerful one leg skate, gliding on other leg	Double poling while skating with one leg	Asymmetrical one side skating	Variable level terrain, transitions and curves
6	Single Dance	Chap. 8, Sec. I	Straight double poling with first of two or more skates	Skating on alternate legs	One double poling per two or more skates	Poling with first skate, with recovery while skating on other leg	Variable level, primarily in high speed terrain
7	Single Dance Hop	None	Same as above prior to quick jump off one ski	Same as above but with rhythmic jump off one ski immediately before pole plants	Same as above but higher frequency and an aggressive jump off one ski	Same as above, with jump off one ski, high frequency, rhythmic	Variable level terrain, flat; to accelerate
8	Double Dance	Chap 8, Sec. II	Straight double poling with each skate	Skating on alternate legs	Double poling with each skate	Symmetrical, high frequency poling for each skate	Variable and level terrain, transitions into uphills; to accelerate

Number	Technique Name	Chapter and Section	Type of Upper Extremity Movement	Type of Lower Extremity Movement	Correlation Between the Extremities	Typical Signs of Identification	Applications to Type of Terrain and Speed
	A	B	C	D	E	F	G
9	Double Dance Hop	None	Straight double poling with each skate	Same as above but with rhythmic jump off one ski immediately before pole plants	Double poling each skate	Symmetrical double poling with pre-jump off one leg, high frequency, rhythmic	Variable level terrain and transitions into uphillls; to accelerate
10	Paddle Dance	Chap. 8, Sec. III	Asymmetric staggered double poling, slight rotation of body	Skating on alternate legs, aggressively	One pole planted slightly ahead of other before skate	Asymmetrical poling and skating	Steeper, tough uphills
11	Mogren's Paddle	Chap. 8, Sec. III, K-1	Same as above but finish poling earlier	Sames as above, but longer, powerful skate impulse on Hang side	Same as above	Sames as above, but longer skate time on Hang side	Same as above, but also in mild uphills
12	Paddle Dance Hop "The Pump"	Chap. 8, Sec. III, K-2	Same as above but more aggressive movements	Same as above, but with rhythmic galloping jump from one ski to the other	Powerful aggressive action with double pole plant and skate jump off one ski	Same as above, but a jump action off one skate leg, very high intensity	Steep shorter uphills, very strenuous, generates very high speed
13	Diagonal Dance	Chap. 8, Sec. IV	Poling alternately by left and right arms	Skating on alternate legs	Diagonal movement of arms & legs	Poling with left arm while skating with right leg	Steep uphills when other techniques become tiring
14	Wide skate step - fast curved downhill	Chap. 9, Sec. IV C-2	Arms wide to control balance	Quick lateral skate stepping, one ski at a time	Aggressive upper and lower body movement	Hard work with arms and legs to retain balance	Fast curved downhill with sharp curves
15	Tight Skate Step in Tuck - Curved Downhill	Chap. 9 Sec. IV C-2	Tuck position, poles tucked under arms	Lateral skate stepping, one ski at a time	Poles under arms, tuck position, legs step laterally	Little movement of upper body, downhill tuck	Curved downhill, mild or steep, to accelerate or maintain speed
16	Skating to Two sides, Low tuck	Chap. 9, Sec. IV, C-4	Tuck position, little or no body movement, poles under arms	Skating on alternate legs	Poles under arms, skating to both sides	In tuck, little movement of upper body, leg action only	Mild downhill, to accelerate or maintain speed
17	Skid Turn- Curved downhill	Chap. 9, Sec. IV, C-3	Tuck, or arms close to body	Skis parallel, skidding and sliding laterally	No leg movement, hip and feet rotation	Spray of snow caused by skidding while edging	Steep, sharp, tricky or icy curved downhills

V. SUMMARY OF FACTORS CONTROLLING SPEED OF MOVEMENT AND ENERGY IN SKI SKATING

To be effective in ski skating a skier should be knowledgeable about, and physically and technically able to comply with, the following:

1   Rhythm, good balance, and continuity of movement.

2. Training of neurological response time, muscle endurance strength and coordination (Ch. 4, Sec. III).

3. Initiation of muscle action starting with the large muscle groups at the mid-section, then superimposing, in the right order, to muscle action of legs and arms (Ch. 4, Sec. IV).

4. Effective forward lean, with little or no bending at the hips, crowning of back and proper orientation of the upper shoulder, hip and trunk alignments (Ch. 11, Sec. I-B-3).

5. Correct NKT (Nose-knee-toe) alignment (same ref as above).

6. Elbows at a 90° rotation about the shoulder during poling, with full arm extension during poling push off (Ch. 6, Sec. IV, Ch. 11, Sec. II-A-3).

7. Pole plant for most techniques immediately prior to downset of ski. Vertical pole plant force component reduces the skier's weight and thereby the static (contact) friction (Appendix, Sec. I-C-6).

8. Legs move close together, during initiation of all techniques, avoid angling knees inward during the skate.

9. Light initial contact with downset of ski to reduce static friction (Appendix I-C-5).

10. Minimized skate ski angle (α) with the direction of skiing (Ch. 11, Sec. II-B-10).

11. Full weight shift from one ski to the other (vertical extension line of body's COG should be over ankle when in balanced position on one ski).

12. Glide on flat ski as long as possible to reduce edging friction and to ski with least energy (Appendix, Sec. I-C-6).

13. Maximize skate force during middle of the skate when there is least frictional resistance (same ref. as above).

14. Adjustment of the skate frequency to environmental factors, such as steepness of hill, snow condition, altitude, temperature, by acknowledging speed (v) in the "Skate Impulse Expression"

$$v = \frac{F(t)}{m}$$ when skiing (Ch. 11, Sec. II-B-4).

In skiing with least use of energy, there are a number of specific often neglected factors that contribute to increased speed of skiing:

♦   Recoil effect from crowning (preloading) the back during poling (Ch. 6, Sec. XI, Ch. 4, Sec. II-D).

♦   Hip movement (Ch. 5, Exercise IV).

♦   Weight shift - Balance (Ch. 3, Sec. I).

♦   Ideal Skate Force Distribution (Appendix, Sec. I-C-7).

♦   Glide on flat ski, applies to all techniques.

♦   Momentum (Ch. 11, Sec. II-B-9).

♦   Vertical movement of COG (Ch. 11, Sec. II-B-6).

♦   Aerial movement of leg and ski (Ch. 11, Sec. II-B-5).

♦   Inertia (Appendix, Sec. II).

CHAPTER 11

Introduction to Ski Skating Mechanics

Figure 11-1

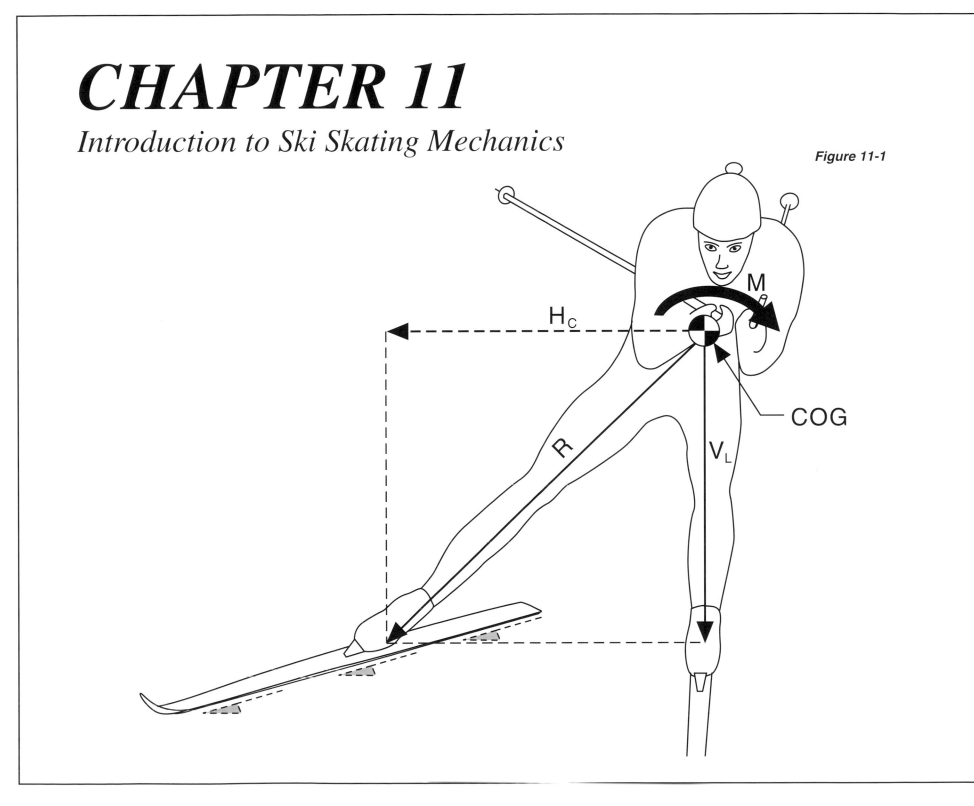

CHAPTER 11

Introduction to Ski Skating Mechanics

CONTENTS

CHAPTER 11

Introduction to Ski Skating Mechanics

INTRODUCTION

Cross Country Skiing Mechanics is a branch of physics which deals with movement, as it applies to the skier's total body, segments of the body, the mind, and the skier's equipment.

To simplify the application and understanding of skiing mechanics for the novice, the author uses numerous easy-to-read graphical illustrations instead of mathematical expressions.

Cross country skiing mechanics in practice involves analyzing:

1. The *skier's physical actions* that stimulate and cause the skier's forward movements (acceleration).

2. *External environmental factors* that influence the skier's deceleration (slow down).

Cross country skiing performed on level terrain at relatively slow speed, is characterized by frequent acceleration (repetitive body movements directed forward) generated by the muscular actions of the skier, which are needed to overcome a continuous snow drag (resistance) created by contact of the ski with the snow. Otherwise, the snow drag would retard the skier to a stand-still over a relative short distance. The skier must repeatedly apply muscle strength to the equipment to propel the body forward.

The factors involved in analyzing a skier's uphill or downhill progress are much more complicated, taking into account a myriad of forces other than simple snow drag, the major ones being the *skier's gravity force components.*

Muscle strength from the back, abdomen, shoulder and arms produce poling forces that contribute to the forward motion in virtually all cross country techniques. In Classic Technique the back, hip and leg muscles create an explosive friction kick force under the ski to accelerate the body forward. During ski skating, forward propulsion by leg action is caused by *continuous gliding skate push forces* acting under an angle with the traveling direction.

Understanding and interpreting skiing movements by applying Basic Force Mechanics is a tremendous advantage during learning, instructing, and correcting technique in order to ski efficiently (with least use of energy). Although technique has to be modified to some degree with the variation of the environment and new equipment innovations, the Laws of Mechanics do not. Any new innovation in skiing, advantageous or not, can be evaluated and critiqued from the basic laws of mechanics of movement, introduced in this chapter, and applied extensively throughout this text for skating techniques.

The mechanics analysis moves through explanations of such fundamental graphics concepts as Center of Gravity (COG), forces, and moments, and extends into practical applications of skiing movements, arriving at the most efficient forms for skiing. This chapter is used extensively as a *theoretical* reference source to clarify techniques in practice, as illustrated and described in other chapters of this book.

I. FUNDAMENTAL GRAPHICAL CONCEPTS

A. *BODY AXES AND CENTER OF GRAVITY (COG)*

1. LOCATION OF COG FOR AN ERECT BODY

When analyzing a skier's movement, it is convenient to describe the position of the total body or segment of the body by establishing body reference lines by means of an *AXIS SYSTEM*.

For a person in a horizontal resting position in balance about a point (a roller in the illustration), establish a body axis through the balance point *(See Fig. 11-2)*. The Z-Z axis is found to be the distance "a" from the bottom of the feet.

The same person is then rotated to the standing position with front and side views, as illustrated, assuming both feet are evenly weighted. A symmetrical vertical Y-Y axis is established for both the front and side view of the body while in the erect position. For the side view, the location of the Z-Z axis is repeated, and for the front view, an axis X-X is established perpendicular to the Z-Z axis.

The intersection of the three axes (X-X, Y-Y, Z-Z) gives a theoretical point called the ***Center of Gravity*** (COG) of a person's body.

The location of COG, a distance "a" up from the feet can also be found by moments and weight calculations. For a person in an ideal erect body position, the body masses on either side of an axis balance each other. COG is defined as a point within a person's body (or within an element of the body) where the Lever Moment (mass times a distance) on one side of the axis is equal to the Lever Moment on the other side of the axis.

COG is the theoretical point where the total mass of a body is assumed to be concentrated. COG can also be visualized as a support point about which the body is in equilibrium regardless of form or position (as an axle for a wheel).

Location of COG for most active skiers in an erect body position is approximately 3 to 5 cm. in front of the spine, level with the third lumbar vertebra. This level is approximately at the waist or belt line.

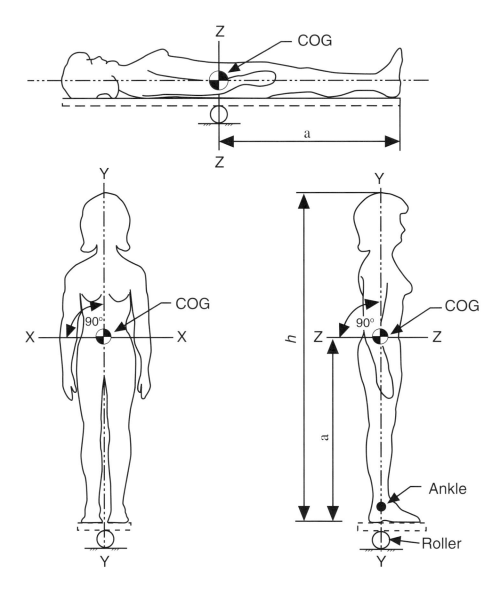

Figure 11-2 *Location of COG for an Erect Person - 3 Views*

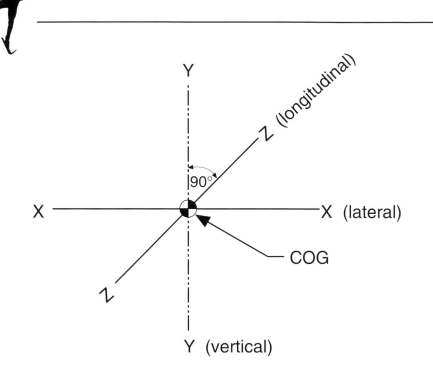

Figure 11-3 *Perspective View of 3 Axes System*

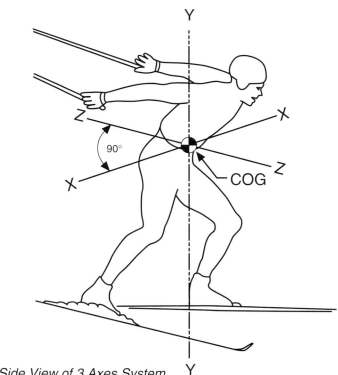

Figure 11-4 *Side View of 3 Axes System*

2. LOCATION OF COG AS BODY POSITION VARIES

As the body changes position and moves, the COG will change location longitudinally, horizontally (laterally), and/or vertically. In this book, COG movement is measured longitudinally as progressive skiing distance movements, and also laterally and vertically as small displacements. This applies to the skier's body as a whole, segments of the body, and skiing equipment.

The study and evaluation of vertical fluctuation and lateral movements of the skier's COG is critical in the analysis of technique and energy use in this book.

3. 3 AXES REFERENCE SYSTEM APPLIED TO SKIERS

With reference to the mechanics of a skier in motion, an axes system having the following fixed established reference lines will be used *(Fig. 11-4).*

- Z-Z axis, longitudinal axis. (The direction in which the skier is traveling.)

- X-X axis, lateral axis. (Skier seen from front or rear view.)

- Y-Y axis, vertical axis. (Skier seen from any side, front or rear view).

The intersection of the 3 axes locates the COG of the skier's body during movement.

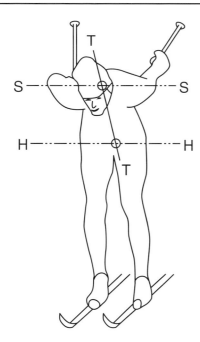

Figure 11-5
HST Alignment in Double Poling
In straight double poling the hip (H-H) and shoulder (S-S) lines are parallel; while during skating, the hip and shoulder alignments are independent of each other.

B. BODY REFERENCE ALIGNMENTS

In addition to the axes defined, three reference lines called alignments are also used. While body axes are fixed lines, the alignments refer to segments of the body that constantly change with body position and techniques used.

1. HIP, SHOULDER AND TRUNK ALIGNMENTS

These alignments refer to the orientation of the three principal parts composing the greater mass of the body, namely:

a. ***Hip (H-H) Alignment***
A line drawn through the center of the pelvis' hip ball joints.

b. ***Shoulder (S-S) Alignment***
A line drawn through the center of the shoulder ball joints. The H-H and S-S lines will vary with movement of the hips and shoulders horizontally and vertically, individually, or together.

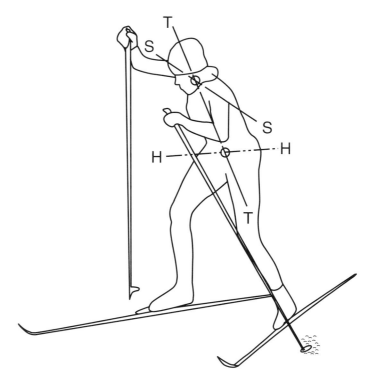

Figure 11-6 *HST Alignment in Skating*
For some cross country techniques, such as the Paddle Dance Skate, the hip (H-H) and shoulder (S-S) alignments are parallel at initiation when legs are together, but during poling there is a marked difference in the orientation of the two alignments. The trunk line (T-T) initially goes through a small forward incline, with little or no bending at the hips, but with crowning of the back. The shoulder line (S-S) is perpendicular to the drive (gliding) ski, and the hip line (H-H) is rotated both clockwise and counter-clockwise.

c. ***Trunk (T-T) Alignment***
This is a line, dividing the trunk symmetrically into left and right sides when viewed from the front and rear. T-T is assumed to intersect the H-H and S-S lines. T-T alignment is also a reference to the amount of forward bending of the upper extremity.

2. DIVISION OF BODY - LEFT AND RIGHT SIDES - UPPER AND LOWER EXTREMITIES

By extending the trunk line (T-T) downward, the body, during movement, is divided into *Left and Right sides*, when viewed from the rear.

The lateral axis through COG, (X-X), divides the body into *Upper and Lower Extremities.* Muscle action for poling primarily involves the upper extremity, while leg work for Classic and skating primarily involves muscle action by the lower extremity.

Figure 11-7
Division of Body

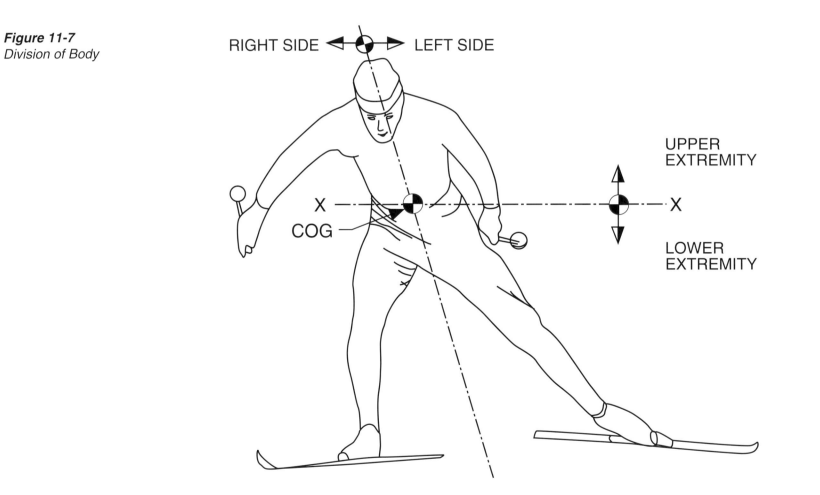

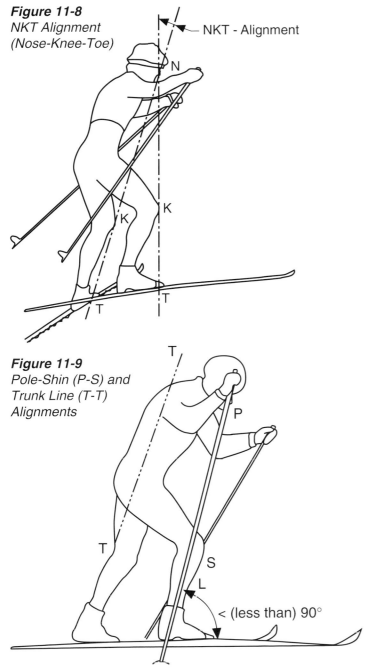

Figure 11-8
*NKT Alignment
(Nose-Knee-Toe)*

NKT - Alignment

Figure 11-9
*Pole-Shin (P-S) and
Trunk Line (T-T)
Alignments*

< (less than) 90°

3. VISUAL ALIGNMENTS FOR GOOD SKATING

a. *Nose-Knee-Toe (NKT) Visual Alignment (Figure 11-8)*

The NKT visual alignment is one of the most efficient self-teaching aids skiers can use to improve and perfect their cross country skiing technique. When *initiating* the skate the skier checks body position by visually lining up the knee and toes with the nose.

When a good NKT alignment, which assures a correct forward lean and lateral position, is combined with a minimum vertical fluctuation of COG (achieved by *minimal bending* at the hips and knees), efficient, energy saving technique results.

The NKT alignment can be used in virtually all situations, when the skier is in balance on one leg (One Point Of Contact). In skating, it often applies to the angulation of both legs simultaneously, as shown.

b. *Pole-Shin (P-S) Alignment (Figure 11-9)*

At the time of the pole plant, the pole and shin should be parallel and inclined forward. For effective transfer of leg action forces to the ski, the angle between the shin and ski should be less than 90° at all times on the level, as well as in the uphills. The same leg and pole should be parallel during downset of the ski when viewing skier from a front or rear view.

c. *Angle of Trunk-Line (T-T) (Figure 11-9)*

This alignment works in unison with the NKT and P-S alignments. Basically, ski skaters should bend relatively little at the hips, and apply forward lean of the whole body, on the level as well as in the uphills *(see Fig. 11-6 also).*

C. FORCES - GRAPHICAL ILLUSTRATIONS

Physically, a skier applies forces to equipment to propel the body forward. Poling forces are used in all techniques, with leg kick in classic and push forces in skating. *To simplify concepts of cross country skiing mechanics of movement and make them easier to understand, the author will apply graphical illustrations.*

1. FORCE LINES - VERTICAL AND HORIZONTAL COMPONENTS

A vertical force line arrow (V) represents a force acting downward or upward. A horizontal force line arrow (H) represents a push or pull force acting horizontally in either direction *(Fig. 11-10)*.

When the vertical force line (V) and horizontal force line (H) are combined, a combined force called the resultant R is obtained.

Such a configuration is called a ***force line triangle*** *(Fig. 11-11)*. The force lines can be drawn to scale, where the magnitude of the force would be indicated by the length of the arrow, and the force direction by the arrowhead.

Force lines are also called ***force components***. When two of the force components are graphically drawn to scale, the numerical value of the third one is found by measuring it.

When applying a force line triangle using different symbols, the components do not have to be vertical and horizontal, as illustrated. A 90° triangle can be used in any space configuration or orientation to illustrate forces and their relationships.

2. WEIGHT OF SKIER AND EQUIPMENT *(Figure 11-12)*

Weight is the earth's gravitational attraction on any body or object. **Weight is also a force.** Internationally, the unit kilogram (kg) is commonly used to measure weight. Weight of a skier can be illustrated graphically by use of a vertical force line.

Weight of a skier is assumed to act at COG, a theoretical point for the whole body, but specifically it also could refer to a segment of body or equipment. The direction of weight is always vertical, toward the center of the earth.

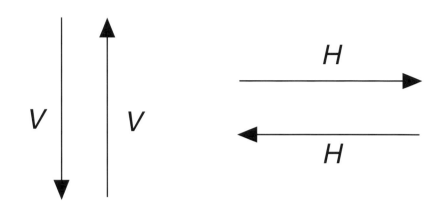

Figure 11-10 *Force Lines*

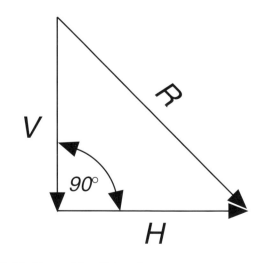

Figure 11-11 *Force Line Triangle*

3. THE FORCE LINE EQUILIBRIUM CONCEPT

a. Vertical Action And Reaction Forces

When a skier is in balance on a pair of skis, as shown in Figure 11-12, the skier's weight (W_B), acting at COG, is assumed to be transferred through the ankles to the skis below. W_B is the **Action Force.** Under each ski there is a force in the opposite direction, which is called a **Reaction Force**. If the skier's weight W_B is supported evenly on two skis, then the reaction force under each ski =

$$V_L \text{ (left)} = V_R \text{ (right)} = \frac{W_B}{2} \text{ or } W_B = V_L + V_R$$

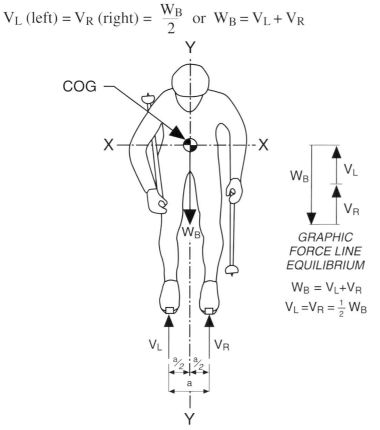

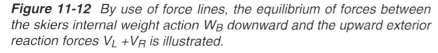

Figure 11-12 By use of force lines, the equilibrium of forces between the skiers internal weight action W_B downward and the upward exterior reaction forces $V_L + V_R$ is illustrated.

b. Pole Force Equilibrium and Pole Force Triangle

When an internal muscle action is applied through the pole shaft, (**pole shaft action force**, P) as in Figure 11-13, an equal **Reaction force** (P_{RE}) is assumed in the opposite direction at the surface level. ($P = P_{RE}$).

In the pole shaft force line triangle, (P) has two force line components, P_V, perpendicular to the ground and P_H, parallel with the ground.

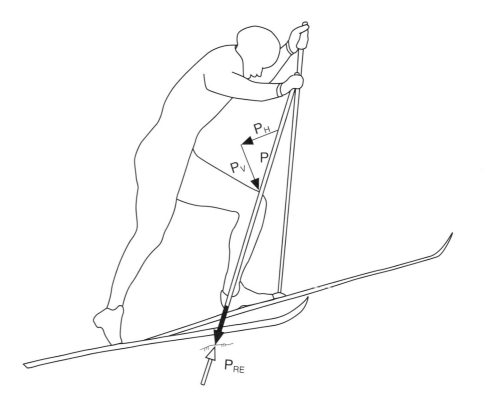

Figure 11-13 Poling Forces

4. VERTICAL LIFTING (UNWEIGHTING) BY POLING FORCES

During effective poling, the vertical poling force components in the two poles (P_{V+R}), reduce (V_{MF}), the additional internal muscle force required to lift the body's weight (W_B) uphill. This is another example of application of the Vertical Equilibrium of Force Lines.

A powerful force on an *forwardly inclined* pole in the uphill has a *double function* in skiing with less use of energy. The force component (P_H) parallel with the ground, contributes to a further increase in the speed forward (Ch. 11, Sec. II-A).

These principles apply to all cross country techniques.

⊕	=	COG (Center of Gravity)
Δh	=	Vertical distance COG moves uphill
W_B	=	Body Weight
P_L	=	Left pole shaft action force
P_{V_L}	=	Left pole shaft force component perpendicular to the ground
P_{H_L}	=	Left pole shaft force component parallel to the ground
$P_{V_{L+R}}$	=	Vertical pole component forces for left and right pole
V_{MF}	=	Additional internal muscle force by lower extremity to lift body vertically, Δh, uphill, assumed to act at COG
V_{MF}	=	$W_B - P_{V_{L+R}}$

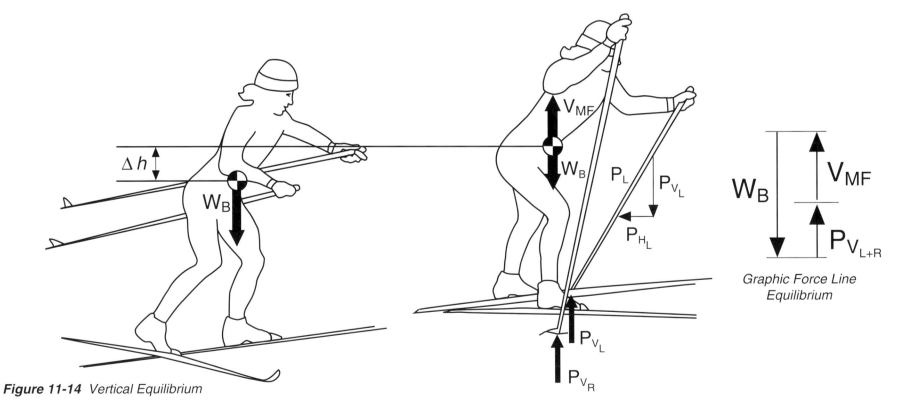

Graphic Force Line Equilibrium

Figure 11-14 *Vertical Equilibrium*

5. CENTRIFUGAL AND CENTRIPETAL FORCES (LATERAL FORCES)

When skiing a curved path there are forces that act laterally (sideways). The terms for these forces, centrifugal and centripetal, are often confused.

An object on a string, when whirled around, exerts centrifugal force which forces the object out from the center. A pulling force is exerted on the string (the centripetal force) to keep it whirling in a circle.

Likewise, the force felt on the body when driving a car too fast through a curve is centrifugal, which forces the car to continue forward in a straight line, unless the force is resisted by the tire friction on the pavement - the centripetal force which keeps it moving around the corner.

During the constant changes in direction in cross country skiing terrain, the centrifugal force tends to keep the skier going in a straight line, unless techniques are applied to change direction. In such instances, the lateral (centrifugal) force has to be counteracted by use of body movement and/or skiing equipment.

6. CENTRIFUGAL (LATERAL) FORCES WHEN BIKING A CURVE *(Figure 11-15)*

An example of centrifugal forces in practice is bicycling a curve as shown. The biker has to balance the vertical weight component (W_B), body + bike, and the centrifugal force (H_C) acting outward of the curve.

The resultant force line (R), from the force line components W_B and H_C, when extended from COG, must act through the wheel rim at the ground level, otherwise the biker will tip over.

In ski skating the skier constantly develops lateral forces similar to the centrifugal forces of the biker.

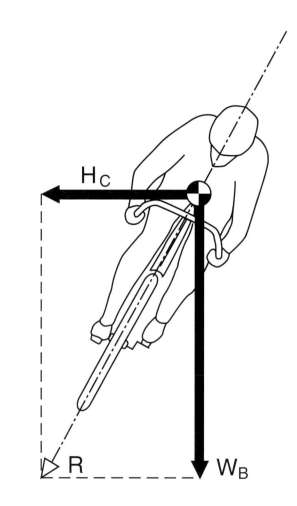

Figure 11-15 *Centrifugal Forces when Biking a Curve*

7. CENTRIFUGAL FORCES WHEN SKIING A CURVE

All changes of direction in cross country skiing on level or variable terrain are done either by skiing a curved path or by use of a skating technique.

When skiing downhill in a curved groomed path the skier's body has to lean forward and inward to counteract the frontal air drag resistance (D), (Ch. 11, Sec. II-C) and the lateral centrifugal force (H_C) which tends to tip the skier over. A tucked body position *(Fig. 11-16a)* is an advantage since the overturning moment = H_C (h) is minimized as the COG of the skier is lowered. ***The skiers ideal incline in a groomed track is when the resultant (R) of the two forces (W_B and H_C) comes between the ankles of the skier.***

To effectively skate any technique at moderate or high speeds along a curved track or path requires good coordination and a consistent weight transfer to the ski innermost on the curve. *Figure 11-16b* shows a skier skating a curve leaning toward the inside of the curve, thus moving the COG inward to a new position. When skiing through a curve, a centrifugal force (H_C), as shown, acts at COG outward from the curve, trying to tip the skier out of balance.

The ***most ideal body position*** occurs when the resultant R of the horizontal force (H_C) and the vertical body weight (W_B) goes through the ankle down to the inner gliding ski. Likewise, when the outer ski is the gliding one in a track, the ideal position occurs when the resultant R goes through the ankle of the outer ski.

Since the radius of the curve (*r*) and the speed is unknown, in order to ski the curve rhythmically and relaxed, the skier must adjust his weight shift inward, to a comfortable position.

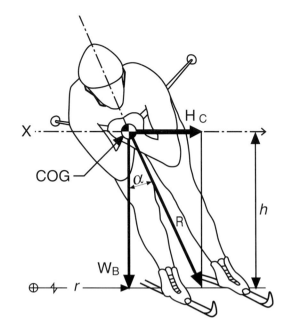

Figure 11-16a *Skiing a Curve in a Groomed Track*

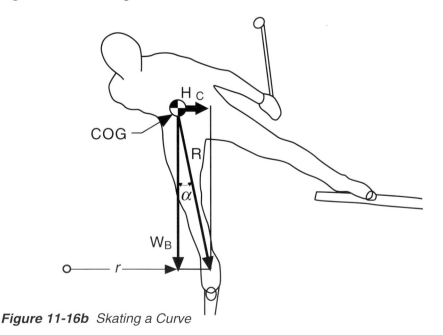

Figure 11-16b *Skating a Curve*

◗	=	COG (Center of Gravity)
W_B	=	Body Weight
H_C	=	Centrifugal Force Acting Outward
R	=	Resultant Force of W_B and H_C
α	=	Angle between R and W_B
r	=	Average Radius of Curve

D. MOMENTS

1. MOMENTS - DEFINITION

In everyday life, segments of the body do physical **work** which theoretically and practically can be expressed in terms of **moments**. Understanding moments and their application to mechanics of movement in cross country skiing, admittedly, is not easy. ***The author here again uses graphical illustration, with a few numerical examples, to explain moments in relation to muscular strength and efficient use of energy in cross country skiing.***

> Moment is defined as:
> A PRODUCT, EQUAL TO FORCE TIMES A DISTANCE

2. MOMENT - EXAMPLE

Figure 11-17 illustrates a moment at the wrist of a hand holding a bar with a weight at the end. The moment of the weight is designated as M = W(a) (Weight times the distance).

The moment at the wrist in this case is a term for muscular resistance caused by the weight and a lever arm. The numerical value can be found by measuring the Weight (W) and the distance (a). As these values vary, so does the size of the moment.

If we assume the weight (W) = 4 kg (kilogram) and the distance (lever arm) = 20 cm (centimeters), the wrist moment M = W(a) = 4 kg x 20 cm = 80 kg cm. If the weight (W) is increased to 7 kg, and the distance is reduced to 15 cm, the M = 7 kg x15 cm = 105 kg cm. We could have a contest among athletes to learn which one could resist (support) the biggest wrist moment.

3. MOMENT AS TERM FOR MUSCLE STRENGTH

Moments essentially are a term for muscle strength, which accordingly can have numerical values. Muscle forces are used continuously in cross country skiing to overcome gravitational forces (weights) and skiing frictional forces (drag).

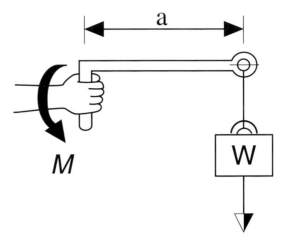

Figure 11-17 *A Moment at the Wrist*

4. PLUS AND MINUS SIGNS APPLIED TO MOMENTS

The numerical value of a moment acting clockwise is designated as + (plus sign) and the counter-clockwise moment is - (minus sign) *(Fig. 11-18).*

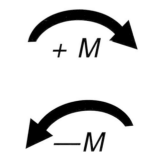

Figure 11-18 *Clockwise and Counter-clockwise Moments*

5. LEVER ARM IN MOMENTS

For simplicity, the illustrations shown in this book indicate lever arms for moments at COG *viewed from one side,* **together with forces** *in the same viewing plane.* It should be noted that the *actual lever arm for the force in the pole shaft is the distance* (a) *from COG perpendicular to the pole shaft (Fig. 11-19).*

Likewise, for glide forces in skating (G), the lever arm (a_1) is the distance perpendicular to the component forces acting in the direction of skiing. The illustration shows actual lever arms for poling and skating forces. In analysis of the most energy efficient technique, *correct lever arm distances from COG become very important in generating effective skate and pole forces.*

6. SYMBOLS FOR SPECIFIC MOMENTS

A symbol for a specific moment has a notation index attached to M. For example, M_I represents an internal muscle moment, while M_E refers to an external moment created by the skiing equipment, poles, skis or other external forces to which the skier is exposed.

The general symbol of a specific internal moment acting at COG is designated M_I, while *local* internal moments pertaining to individual segments of the body have a different notation index attached. For instance, M_e refers to a *local internal moment* acting at the elbow.

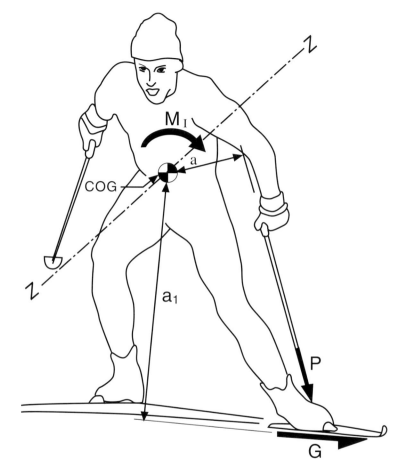

Figure 11-19 *Lever Arms For Poling And Skating Forces*

◓	=	COG (Center of Gravity)
a	=	Lever arm for pole
a_1	=	Lever arm for skate gliding force (G)
M_I	=	Moment of pole and skate forces at COG
P	=	Force in pole shaft
G	=	Skate gliding forces

7. MOMENTS ABOUT JOINTS *(Figure 11-20)*

To simplify expressions of muscle strength and energy, the theory of internal moments can be applied at a flexible joint, such as the ankle, knee, and hips for the lower extremity, and neck, shoulder, elbow and wrist for the upper extremity. A joint can be considered to be a hinge; when isolating a segment adjacent to the joint, the summation (equilibrium) of all moments and all forces for the segment involved is equal to zero.

8. INTERNAL MUSCLE STRENGTH (MOMENTS) AT JOINTS

Muscles are attached to the joints (Ch. 4, Sec. II-C and *Fig. 4-3*), with very short *internal* lever arms. When activated, muscle forces multiplied with the lever arm are equal to the internal muscle moment at the joint. The potential muscle strength (moment) at a joint is directly related to the size of the muscle group involved and the internal lever arm.

9. SUMMATION OF MOMENTS (MUSCLE STRENGTH) AT LOWER EXTREMITY TO ACTIVATE LEG SKATE ACTION

During the skate *(Fig. 11-20)*, muscle moments for the lower extremity are generated at the lower back (M_b), the hip (M_h), the knee (M_k), and at the ankle (M_a). The author assumes, in order to simplify this subject, that the summation of all these *internal* muscle action moments ($M_b + M_h + M_k + M_a = \Sigma M_{IL}$) acts at COG. The *external* moment M_{EG} = a skate force (G) times the distance (a_2) to COG. $M_{EG} = G(a_2)$.

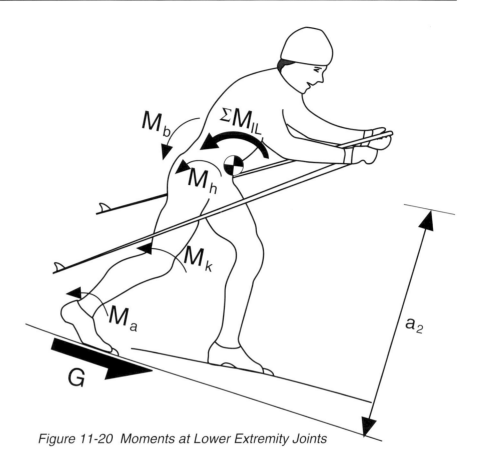

Figure 11-20 Moments at Lower Extremity Joints

◕	=	COG (Center of Gravity)
G	=	Effective Skate action force(s) under the ski during skate
a_2	=	Distance from COG perpendicular to ski
ΣM_{IL}	=	Summation of all internal muscle moments for lower extremity
M_{EG}	=	Skate force (G) times the distance (a_2) – external skate moment.
t	=	Endurance time of skate action

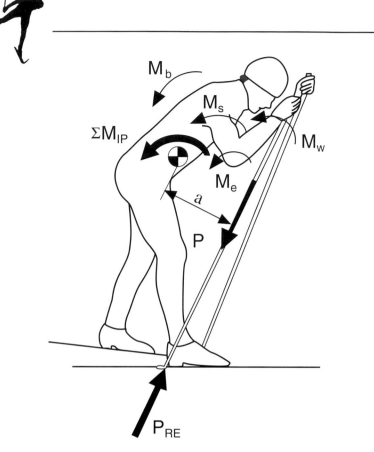

Figure 11-21 *Moments at Upper Extremity Joints*

⊕ = COG (Center of Gravity)

a = Distance from COG perpendicular to pole

P = Poling force in pole shaft

ΣM_{IP} = Summation of all *internal* muscle moments for poling for upper extremity

M_{EP} = Poling force (P) times distance (a) = *external* poling moment

ΣM_{IP} = M_{EP}

10. SUMMATION OF MOMENTS (MUSCLE STRENGTH) AT UPPER EXTREMITY TO ACTIVATE POLING FORCES

During poling, the moment (M_{IP}) would represent the total muscle action behind the poling force (P) for muscle groups within the upper extremity. These consist of muscle moments activated at the upper back and abdomen (M_b), the shoulder (M_s), the elbow (M_e), and at the wrist (M_w), as shown in the illustration.

$$\Sigma M_{IP} = M_b + M_s + M_e + M_w$$

The *external* moment M_{EP} = Poling force (P) times its lever arm distance (a) to COG, $M_{EP} = P(a)$

11. EQUILIBRIUM OF FORCES AND MOMENTS AT COG

The analysis of physical movement is simplified when assuming forces and moments act at COG. This is particularly helpful when studying the equilibrium of a skier in motion, since COG is *the theoretical balance point*, where summation of all *external action and reaction forces* therefore can be assumed equal to zero:

V = 0   Summation of Vertical Forces

H = 0   Summation of Forces Acting Laterally

Z = 0   Summation of Longitudinal Forces
(in skiing direction)

Likewise, there has to be moment equilibrium about COG:

Internal Moment = External Moment

$$M_I = M_E$$

$$M_I - M_E = 0$$

For a skier who is stationary or in movement there always has to be moment equilibrium; the *internal* and *external* moments must balance each other.

12. SUMMATION OF INTERNAL BODY ACTION MOMENT (ΣM_I) = SUMMATION OF EXTERNAL REACTION MOMENT (ΣM_E)

A skier's forward movement is created by applying ***internal muscle strength*** to the equipment (poles and skis). Muscle strength ***can be expressed numerically*** by use of ***moments***. (See Ch. 11, Sec. I-D-2) The total muscle strength involved is expressed as ΣM_I (Summation of ***internal*** moments involved). Likewise, external moments are identified by reaction forces applied to skiers equipment times their lever arms. The external moments caused by reaction forces is expressed as ΣM_E (Summation of ***external*** moments).

In this text, for every analysis made in mechanics of movements in skiing, this condition always applies:

$$\Sigma M_I = \Sigma M_E$$

The Summation of Internal (Body) Moments =

The Summation of External Reaction Moments.

CHAPTER 11
II.   Application of Mechanics To Skating Movements

In the following section, some *basic concepts of force lines* are applied to skiing mechanics and technique.

A.   POLING TECHNIQUE

1.   POLE ANGLE

a.   Force Line Triangle Concept Applied To Poling

The force line triangle concept, explained in Ch. 11, Sec. I, can be applied to poling, where P (the resultant) is the force in the pole shaft *(Fig. 11-22)*. P can be divided into two force components, where P_V is perpendicular, and P_H parallel to the ground during the pole plant and poling.

This graphical force line triangle visually shows that the P_H force, the component that is parallel to the ground, is one of the two forces (from two poles) contributing to the skier's forward movement.

b.   Application Of Force Lines To Determine The Most Efficient Pole Plant Angle.

The force line triangle concept can be applied to some practical examples to study forces created in the pole. Forces are assumed to act in a vertical plane when looking at the skier from the front. The graphical illustration shows that the only poling force contributing to the forward motion at the instant of the pole plant is the force component P_H in the force line triangle. The following discussion refers to forces in *one* of the two poles.

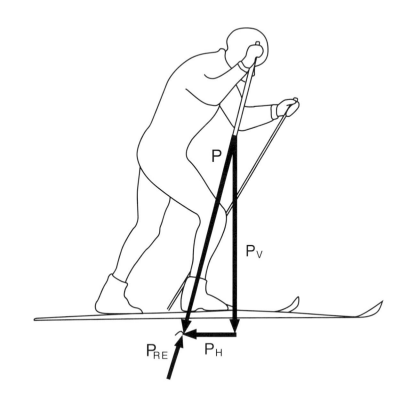

Figure 11-22 *Skier with Poling Force Triangle*

P	=	Pole shaft force
P_{RE}	=	Pole reaction force at surface
P_V	=	Component force of P, perpendicular to the ground
P_H	=	Component force of P, parallel to the ground

c. Inefficient Perpendicular Pole Plant (Figure 11-23)

An inefficient, energy wasting situation exists when the skier plants the pole perpendicular to the surface. The force lines clearly show that in this case the component parallel to the surface of the poling force does not contribute to the forward motion at the instant of the pole plant ($P_H = 0$). The total pole plant force dissipates into the ground, even if the skier's whole body weight is on the pole.

The force line concept suggests that the pole should always be planted with an incline backward at an angle less than 90°, since force (P) applied to a pole perpendicular to the ground will be a waste of energy. ***This applies to all cross country techniques, including skating.***

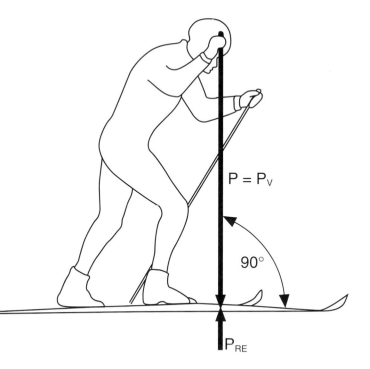

Figure 11-23 *Inefficient Pole Plant during Skating*

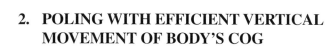

2. POLING WITH EFFICIENT VERTICAL MOVEMENT OF BODY'S COG

During poling, the skier's COG constantly moves vertically, slightly forward, and for all skating techniques, also laterally. As the skier's body changes position with movement, the location of the COG also changes *(Fig. 11-24, 25)*.

To understand and evaluate the cross country skier's poling technique and use of energy, visually locate the COG for the different body shapes of the skier in motion.

The skier's body weight W_B is assumed to be located at COG (the intersection of the axes system, namely the Y-Y, X-X, and Z-Z axes seen in Figures 11-4 and 12). As the skier lowers (flexes) his upper body, the COG moves downward, and when the skier erects his body, the COG moves upwards. The amount of vertical fluctuation (Δh) of COG varies with different techniques and each skier's efficiency of execution.

In skating, the COG also moves a considerable amount laterally, which makes the skiing path longer. Extra energy is needed to ski this extra distance.

Moving arms up and down causes small vertical movements of COG, while bending the body 90° forward, as done by many skiers during ***double poling*** in several skating techniques, involves moving a greater body mass and causes fluctuation of COG that has ***considerable impact*** on use of energy.

It is obvious that moving the COG vertically up and down for 1/2 to 3 hours, as happens in cross country skiing, demands a lot of energy. It may be compared to doing weightlifting where the W_B is the weight of the skier and Δh the lifting height. The energy used during movement can be found by multiplying the body weight W with the vertical distance of movement Δh at COG and time (*t*) of movement.

$$E = W_B (\Delta h)t.$$

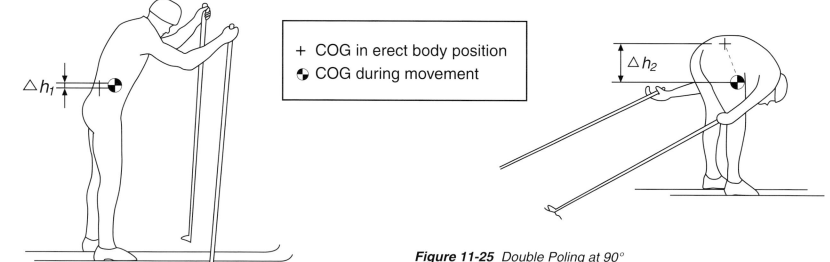

+ COG in erect body position
◕ COG during movement

Figure 11-24 *Double Poling, Erect*
Slight lifting of COG (Δh_1) caused by lifting of arms requires some energy

Figure 11-25 *Double Poling at 90°*
Significant lowering of COG (Δh_2) caused by bending upper body 90° or more, then lifting the body again to an erect position demands substantial energy

TESTING OF ENERGY DEMAND DURING VERTICAL MOVEMENT OF COG

The vertical movement of COG for the skier tested in the wind tunnel, (Ch. 11, Sec. III), weighing 80 kg. with a height of 185 cm. was calculated to be 22 cm, measured from erect body position with arms forward, and forward bending of trunk line 90° to horizontal position with arms down.

The vertical work (energy) involved in this case by lifting the body from the low position back to the erect position =

$$W = W_B (\Delta h) = 80 \text{ kg. } (22 \text{ cm}) = 1760 \text{ kgcm}$$

By crowning the upper back approximately 45° the work (energy) performed was reduced to approximately 1000 kgcm. It is the author's opinion that a tremendous amount of energy can be saved without reducing the average speed of skiing during a long tour or race, if a skier avoids excessive bending at the hips during poling.

3. DOUBLE POLING WITH MAXIMUM EFFICIENCY

Maximum efficiency in double poling is achieved by taking advantage of the poling components P_{HR} and P_{HL} from the right and left arms *(Fig. 11-26)*.

a. Use an efficient pole plant angle.

b. Avoid excessive vertical movement of COG.

c. Crown the upper back (with abdomen in) to maximize the larger muscle groups of the trunk, at the back and abdomen.

d. Keep elbows locked at approx. 90° until elbows reach the side of the body; the elbows then open up, with rotation about the larger shoulder muscles (See Ch. 6, Sec. IV).

e. Let legs glide forward to increase momentum and speed during final pole push-off.

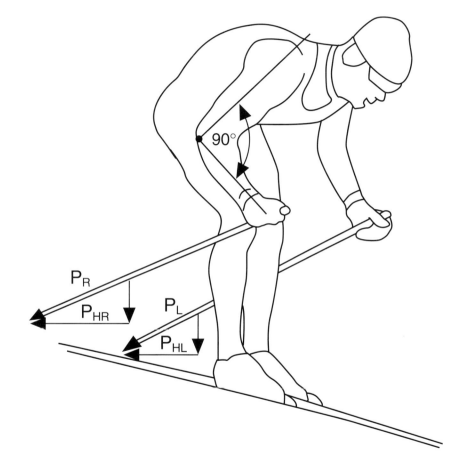

Figure 11-26 *Double Poling with Maximum Efficiency*

B. SKI SKATING TECHNIQUE

1. BASIC DIFFERENCE BETWEEN THE MECHANICS OF CLASSIC AND SKI SKATING

The difference between Classic and skating technique is primarily in how the forces are applied by the lower extremity to the ski.

In Classic *(Fig. 11-27)*, the skis are parallel, close together and a leg kick traction force (T) locks the ski to the snow and propels the skier forward. In the diagonal, double poling with leg kick, and the herringbone strides, static friction forces are created between the base of the ski and the snow to prevent backward slippage when the center of the ski grips the snow. Such grip is created by special wax applied to the ski base, or by building a ski base that prevents backward slippage, which always increases the forward gliding friction. The frictional grip kick in Classic is a short explosive one lasting for as little as 0.1 second for a racer. During this instant kick, the speed of the kick ski = 0. The traction force $T = F_T$, a force assumed acting at the skier's COG; F_T causes the forward movement of the skier.

In ski skating this "locking" or friction grip does not take place. The philosophy of modern skating is actually the opposite, namely, to glide wax the full base length of the skis for minimum frictional resistance. The illustration *(Fig. 11-28)* of a skater terminating the skate push shows how skate glide forces acting parallel with the ground cause the skier's forward movement.

It is impossible for a forward gliding skate ski to create friction forces in the opposite direction, as in Classic skiing. Ski skaters push off only in **one plane** which is at a right (90°) angle to the gliding direction of the skate ski. During ski skating, the COG moves laterally as well as vertically, and the body's COG in this respect moves a longer distance than during Classic skiing in a parallel track.

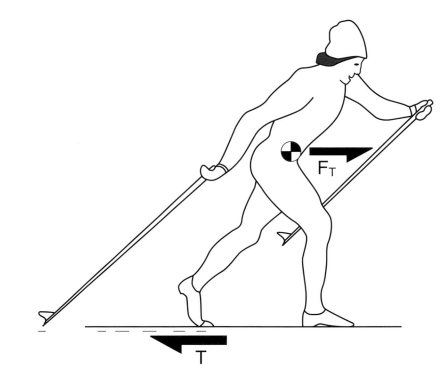

Figure 11-27 *Diagonal Skier*

2. HOW SKATE GLIDE FORCES MOVE SKIER FORWARD

During skating *(Fig. 11-28)*, the skier's forward propulsion force (F_B) in the direction of skiing is created by an outward (lateral movement) angulation (α) of the skis with the skiing direction Z-Z. An outward skate push against the left ski, perpendicular to the gliding direction creates many small force components (G_1, G_2, G_3, G_4, $G_5 = \Sigma G$) in the skate ski direction during the glide. The summation of these small variable size forces = total force (ΣG) of leg action for the left skate. These force components acting at an angle (α_1) with the skiing direction over a relatively longer period of time (approximately 1 sec. on level ground) give the skier the continuous forward glide during skating.

For the gliding skate forces of the left ski to be effective in the direction of the skiing course Z-Z, F_B is reduced and becomes = ΣG (cos.α). *(See Force Line Triangle for Skate Action, Figure 11-29)*. F_B with point of action assumed at COG causes the forward movement of the skier.

Figure 11-28 *Back View of Ski Skater with Force Lines*

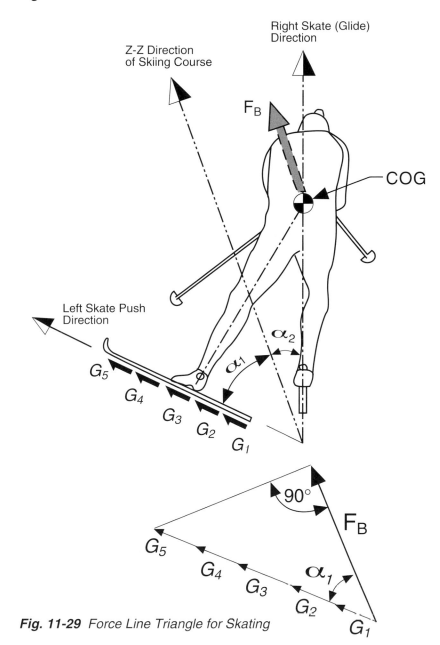

Fig. 11-29 *Force Line Triangle for Skating*

3. LATERAL AND VERTICAL FORCES FOR ICE SKATER IN PERFECT BALANCE

In Figure 11-30, an ice skater in perfect balance illustrates forces, moments, and ideal gliding balance. The ski skating concept was originally derived from studying ice skater's patterns of movements. The force line concept is simpler to apply to an ice skater than to a skier whose forces are supported by a wider base (skis), which can be flat or edged (canted), depending on a skier's foot rotation.

The ice skater is terminating a powerful skate push with the right leg. The direction of the push is the line extended from the body's COG through the ankle to the right skate blade. The line extension of the body weight including any impact action (W_B) at COG is through the ankle to the left foot.

The body weight and impact action (W_B) is balanced by the vertical force component through the right blade (V_R), and V_L through the left blade. The centrifugal force acting outward at COG is counteracted by a powerful skate leg push (H_R) acting perpendicular to the right skate, which makes the skater glide on the ice in the direction of the left skate.

The skater illustrated is in an ideal gliding balance, since the extension of the force lines from COG goes through both the ankles and the skate blades, while simultaneously the force of gravity + impact (W_B) acts in line with the reaction force V_L for the left skate blade.

Internal muscle energy, assumed concentrated at COG, is expressed in terms of a moment (M_I). For the ice skater shown, the following basic equilibrium concepts can be expressed and illustrated:

I. Force Line Equilibrium

$W_B = V_R + V_L$

$H_C = H_R$

II. Moment Equilibrium

$M_I = V_R(a) - H_R(h) = 0$

$V_R(a) = H_R(h)$

This is an ideal situation because there is no internal muscle moment at COG caused by an unbalanced body position; i.e. skating with least use of energy.

It should be noted that the *inertia* from the powerful forward diagonal movements of the arms in ice skating also contributes to the forward movement, but this also demands muscle energy (Appendix, Sec. II). Free movements of arms are used to a lesser degree in ski skating, although there are many opportunities where they can be applied efficiently such as on the flats and in mild downhills (Ch. 5 and Ch. 8, Sec. IV-F).

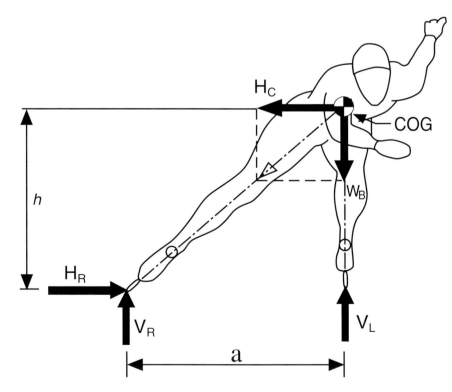

Figure 11-30 *Ice skater from Front with Force Lines*

4. LATERAL MOVEMENT FORCES DURING SKATE PUSH-OFF

The skier illustrated, in an unbalanced skate position *(Fig. 11-31)*, has just terminated a strong leg push (H_R) onto the right ski to counteract the lateral (centrifugal) force (H_C) acting outward at COG.

To move the skier back to a balanced position, the muscle reaction forces on the skate ski (H_R) have to be greater than H_C. This difference in force of movement, (H_D), moving the body to the left, is shown acting at COG.

Lateral Force Line Equilibrium

$$H_R = H_C + H_D = 0$$

Lateral Body Movement Force (Moving body to the left)

$$H_D = H_R - H_C$$

Contrary to Classic parallel skiing, during skating the body's COG constantly moves laterally *(Fig. 11-32)*. The amount of lateral movement varies with:

1. The skate angle α
2. The individual
3. The steepness of the terrain
4. The glide on the ski
5. The speed
6. The source and amount of energy available

With so many variables, lateral movement is very important. The skate angle, α, directly controls the amount of lateral movement and also effects all other factors. If two skiers skate at the same speed in the course direction, the one who skis the longer path with a greater skate angle has to use more energy to keep up because of the longer distance skied. Ideally a skier should try to minimize lateral movement and skate with optimal (most efficient) skate angle (also see this Chapter, Sec. II-B-10).

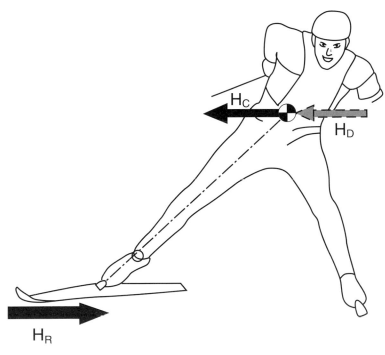

Figure 11-31 *Ski Skater from Front with Lateral Force Lines*

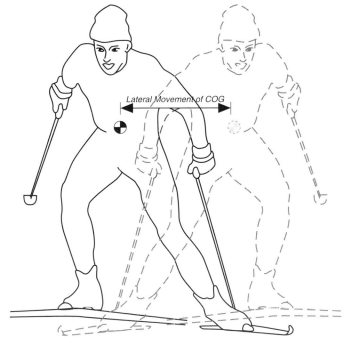

Lateral Movement of COG

Figure 11-32 *Lateral Movement in Skating*

5. ENERGY REQUIREMENTS FOR AERIAL MOVEMENT OF LEG DURING SKATING

In Figure 11-33, the skier is skating in a downhill tuck position at high speed in ideal balance, on the left foot with no counteracting lateral (centrifugal) forces acting on the body. The right leg which has finished the skate is being moved inward toward the left leg.

To support the weight (W_L) of the right leg in such a position requires muscle energy, which can be expressed as internal moment (M_I), assumed acting at COG.

The external leg moment ($M_E = W_L(a)$), holding the right leg outwards, is balanced by the internal muscle energy moment (M_I).

During inward recovery from skating movements, the leg should be kept fairly straight, with the ski following a path parallel and as *close to the ground* as possible. Height (*h*) should be minimized. Unnecessary vertical lifting of the legs demands extra energy, as well. Energy requirement for lifting of leg = $W_L(h)$.

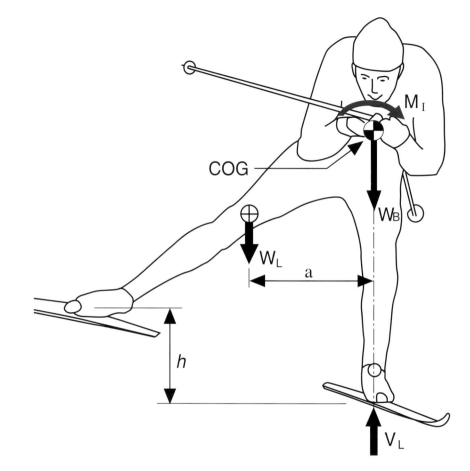

Figure 11-33 *Ski Skater in Downhill Tuck*

6. VERTICAL MOVEMENT AND ENERGY EFFICIENCY IN SKI SKATING

During each skate cycle (between pole plants, see Ch. 8) the body's COG moves up and down. The amount of vertical fluctuation of COG directly reflects the energy expended by the skier, and is therefore of primary concern. Stages for Low Center of Gravity (LCOG) and High Center of Gravity (HCOG) during a skate cycle are shown in the illustration.

The energy spent during vertical movements of the body is a function of four factors:

a. Weight (W_B) of the skier
b. Amount of vertical fluctuation (Δh) during a cycle
c. Average time of each cycle
d. Skating frequency (Number of cycles per minute)

To ski energy efficiently and maintain speed, the ski skater should strive for minimizing the vertical fluctuation (Δh) by keeping the level of COG relatively high (HCOG) during the skate cycle *(Fig. 11-34).*

Factors effecting Δh are the amount of forward bending of the upper extremity and bending at the knees. Guidelines for maintaining movement with HCOG are:

a. The angle of the Trunk Line (T-T) with the horizontal should not be less than 45°

b. The angle at the knee should not be less than 115°

Bending the upper extremity further than 45° and/or bending the knees deeper than 115° requires additional energy that could better be used by the skier at some other place along the course to increase average speed.

Moving the COG up and down in skating may be compared to weight lifting, where W_B is the body's weight and Δh the lifting height and the time of movement = t

$$Energy = W_B(\Delta h)t$$

Figure 11-34 *Low and High Centers of Gravity*

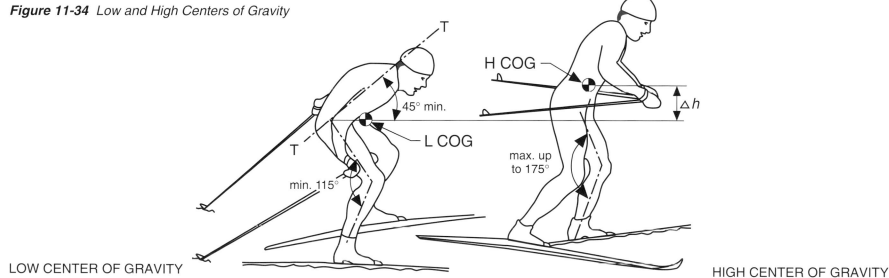

LOW CENTER OF GRAVITY   HIGH CENTER OF GRAVITY

7. MAINTAINING MAXIMUM EFFICIENCY THROUGH A CURVE (Skiing With Less Energy)

Since there are many, many curved sections throughout a ski touring or racing course, it is important that the skier knows how to ski curves in the most efficient way. If the curve has a small radius, it may be advantageous to skate with a shorter stride length, thereby reducing the amount of friction created by edging the front, tails, and midsections of the skis. In skating a sharp curve, shortening the cycle and increasing the frequency usually results in a higher speed without an increase in use of energy. Maintaining maximum speed and efficiency through a curve requires advanced cross country technique.

Besides having the COG shifted inward when skiing a curve, the skier also must maintain a forward lean to counteract excessive snow drag and aerial body forces, which tend to move COG backward.

The most ideal body position for the best balance is when the resultant (R) of the horizontal force (H_C) and the vertical body weight (W_B) goes through the ankle down to the inner gliding ski *(Fig. 11-35)*.

When skating a curve rhythmically and relaxed, the skier must adjust his weight shift inward to a comfortable balanced position.

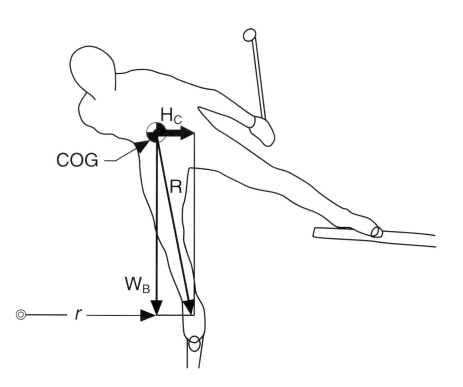

Figure 11-35 *Ski Skater on One Leg*

8. DYNAMIC EXPRESSIONS FOR SKIING A CURVE

When skiing a curved path or track, there is a horizontal force (H_C) acting at COG of the skier toward the outside of the curve. If the skier's path is is assumed to be radial = r, according to laws of physics, the numerical value of the centrifugal force can be expressed as follows:

$$H_C = \frac{W_B v^2}{gr} = m \frac{v^2}{r} \quad \text{where}$$

W_B = weight of skier

m = mass of the skier

g = gravity acceleration force

v = the average speed through the curve

r = the average radius of the curve

From the expression, the horizontal centrifugal force (H_C) is:

1. Proportional to the weight (mass of the skier, m)

2. Proportional to the square of speed, v^2

3. Inversely proportional to the radius of the curve, r

In other words, if the skier's speed (v) increases from 4 meters / sec to 8m/sec, the centrifugal force quadruples, which means the movement of the skier's COG toward the inside of the curve should actually be increased four times to keep the skier in balance. If the radius throughout the curve becomes smaller, the lateral movement of COG becomes even greater.

9. IMPULSE AND MOMENTUM EXPRESSION IN SKATING VS. CLASSIC

In ski skating the theoretical impulse and momentum expression can be applied to skaters' movements as follows:

$F(t) = mv$ and $v = \dfrac{F(t)}{m}$ where:

This expression is derived from the basic formula F=ma, where F is assumed to act at skier's COG.

$F(t)$ = Impulse

$m(v)$ = Momentum

F = Effective average skate force in course direction applied at skier's COG

t = time of skate push

m = mass of skier = $\dfrac{W_B}{g}$

v = average velocity of skier = $\dfrac{v_0 + v_1}{2}$

v_0 = Speed before skate push

v_1 = Max. speed achieved

a = acceleration of skier

While a Classic leg kick immediately contributes to forward movement, the downset of the skate ski itself does not contribute to the forward speed. In the impulse expression, the skate time (t) is more significant than in the Classic leg kick where (t) may be 0.1 second only. In skating the force is relatively small, but multiplied with a time (t) that is 1 second or more, the impulse speed (v) can easily become faster (greater) than obtainable with classic technique.

The impulse expression has wide application in cross country skiing. For example, the **momentum** (mv) has application during the continued glide after the poling or skate action, represented by $F(t)$, has been completed.

10. SKATE ANGLE AND GLIDE DISTANCE — CRUCIAL FOR EFFICIENT SKATING

In One-Side or Two-Side ski skating (Ch. 7 and 8), one or both the skis are oriented at an angle with the course direction. The skate illustration *(Fig. 11-36)* shows the skate angle α_2 for the left ski, and angle α_1 for the right ski, with the direction of travel Z-Z.

The skater has to adjust the skate glide distances, the skate angles and frequency (number of skates per time unit) to ski most efficiently (with minimum lateral movement of COG), at optimal speed.

The skate angle (α) depends to large degree on the terrain and the speed at which the skater is moving.

In *steep uphills* where the speed is slow:

a.   The skate angle (α) becomes larger
b.   The speed is slower
c.   The skate glide distance is shorter
d.   The frequency is higher

When skating *downhills*, effective (fastest, with least use of energy) skating technique is by use of:

a.   A small skate angle
b.   And a long skate glide distance, where the skate frequency is less.

To ski at a high speed on variable flat terrain, the skier shown would adjust the skate angle (α) to become smaller with less frequency. For a slower speed, the skater would increase the angle, and also increase skate frequency.

Increasing the skate angle (α) will produce a *slower speed* because of the *longer* actual *overall distance*, since the:

Actual skiing distance in the direction (Z-Z) of travel (S) =

Length of skate glide (L), times cosine to the skate angle, (cosα)

Skiers therefore should strive to skate with optimal smallest angles and long glides which is more efficient. (Also see Ch. 11, Sec. II-B-2 and B-4)

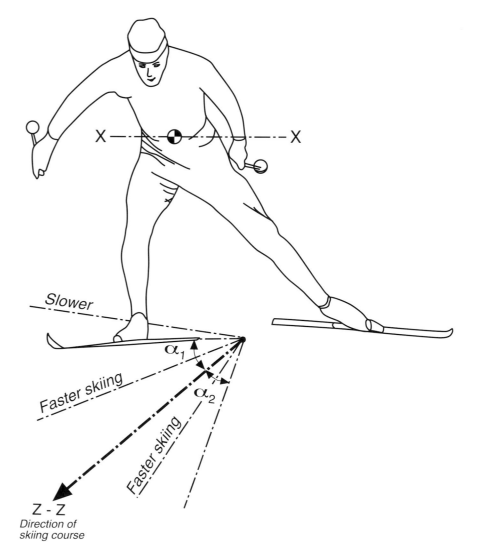

Slower

Faster skiing

α_1

α_2

Faster skiing

Z - Z
Direction of skiing course

Figure 11-36 *Ski Skater from the Front with Skate Angles*

C. DOWNHILL DYNAMICS

A study of cross country international race courses shows that 30% to 50% of the length of the courses are downhill skiing. This suggests that knowing how to maximize the speed and master the difficulties encountered in a downhill is of equal importance as the techniques used on other sections of a race course.

The technique suggested by this author for cross country downhill racing is based upon the most efficient use of energy while maintaining a body position that gives the highest and safest speed downhill. In most downhills, the cross country skier is in a recovery or resting stage, and a body position that is the fastest sometimes may be too strenuous.

1. CRUCIAL BODY POSITION

In cross country downhill racing the body position is crucial in determining optimal speed. If speed in a downhill exceeds a skier's capability, it may be controlled by skiing with a more erect body position, thereby creating a greater frontal aerial resistance with body and poles. ***The speed in a downhill is in inverse proportion to the projected body area*** seen from the front of the skier. In other words, the smaller the frontal projection area of the body and the poles, the faster the potential obtainable speed.

2. ANALYSIS OF SKIER IN HIGH TUCK

Figure 11-37 shows a skier in a semi-crouched body position called a high tuck. This position is the most common for downhill cross country skiing, used by experts as well as novice skiers. The skier is striving for the most restful position while maintaining high speed, keeping the trunk and poles parallel with the skis, and the legs fairly straight with a slight flex at the knees.

Figure 11-37 *Skier in High Tuck*

3. SYMBOLS AND FORCES IN DOWNHILL DYNAMICS

When skiing from a level track to a mild downhill a certain slope is needed before the skis start gliding by themselves. This is due to several resistant forces that act against forward motion. There is also one major force, gravity, which creates downhill motion alone (excluding such external aids as poling and vertical flexing of the body).

The following expressions and Figure 11-38 describe the dynamics of the principal forces that resist the skier's downhill motion as well as the forces that cause the skier to glide downhill. Physical data of the skier and the environment are also factors that have to be considered.

Y-Y = Vertical Axis

X-X = Horizontal Axis

α = Angle with the horizontal (steepness of the hill) - used in the force triangles shown (Unit in degrees)

W_B = Weight = mg (mass times gravity acceleration) of the skier and his equipment acting vertically through the ankle (g varies with elevation) (Unit in kg.)

H = $W_B (\sin \alpha)$ = the downhill component of W_B acting parallel with the skis (Unit in kg.)

N = $W_B (\cos. \alpha)$ = the component from the weight (W_B) acting perpendicular to the skis (Unit in kg.)

W_B, H and N are Force components in a graphical triangle as described in this Chapter, Sec. I-C-1.

U = Uplift force, acting opposite to N, but in the same direction. U is a factor of significance only during very high speed (Unit in kg.). Wind Tunnel tests results (Ch. 11, Sec. III) incorporate all factors under U and D.

F = $N(\mu)$ = the friction under the skis, acting uphill, parallel with the skis (μ is the friction coefficient having no unit) (Unit in kg.)

D = $1/2C(p)(A)(v^2)$ = air drag resistance caused by the skier and his equipment (Unit in kg.) where:

C = factor referring to the streamline of the body shape of the skier, his equipment and clothing, having no unit

p = density of the air, which varies with elevation and temperature (Unit in $kgsec^2/m^4$)

A = Actual net aerial exposure of the skier and his equipment projected perpendicular to the skis, seen from the front of the skier (Unit in m^2)

v = Velocity or speed of skier relative to the surrounding air, acting in the direction of skiing, parallel to ground or slope of hill (Unit in m/sec)

The forces the skier is exposed to can be grouped as follows:

- **Resistance forces** acting on skier and his equipment

  a. Snow (friction) drag (F)

  b. Aerial resistance (D)

- **Forces causing the downhill movement**

  Skier's gravity force component (H)

All forces shown in this illustration are assumed concentrated and acting in a vertical plane through the skier's Center of Gravity (COG).

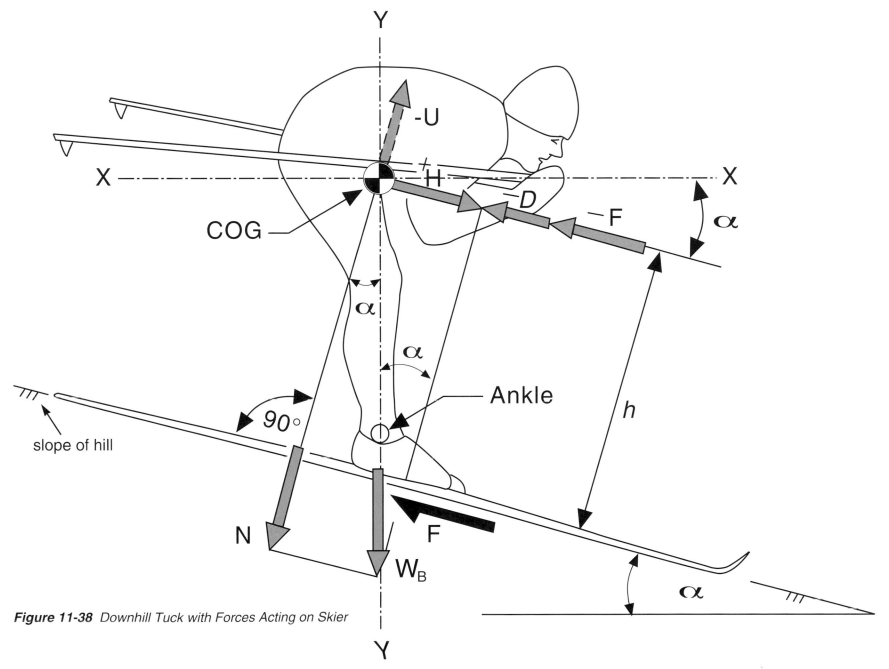

Figure 11-38 Downhill Tuck with Forces Acting on Skier

4. RESISTANCE FORCES

a. Snow Friction (F)

Friction between the skis and the snow acts against the direction of motion. A formula commonly used to express the friction force is: $F = \mu(N)$, where μ is defined as the average coefficient of skiing friction and N is the force component of the skier's weight W_B, perpendicular to the skis. The smaller the coefficient of friction, the smaller is the resisting friction force between the skis and the snow.

The uplift force U acts opposite to N and in the same line of direction. The uplift will slightly reduce the size of F, and the friction force becomes $F = \mu(N-U)$. U is a factor of significance only during very high speed (Ch. 11, Sec. III-E)

b. Drag or Air Resistance (D)

The aerodynamic formula for the drag or air resistance a cross country skier encounters, when skiing downhill is:

$$D = 1/2(p)(C)(A)(v^2)$$

This expression states that when the speed (v) doubles, drag resistance (D) quadruples. The drag resistance can be significant, even in cross country skiing, where the speed in mild to steeper downhills may vary from 10 to 20 m/sec (36 to 72 km/hr).

A is the computed front projected net area of the skier in a plane perpendicular to the skis. From the equation it can be seen that the smaller the exposed area A, the smaller the drag D, a very important factor in skiing downhill.

The speed of the skier (v) in m/sec is relative to the air surrounding the skier. The formula accounts for wind acting on the skier that could increase or reduce the velocity.

5. FORCES CAUSING DOWNHILL MOVEMENT (H)

During downhill skiing, the skier's weight has a gravity force component at COG, that acts downhill parallel with the skis or slope of the hill. This component, H, shown in the illustration has to exceed the two resisting forces (F+D) to move the skier downhill.

$$H = W_B(\sin \alpha)$$

This equation states that the downhill force component H is proportional to the weight (W_B) of the skier and the steepness (α) of the slope. The greater H is, the higher the potential speed of the skier. If other factors are equal, a heavier skier should be able to obtain higher speed in the downhill.

When airborne during skiing downhill, as sometimes happens at high speed, the effect of the component along the slope of the hill disappears and accordingly, speed is immediately reduced. If the skier is airborne a long time, he would eventually free-fall vertically, with no forward movement.

6. CONDITIONS FOR GLIDING DOWNHILL

In studying the forces that act on the skier illustrated *(Fig. 11-38)*, the force F+D is acting against (resisting) the downhill motion. H, a component from the Mass or Weight of the skier, is the **only force that acts downhill** in the direction the skier is traveling.

To glide downhill with increasing speed without the help of poles and leg work, H must be greater than (>) F+D. $H = W_B (\sin \alpha)$, therefore if α, the slope of the hill, is very small or flat, the skis cease to glide. To overcome friction, a certain steepness of the hill is required before the skis start gliding downhill.

The relationship H < F+D (< means smaller than) states that the skier cannot glide downhill because the hill is too flat. If there is no wind or other external forces acting on the skier under slow speed, the factor D can be ignored, and the condition for gliding downhill is the H > F; a skier's gravity force component H has to be greater than the snow friction (F).

As the skier picks up speed, the drag (D) has to be accounted for. In steeper hills H becomes substantially larger than F+D, and the speed v increases accordingly.

D. LEVEL AND UPHILL DYNAMICS

1. LEVEL TERRAIN DYNAMICS (*Figure 11-39*)

When skating on the level, the H force component from gravity (weight) of the skier = 0. The skier in this case has to use more energy to maintain a certain speed to overcome F+D (Friction and Drag forces). If the energy can sustain the speed for only a short time, the speed (v) has to be reduced, and accordingly also the Drag Force (D), and the skier could take a more erect body position that demands less energy.

2. UPHILL DYNAMICS (**Figure 11-40**)

In uphills the gravity force component H = W(sinα), illustrated in Figure 11-38 as positive in the downhill will become negative, acting against the skier's movement uphill. To overcome the gravity and friction components H and F in the uphill demands tremendous energy and the skier has to reduce speed comparable to downhill and level skiing. The drag force D in this case also will be reduced considerably and the skier therefore can select a more upright body position to reduce energy consumption.

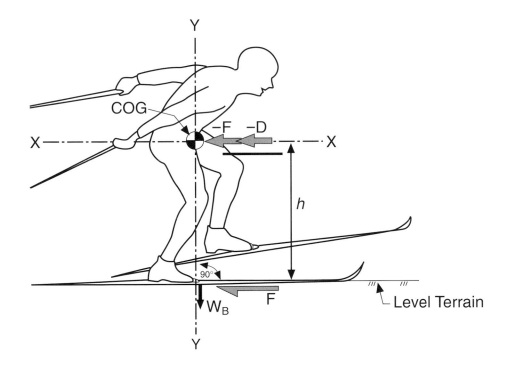

Figure 11-39 *Level Terrain Dynamics*

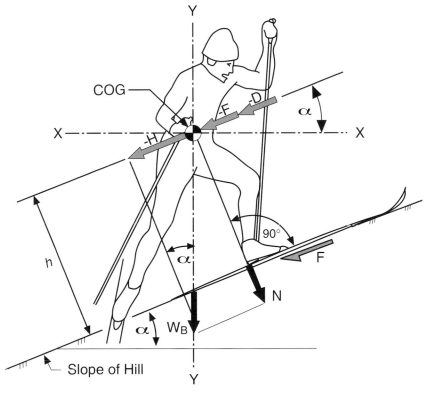

Figure 11-40 *Uphill Dynamics*

E. SUMMARY AND EFFECT OF FORCES IN SKATING DYNAMICS

The difference in energy consumption for the three different types of terrain described below is primarily in the effect of gravity (weight) of the skier, W_B.

1. STRAIGHT DOWNHILL

In Straight Downhill Skiing *(Fig. 11-38)* the positive (+) component H (derived from W_B) is greater than the sum of the resistant forces (the drag force D and the skiing friction force F), and accordingly there is no muscle energy needed to propel the skier forward. The force component H increases with the steepness of the hill, designated by the angle α. The drag force D also increases with speed, while there is relatively little difference in the friction F.

The drag force D can be reduced by minimizing the frontal catch area A of the skier by skiing in a tuck body position (see Ch. 11, Sec. III), however, low tuck is more energy demanding in itself, so skier has to compromise, depending on the energy sources available.

2. SKATING ON THE LEVEL

When Skating On The Level *(Fig. 11-39)*, the force component H = 0, since the angle α = 0, a skier has to use muscle energy to overcome the skiing friction F to maintain a certain speed. The speed on the level is normally considerably less than in the downhill, and the drag forces D accordingly are also less so the skier may take a more erect body position which demands less energy. However, during fast skiing conditions on level terrain, such as in high speed skating without use of poles., the drag forces D may also be a concern, and in order to reduce D, the skier may "crouch" more to minimize the frontal body catch area A.

3. SKATING UPHILL

Skating Uphill *(Fig. 11-40)* is very energy demanding, since the skier must overcome all three resistant force components H+D+F. F (friction) will vary depending on efficient skiing technique, as discussed earlier in the text. Since the speed is relatively slow in the steep uphill, the drag force D is not very critical, so the skier takes a more upright body position to save energy. The gravity force component H, derived from W_B, is directly related to steepness of the hill and controls the speed of uphill skiing as far as energy demand is concerned.

CHAPTER 11

III. Scientific Testing In Wind Tunnel For Ideal Body Positions In Cross Country Skiing

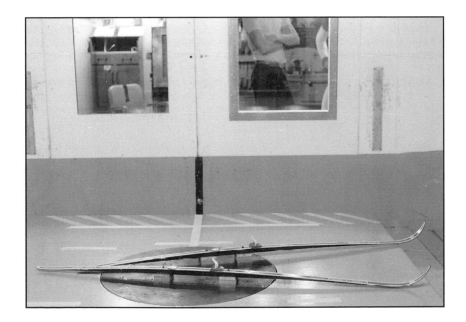

Figure 11-41 *The photo taken inside the tunnel shows a pair of cross country skis bolted to a sensitive platform disk at specifically calculated points at the toe and heel of the bindings. The skier was stationary on the skis, as wind was forced through the tunnel onto the skier, at speeds of up to 50 mph (80 km/hr.). Data of wind forces acting on the skier, and the equipment, as he assumed body positions that simulated actual cross country skiing conditions, were transferred through the skis to the sensitive disk which relayed numerical data of timing, forces and moments to a complex computer.*

The author's purpose in conducting complex wind tunnel testing was to ***determine ideal (most efficient) body positions for various cross country ski techniques to generate maximum speed of skiing*** and also to determine how body positions respond to different speeds.

During the last 5 years the average speed of ski skating has increased dramatically, and in certain terrain such as fast flats and mild downhills, the maximum speed obtainable is determined by body position as well as choice of technique. A skier's body position and attainable ski skating speed are directly related, and both factors are also governed by the available energy resources of the skier, regardless of ability.

With special permission of the Kristin Aeronautical Wind Tunnel at the University of Washington, Seattle, WA, USA, the author performed extensive scientific testing of ***drag forces, speed, uplifts, and moments*** for different body positions simulating various cross country skiing movements. The preparation and organization of such testing is complex, and the computer data results, to be useful, have to be applied to similar situations on snow skiing. The 50 page computer printout of the test data was interpreted and refined by the author into practical, meaningful results and finally converted into simplified graphs, with accompanying photo illustrations taken during the tests, demonstrating the most ideal and efficient body positions for the different cross country ski techniques for certain speeds.

When testing in the wind tunnel, the skier was stationary on skis, which were anchored to a platform disk at the toe binding and heel *(Fig. 11-42, 43)*. Wind was forced through the tunnel onto the skier at different controlled pressures. The sensitive platform disk relayed information to a computer, which gave a printout of the detailed numerical data which the author compiled and evaluated.

The skier tested here, an elite competitor coached by the author, weighed 80 kg, with a height of 185 cm. The skier's suit was made of form fitting lycra. There is relatively little difference in the resistance of the clothing used today by elite skiers in cross country skiing.

A skier tested in a large-scale wind tunnel under these circumstances must be mentally and physically capable of tolerating long exposure to variable wind pressures with magnitudes that often exceed what is experienced during skiing. Safety precautions for the skier were a concern.

The following results of the author's wind tunnel tests for different body positions simulating those of cross country skiing, should be reviewed together with the force analyses of downhill, level and uphill skiing in the previous section in this chapter. (See Ch. 11, Sec. II-C,D)

Figure 11-42 *Skier on Skis Anchored to Platform Disk in Parallel Position*

A. DRAG FORCES, BODY POSITION AND SPEED

The drag force resistance (D) is in proportion to the frontal catch area (A) of the skier (See Ch. 11, Sec. II-C-3). By reducing the drag force, potential speed becomes greater. This can be accomplished by using a body position that minimizes the frontal catch area, as in a crouched (tucked) position. However, more crouch or forward bend also demands more energy output so a skier might compromise and select an ideal body position comparable to the skier's energy resources.

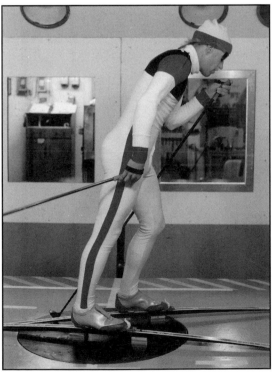

Figure 11-43 *Skier on Skis Anchored to Platform Disk in Skate Angle Position*

The maximum average speed obtainable today *on the level* using classic diagonal is 7 m/sec (25 km/hr) with a possible 8 m/sec (29 km/hr) in double poling, considerably less than the potential maximum skating speed of 10 to 12 m/sec (36 to 40 km/hr). In a downhill speed is considerably higher. Therefore, when analyzing the wind tunnel test data and results, the Downhill, Double Poling, and Skating techniques are discussed separately.

INTERPRETATION OF ILLUSTRATIONS AND RESULTS

The tests illustrate Body Positions and Graphs (results) consisting of two series, each having six body positions as follows:

SERIES 1 - BODY POSITIONS 1 THROUGH 6

    B. Downhill Body Positions, Graph I

    C. Double Poling Body Positions, Graph I

SERIES 2 - BODY POSITIONS S1 THROUGH S6

    D. Skating Body Position, Graph II

In addition, UPLIFT FORCES *are graphed and illustrated by* BODY POSITIONS *from both* SERIES 1 AND 2.

    E. Uplift Forces in Series 1 and 2, Downhill (Graph III) and Skating (Graph IV)

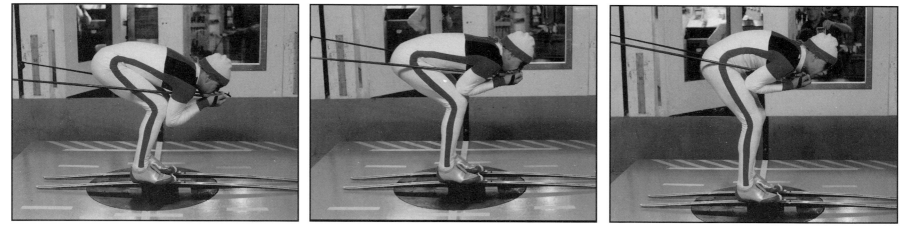

POSITION 1   **POSITION 2**   **POSITION 3**

B.   *DOWNHILL BODY POSITIONS 1 through 5 (GRAPH I)*

The results of the wind tunnel tests (plotted on Graph I) show that the ideal energy efficient body position in cross country downhill skiing for the *average* racer is the **High Tuck**, shown in Positions (**3**, **4**), where elbows are kept above the knees. At a speed of 15 m/sec (54 km/hr) there is a relatively minor difference (from 5 to 5.5 kg) in the drag forces for these positions. As the body becomes more erect in (**5** ,**6**), the drag forces for this speed increase substantially to 6 and 8 kg.

For the **Low Tuck** (**1**) (elbows on or below the knees) the drag force at the same speed is considerably less, only 3.2 kg, but this position also **demands more energy**. Skiers with surplus of energy or near the finish of a race may select this body position with advantage. With a drag force of 5 kg in the low tuck (**1**), the maximum potential speed becomes 18.5 m/sec (67 km/hr). It should be understood that to reach such a high speed, a fairly long downhill is needed.

(**2**) has a drag force of only 3.5kg, but is also energy demanding. (**3**) with *poles in front* has a slightly higher drag than (**4**) with **poles in back**, both in the same body tuck.

C.   *DOUBLE POLING BODY POSITIONS 4, 5, & 6 (GRAPH I)*

During double poling the body trunk line moves from the erect Position 6 to a 60° forward lean similar to (**5**). Although many elite skiers lean 90° forward (**4**) during the final push-off, the author recommends less bending of upper body with higher frequency as more efficient for the average racer. Lowering COG by bending 90° demands more energy and reduces frequency (Ch. 6).

Graph I shows relatively low drag forces for (**4, 5, 6**) at speeds under 8 m/sec (drag forces from 1.5 to 2.5 kg), although there is approx. 40% more drag in the erect body (**6**), than in (**5**). In ski races there are often only seconds between the top skiers, therefore efficient body positions in double poling become imperative even at speeds of 6 to 8 m/sec. Maintaining a slight crowning of the upper back, as in (**5**), together with preloading of muscles for the upper extremity, with correct sequence of muscle action, should be more efficient and give potentially greater speed during high frequency double poling.

The graphs can also be analyzed in the reverse order by assuming a fixed drag force = 2 kg, which gives a maximum obtainable speed in (**6**) of 6 m/sec, while in (**5**), with the same drag force, the maximum obtainable speed becomes 8 m/sec, which is a substantial percentage of difference. In (**4**), with poles low behind back, the potential speed becomes 9.2 m/sec., a 15% further improvement.

POSITION 4

POSITION 5

POSITION 6

GRAPH I
Downhill & Double Poling

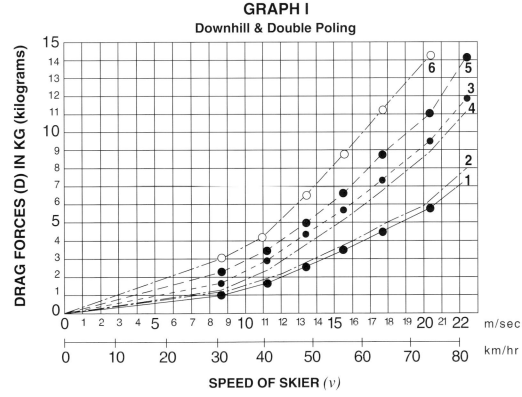

DRAG FORCES (D) IN KG (kilograms)

SPEED OF SKIER *(v)*

GRAPH I

*Graph I illustrates plot lines of speed and drag forces for all six Body Positions, at speeds varying from 0 m/sec. up to 22 m/sec. (80 km/hr), starting with Position **1** at the bottom, ending with Position **6** at top.*

*In the Graph I photos above, the COG of the skier is gradually lifted from body Position **1** (Low Tuck) to Position **6** (Erect body position). Body Positions **1** through **5** are used for downhill tucks. Body Positions **4** through **6** are similar to postures used in double poling.*

POSITION S1

POSITION S2

POSITION S3

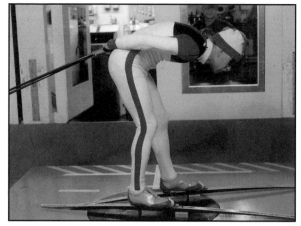

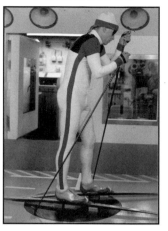

D. SKATING BODY POSITIONS (GRAPH II)

During skating, the angulation of the skis, as well as the outward spread of the legs and arms, causes an increase in the drag forces when compared to the Downhill Position in Graph I. This is another reason why a skier's skis, legs and arms should come together during the skating recovery.

As speed increases to 10 m/sec or more, drag forces become more significant. Skating is often practiced in mild downhills, and skilled skiers also apply the technique in steeper downhills to further increase speed. As skating speed increases, the graphs clearly show that body position becomes very important.

Bending forward to the 90° position as shown in Positions (**S1**) and (**S2**) clearly reduces the amount of drag, but at the same time this position demands more energy. Movement of arms up and forward to do poling increases the drag forces substantially, indicating

that it is *an advantage during high speed to skate with poles and hands on the back* as shown in (**S2, S4**), as practiced by ice and inline wheel skaters.

At a fixed drag of 3 kg, the potential approx. *speed* in:

Position S3	= 7 m/sec.
Position S5	= 8 m/sec.
Position S4	= 9 m/sec
Position S6	= 10 m/sec
Positions S1 and S2	= 12 m/sec.

This comparison suggests that obtaining a skating speed of 12 m/sec on the level, the same as the maximum for long distance ice speed skating, is possible on the level and in mild downhills, when taking a body position similar to ice speed skating. To accomplish this, snow and grooming conditions would have to be ideal, with possible use of the latest "short ski" equipment.

POSITION S4

POSITION S5

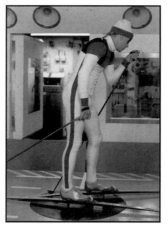

POSITION S6

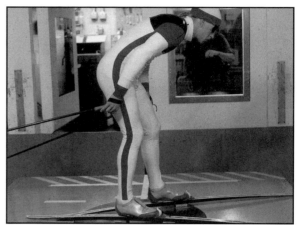

GRAPH II
Skating

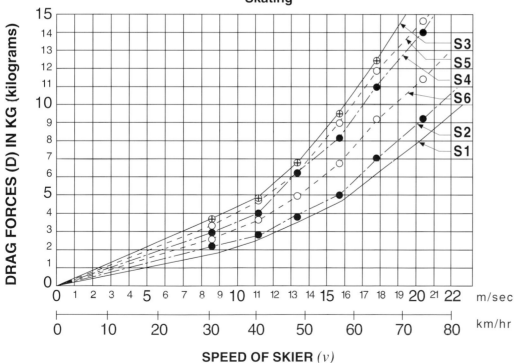

GRAPH II

Graph II illustrates plot lines of speed and drag forces for six Skating Body Positions at speeds from 0 m/sec. up to 22 m/sec. (80 km/hr).

*The Body Positions **S1**, **S2**, and **S6** would be comparable to skating in a tuck, while Body Positions **S3**, **S4**, and **S5** would simulate skating in erect body position. In high speed skating in a tuck without poling assistance, it is an advantage to keep the poles behind the back with the baskets close to the skis.*

POSITION 1   **POSITION 2**   **POSITION 3**

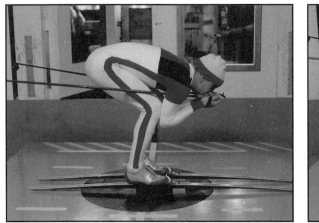

E.   UPLIFT FORCES VS. SPEED IN DOWNHILL (GRAPH III) AND SKATING (GRAPH IV)

Uplift is a force phenomena that becomes significant in ski skating at a high speed. (Ch. 11, Sec. II-C-3-4) This force acts upward, caused by wind and turbulence catching the underside of the body, especially the frontal exposed area from the waist up.

In a fast downhill the Uplift Force is a disadvantage since it counteracts (negates) the gravity component which produces the skier's speed. The graphs illustrate that by applying high and low tucks in a downhill, Positions (**1, 2, 3**), the uplift forces are minimized and barely noticeable at a speed of 80 km/hr which is the maximum downhill speed presently obtainable in cross country skiing.

GRAPH III
Uplift In Downhill

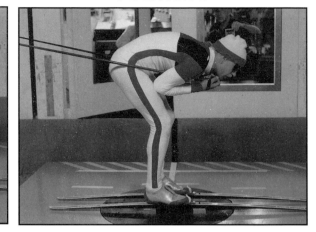

Graph III uses same Body Positions as Graph I

POSITION S6

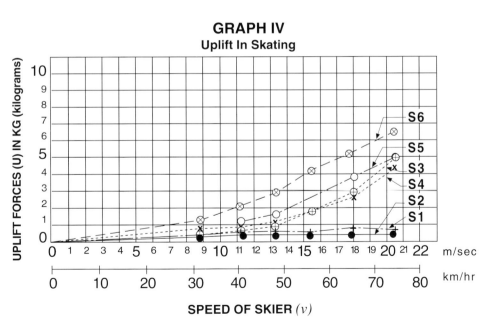

GRAPH IV
Uplift In Skating

Graph IV uses same Body Positions as Graph II

In skating on variable terrain, uplift is sometimes a *positive advantage* since it unweights the skier, meaning that the gravity forces become slightly less, and the normal friction between snow and skis is slightly reduced. Body Position (**S6**) with slight crowning of the upper back suggests an ideal form during skating for maximum uplift.

F. OTHER DRAG FORCE CONSIDERATIONS

When skiing a course in windy conditions, drag and body position are an important consideration for any cross country technique. During a tail wind (from the rear) the skier's desirable body position would be just the opposite of what it is for a head wind. During a strong tail wind a large catch (body) area is an advantage, consequently the skier should take a more erect body position.

In relays, mass start competition, and when skiing in a "pack" of skiers, drag is reduced by drafting (skiing closely behind another skier), a practice which is well known and illegal in some bicycle racing, however, drafting is permitted in cross country ski competition, in any technique.

APPENDIX

The Appendix contains additional and supplementary material to the subjects discussed in this text. Many chapters have references to the Appendix where the subject matter is further analyzed and explained in greater detail.

The Appendix also represents opinions of the author which may rely on theories and examples from science, the study of mechanics, and the environment, in order to verify that indications and statements made and suggestions given have a basis for being correct.

Cross country ski skating, being just a few years old, is in its infancy, and will most likely have more variations and changes in the future. Many theories applied in this text may have bearing on such outcomes.

I. THE MECHANICS OF SKIING FRICTION

A. *INTRODUCTION: ENERGY AND FRICTION*

In cross country skiing, 70% or more of a skier's energy is used to overcome friction. Understanding skiing friction is therefore an important factor in skiing, for all levels of skiers. However, the research done by the author suggests that there is very little information on the effect of friction on modern cross country skiing.

Friction is a phenomena that appears in nature in many forms, and acts as resistant forces on a skier and his equipment in the form of:

♦ Snow friction (also called snow drag)
♦ Aerial resistance (also called air drag) (See Ch. 11-II-C-4)

The following section discusses the basic theory of *snow friction*, its effect on cross country skiing, and *how to ski with least frictional snow resistance.*

B. *SNOW AND SKIING FRICTION*

1. FORMATION OF SNOW

Snow is the name of a shimmering little lightweight ice crystal that is formed at higher elevations when there is excessive water vapor in the atmosphere and the temperature drops below freezing. The original ice crystal is very tiny, 1/10 of a millimeter or smaller, and as it crystallizes, appears as a six-sided flake. Each of these flakes is so unique in shape that it is said that no two are exactly alike.

The flake is attracted by the earth's gravity and starts falling toward the earth at a very slow speed, 10 to 20 cm. per second, depending on airflow and temperature. As these crystals fall through the air, they pick up more moisture and expand. Several ice crystals may join and can clearly be seen coming through the air at a much higher speed, which may be several meters per second, depending on how much vapor they picked up on the way down. When the air temperature is several degrees below 0°C (centi-grade), snow falls at a slow pace. As the temperature gets close to 0°C or above, the snow picks up more moisture and comes down faster, due to the higher density of the flakes.

The fresh falling snow crystals reflect light and make the snow appear white as it piles up on the ground, unless the air or ground is polluted. Microscopic plants may also alter the color of the snow, such as in the Arctic and Greenland where snow appears to have a greenish or reddish color.

If the ground is moist, the first snow settling may melt right away. However, if the ground is already frozen or dry, snow covers the surface very quickly. Snow changes its physical characteristics as soon as it hits the earth's surface. After several days on the ground, melting, crushing and compacting make it into small granules of ice, called "corn" snow, which gives a very good skiing glide.

Snow, in general, is very porous. New fresh snow is very lightweight. A volume as large as one cubic meter in a container may be easily lifted. Initially, settling snowflakes may have a density of less than 0.1. As snow piles up on the ground in layers and becomes compacted, the air volume decreases and the lower layers become considerably denser; older corn snow may have a density three times that of new snow. The densification continues rapidly up to a value of 0.55, which is the dividing point between old corn snow and "firmed", compacted snow.

The phenomena of "snow" is something that only 1/3 of the earth's population is acquainted with. Snow appears year round in the cold polar region, and in the winter time in the temperate zones of the earth, remaining year round in the mountains at high altitudes on glaciers, making it possible to cross country ski in the summertime in many areas. Several countries in the Southern Hemisphere which are close to Antarctica, such as parts of New Zealand and Australia, have snow and the opportunity for cross country skiing during the summer.

2. HOW SNOW EFFECTS SKIING

For a cross country skier, knowledge about snow is of great value, since the consistency of snow, to a large extent, determines the preparation of skis, and the success of the skiing venture. *In skiing terminology there are many different names for snow, characterized by its look, feeling and how it effects the glide and grip of the skis.*

Moisture content and density of snow primarily determine the type of skis chosen and wax preparation used for achieving the best gliding characteristics for the skis. When fresh snow is at a temperature above freezing and therefore moist; snowballs can be made. This type of snow, named *"cram"* gives a very poor ski glide. With a temperature below freezing, fresh snow usually contains very little moisture and is quite dry. It is almost like squeezing baking flour, and doesn't make snowballs. This *"powder"* snow gives a better glide.

As snow settles for some time on the ground, it goes through a structural transformation which meteorologists call metamorphosis. The snow becomes compacted, and, depending on temperature and moisture, may remain soft and powdery in cold weather, or become firm, like brittle ice, called *"skare"* snow, by freezing, thawing and acquiring moisture.

Snow compacts when skied upon, but there are still a lot of air pockets left in it. It forms a unique structure of many small crystals with spaces between that *bridge* the support of the ski. When the skier is gliding on snow, the skis are really in contact with a relatively few number of crystals. The number of crystal contact points varies with the snow structure and moisture content, which, in turn, directly effects skiing friction.

New fallen snow at +0° Centigrade contains a lot of moisture, compacts easier, becomes *dense* with less air volume and provides many more contacts under the ski. Dense snow creates much more friction between the skis and the supporting snow crystals than porous snow does.

Older snow, also called *"corn"* snow, having gone through metamorphosis with the snow crystals becoming much larger by thawing and freezing, has much *fewer contact points* with the gliding surface of the ski. Skiing on such snow means fewer crystals are supporting the ski and there is less friction, resulting in a better glide characteristic.

3. FRICTION, ENERGY AND WAXING - IMPORTANT FACTORS IN SKIING

Friction in cross country skiing is a *physical phenomena* that skiers and skiing manufacturers have confronted ever since the making of the first skis. Friction is a necessity for the cross country kick in Classic skiing, and a problem when gliding, particularly when skating.

Friction between the base of the ski and the snow is very complicated to analyze since environmental factors of weather, snow consistency, temperature, moisture in the air and the snow constantly change. Friction also varies with the skier's skill, type of technique used, elevation, and wax selection. The materials that the ski base and sides are made of and the flex of the skis are the only unchangeable variables.

The energy used by a cross country skier to overcome friction, according to research by the author, amounts to 70% or more of the total energy spent by skiers in competition. Friction, therefore, is by far the most important factor to be considered when evaluating energy use by a skier. The significance of skiing with least frictional resistance is also important for the beginning tourer who normally has much less stored energy for the skiing venture. Probably more first-time skiers have been "turned off" by cross country skiing because of too slippery or too sticky skis than for any other reason.

As moisture in the snow evaporates, the size of the snow crystals becomes larger with more air pockets between. Friction decreases and the glide characteristic of the skis improve. This situation frequently takes place when there are freezing temperatures overnight and a few plus centigrade degrees in the day. After a few days of this, there will be a significant *decrease* in skiing friction.

There is a theory suggesting that the glide of the ski on the snow tends, to some degree, to melt the snow crystal contact points with the ski base, creating a very thin, lubricating film of water. This condition is called **"wet friction"**. As the temperature becomes very cold, there is less lubrication and therefore, there will be a substantial increase in friction under the skis. Below -50°C, such melting of the crystals terminates completely, and the extremely high friction can be compared to skiing on fine sand. This is defined as **"dry friction"**, with no lubricant between the contact base of the ski and the snow (see Appendix I, Sec. C-3).

Waxing Skis for Minimum Friction

The porous base of a pair of unprepared skis easily absorbs air, gases, water, dirt, pollution and other substances which increases skiing friction. To prevent this from happening and also to be able to adjust to all other variables effecting the ski's glide, skiers wax the ski base and sometimes the sides of the skis with waxes suitable for the specific environmental condition.

In ski skating, glide wax only is used, concentrating only on obtaining the most slippery ski and fastest glide. The Classic (traditional) technique also requires a frictional, mechanical or wax grip to prevent backward slippage during the leg kick. Many Olympic and World Championship races have been won by the "luck" of selecting a small variation in wax.

Snow crystals change (metamorphose) after the falling snow has reached the ground. To select the best wax for minimum friction when skiing, snow can be analyzed according to:

a. Moisture content in the air
b. Air temperature close to the snow surface
c. Snow temperature
d. Size of snow crystals
e. Moisture content in the snow
f. The cushion effect of the track or snow

As the six conditions above vary, so too will the frictional resistance between the ski base and the snow crystal contact points, with a large difference in friction for corresponding variations in snow conditions.

> Glide and kick wax tests made apply specifically to the type of snow, compaction, temperature, and humidity that exists at the time of the testing.

C. THE AUTHOR'S THEORIES OF THE EFFECTS OF SNOW FRICTION ON SKIING

1. GRAPHICAL ILLUSTRATION OF FRICTION

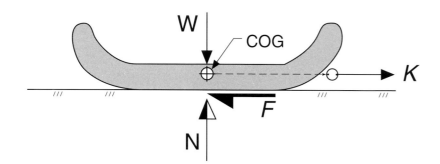

Figure A-1 *Body, Surface and Friction Force*

$$
\begin{aligned}
W &= \text{Weight of body} \\
N &= \text{Reaction Force} = W \\
F &= \text{Friction Force} = \mu N = K = \text{Pulling force} \\
\mu &= \text{Coefficient of Friction} = \frac{K}{N} = \frac{K}{W} \\
K_S &= \text{Static Pulling Force (Variable)} \\
K_G &= \text{Gliding Pulling Force (Even Speed)}
\end{aligned}
$$

$$
\mu_S = \frac{K_S}{N} \qquad \mu_G = \frac{K_G}{N}
$$

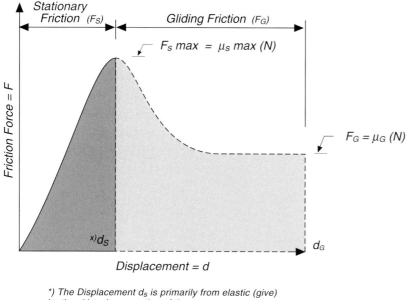

*) The Displacement d_S is primarily from elastic (give)
by the ski and compaction of the snow

Figure A-2 *Graph of Coefficient of Friction*

When pulling or pushing an object on top of a surface, motion is resisted by a friction force (F) between the body and the surface that acts in the opposite direction to the motion *(Fig. A-1)*. If the weight of the body = W is moved along the surface at a slow, even speed by a pulling force = K, there is a state of equilibrium between the vertical and horizontal action and reaction forces, K = F and W = N (see Ch. 11, Sec. I-C-3).

The quality of smoothness between the body and the surface below is identified by its coefficient of friction = μ. (μ = K/W = F/W, or F = μW). From basic theory derived from experiments, the coefficient of friction (μ), at relatively slow speeds as experienced most often during the glide in cross country skiing, varies little with the skiing speed or velocity. Frictional forces also exist when there is a pulling or pushing force, with no relative motion between the body and the gliding surface.

Experiments have shown that the initial force (F = K) needed to initiate motion is *greater.* In other words, when a body begins gliding uniformly along the surface, the friction force (F$_G$) becomes *less (Fig A-2).* These two friction forces can be defined as:

♦ STATIONARY FRICTION (Also called *adhesive* or *contact* friction in this text), the friction force needed to initiate motion of the body = F$_S$

♦ GLIDING FRICTION, the friction force when the body glides uniformly = F$_G$

The phenomena of skiing friction, as encountered during cross country skiing, when skiing on the level on a flat ski base is similar to the illustration of Figure A-1 on the preceding page.

Skiing friction is caused by the relatively few contact high points (snow crystals) between the porous ski base and the surface below. *If the weight (W) on the ski increases, so does the number of contacts, and the friction force F also increases (F= μW).*

Seen in the graph *(Fig. A-2),* the friction Force F$_S$ increases to maximum at the end of the Stationary Friction and quickly decreases as the Gliding Friction F$_G$ begins, before becoming constant, and remains so to the end of the glide (d$_G$) when skiing on a *flat ski base.*

2. STATIONARY (STATIC) FRICTION

a. Stationary Friction And The Classic Kick

In analyzing friction which takes place during cross country skiing, the theory already described can be utilized. Several of the cross country Classic techniques use a *short static friction kick or grip* between the ski and snow to increase or maintain the forward speed or momentum. The kick is "stationary" a very short time, lasting perhaps only 0.1 seconds for a top racer and many times longer for an ordinary skier.

The springy, elastic quality of a typical pair of cross country skis can be explained as follows. When gliding on a pair of skis that are both equally weighted, the midsection of skis are arched (have a camber), and have relatively little pressure against the snow. When exposed to additional vertical pressure, such as during the kick phase, the midsection of a ski, along with the tip and tail is in frictional contact with the snow crystals below.

So, if the midsection of the ski base is grip waxed, chemically, or mechanically (with steps or scales) prepared in such a manner that its coefficient of friction is considerably greater than for the glide-waxed tip and tail areas, static *(adhesive or contact)* friction will permit a powerful backward gripping kick force at the midsection that accelerates the skier forward (Ch. 11, Sec. II-B-1).

The kick utilizes what is defined as *STATIONARY Friction,* also called Adhesive, Contact, or Static Friction, (while the resistance between the ski and snow during the glide is the *GLIDING Friction,* also called Dynamic or Kinetic friction). *Classic cross country skiing, depends to a large extent on a combination of these two types of friction to create forward motion.*

The effect of stationary friction and the quality of the kick in practice can be evaluated as follows:

1. If the skis are slippery (slide backwards) during an effectively executed kick, there is too little Stationary friction.

2. On the other hand, if the skis are sticky during the kick, there is too much Stationary friction, which will reduce the forward glide.

Well known U.S. racer, Bill Koch, won several World Cup cross country races in the early 1980's by innovatively roughening up the mid-section of his skis' polyethylene base and applying a silicone spray which worked as a kick zone grip. This procedure reduces or eliminates icing of the kick zone under difficult (sticky) snow conditions, and has a dual effect of serving as a grip during the kick, and reducing friction during the glide.

b. Stationary Friction And Skating

Ski skating is normally concerned about the Gliding Friction. However, every time the downset of the ski takes place, stationary Friction occurs, which instantly demands much more energy, How to skate with least stationary friction is one of the most important aspects of efficiently learning modern ski skating, in particular, for those involved in racing (See following Sec. 7).

3. GLIDING OR DYNAMIC FRICTION

a. Types Of Gliding Friction

The theory of Gliding Friction is much more complicated than described for Stationary friction, so for practical reasons the author tries to simplify this concept.

When a ski glides on the snow, theory suggests that the gliding friction develops heat between the ski base and the snow that, to some degree, melts the contacts of the supporting snow crystals and creates a thin liquid film that acts as a lubricant between the base and the snow.

Tests indicate two types of Gliding friction:

♦ *Wet or Viscous Friction,* in which a substance(s) between the contact surfaces acts as a lubricant, takes place at high cross country speeds and at normal skiing temperatures.

♦ *Dry Friction*, in which the contact surfaces are unlubricated, occurs primarily at stationary or very slow speeds and at very low temperatures.

b. Factors Effecting Gliding Friction

In analyzing the many factors effecting Gliding friction, the following items should be considered, prior to waxing the skis:

• The Mass (weight) of the skier and his equipment.
• Areas of the sliding ski base supporting weight during skiing.
• Speed of the skier.
• Temperature of the air and snow.
• Roughness of the ski base.
• Chemical and mechanical composition of the ski base.
• Consistency of the snow or ice crystals, amount of moisture in the snow, and amount of surface pollution on the snow.
• Air resistance and drag acting on the skier.
• Elevation above sea level (gravity acceleration).
• Skiing terrain.
• Compactness of snow.

c. Shear, Cohesion And Rolling Resistances Of Snow Crystals

The author suggests that *Shear and Cohesion Resistances* between the snow crystals also contribute to the friction between the gliding ski and snow found in most skiing conditions. *Shear* refers to the snow crystal's structural resistance to breaking apart. *Cohesion* is their tendency to adhere to each other. These usually low resistances, which cause friction, become substantially greater during conditions when icing under the skis occurs and snow sticks to them.

High friction takes place at plus 0° C, in falling snow with high humidity, when numerous small crystals support the gliding ski base. Such snow, like moist flour, will have little air content and a soft cushioning effect and uneven bearing on the skis. Such a condition has more particle contact points and increased *dynamic shear and cohesion resistance*, even if rills (fine grooves) are set into the ski base to increase the air flow between the ski base and the snow.

Low Friction occurs slightly below minus 0° C, with low humidity, and stiff cushioning, when larger and fewer crystals support the gliding base. These large crystals will have relatively high particle pressure with overall less dynamic *shear and cohesion resistance*, explaining the low friction..

During *"skare"* conditions, the ice crystals may also tend to roll, meaning there may also be some *rolling friction,* a condition with even less friction.

4. VARIATIONS IN FRICTION WITH WEIGHT OF SKIER

As weight on the skis increases, the snow compacts, the number of friction contacts for the gliding surface increases, and consequently the friction force ($F = \mu W$) increases as well.

This theory applies to skiers of different weights for gliding or testing a waxed pair of skis. The friction under pairs of skis of the same length, on a level surface, should therefore vary with the weight (mass) of the skiers.

This does not mean that a heavier skier is always at a disadvantage in gliding friction. In downhill skiing (Ch. 9), there is an advantage with increased body weight (mass). As body weight and the slope of a hill increases, the component of body weight acting parallel to the slope causes downhill speed to increase accordingly. Also, the heavier skier may have some advantage on the level by applying specific techniques to create increased momentum (mv), which is related to the mass of the skier (m) and velocity (v).

The heavier skier could use skis with slightly larger gliding base areas, which accordingly would reduce the number of frictional contact points per area of the ski, and overall frictional gliding resistance. Likewise, a lighter skier could use shorter, lighter skis, with a shorter gliding base area and still have skis that are comparable with less frictional gliding resistance. Skiing with lighter skis requires less energy and allows for more flexibility. The skier therefore has to compromise in the selection of size and weight of skis. Terrain and compactness of snow, of course, also determine ski selection.

5. DOWNSET, WEIGHTING OF SKI AND FRICTIONAL ENERGY

The following theories of the author should be considered to reduce overall frictional resistance when practicing all cross country techniques. A skier should be aware of differences in effects of *Stationary* (adhesive) and *Gliding* (dynamic) friction, and apply the technique which has an advantage with respect to energy and speed.

a. As a practical guideline, in the following equations, the coefficient of *Stationary* friction has been assumed to be *twice* as high as for *Gliding* friction.

b. In practice, the higher coefficient of *Stationary* friction is encountered ***instantaneously every time the ski (being airborne) is set down for a new base contact with the snow***. This is particularly noticeable in a steep uphill during both Classic and skating techniques, when snow and/or wax conditions give a poor glide.

c. If the initial weight on the ski during base contact with the snow is light, *Stationary* friction will be relatively small.

d. As soon as the ski starts gliding, more body weight is shifted over to the gliding ski. **A smooth, gradual (not jerky) transfer of body weight to the gliding ski has less overall frictional resistance,** because as soon as the ski starts gliding, the coefficient of *Gliding* friction (μ_G), half that of *Stationary* friction, μ_S, comes into effect. Skiers should have this in mind when practicing Classic or skating techniques, since considerable energy can be conserved by applying this procedure, and energy conserved can be used to increase average speed.

$F_S = (W_S)(\mu_S)$ where F_S = *Stationary* Friction

W_S = Stationary weight on ski

μ_S = The Coefficient of *Stationary* friction

EXAMPLE:

If the body weight distributed evenly over the ski = 75 kg, and the *Stationary* coefficient of friction = 0.1, the instant friction (F_S) = 75(0.1) = 7.5 kg. Compared with a gradual weight shift where W_S = 25 kg, F_S = 2.5 kg. In this case, the stationary friction F_S is reduced to 1/3, or a considerable saving of energy.

6. FRICTION DURING SKI SKATING

a. Minimizing Friction During Transfer Of Body Weight

Figure A-3
Skier Applying Weight To Pole Before Downset Of Ski
*The above photo shows **Gunde Svan** with his full weight on the Hang Pole immediately prior to downset of the Hang Ski, which will reduce weight on the ski and minimize stationary friction.*

To skate with least frictional energy it is important to minimize the static (stationary) contact friction during downset of the ski (Appendix I, Sec. C-2). The contact friction is approximately double the gliding friction. There are two ways to accomplish minimization of friction:

1. Skier plants pole and applies weight to it immediately prior to, or simultaneously with, downset of the ski. An immediate "hang" on the pole will reduce body weight applied to the ski, reducing contact friction.

2. Apply substantially the same principle as above, for a slightly longer time period, by gradually and smoothly transferring weight to the ski during downset of the ski; and additionally weighting the ski as glide is initiated. This is accomplished by starting the glide on the lead ski earlier, while most of the body weight is on the other trailing ski, then using a smooth, spring action in the knee and a foot roll up onto the toe.

An example of such skating is illustrated in Figure A-3. The Hang pole is planted and weighted during the Paddle Dance, immediately prior to downset of ski. To accomplish this, the elbows for both arms are at 90°, poles and hands are close to the body and the legs are close together.

b. Use Of Alternate Techniques In Steep Uphills

Skating steep uphills requires a great deal of energy. **When angled to the hill, the skis travel a longer gliding distance** with less forward gain. The smaller the angle between the skis, the less is the actual skiing distance and total uphill frictional energy used (Ch. 11, Sec. II-B-4,10). However, this demands more efficient power on the poles to maintain or increase forward speed.

In steep uphills, therefore, the skier who does not have an abundance of energy, should consider and practice other alternative techniques such as herringbone or Diagonal Dance skating. A study by this author suggests that the use of effective herringbone technique in steep uphills requires less energy than Diagonal Dance. Very little frictional energy is used during herringbone technique, since there is little or no gliding taking place by the skis. The energy used is primarily vertical lifting of the body and equipment. During Diagonal Dance, this lifting also takes place, in addition to the frictional resistance of the glide on the skis.

The comparison should also take into account that the two techniques use different types of rhythmic hip motion. Greater muscle forces are acting over a shorter period of time in the herringbone, while the opposite is true during the Diagonal Dance, namely smaller muscle forces are acting over a longer period of time.

c. Theory On How Coefficient Of Friction Varies During Skating

The following graph, Figure A-4, is an attempt by the author to illustrate how the coefficient of friction μ varies throughout a skate stride. It is important for the reader to understand that the interval of time between the two types of friction discussed (Stationary and Gliding) is infinitesimally small, but significantly different physically. Effective skating technique (skiing with less energy) is accomplished by *minimizing* the stationary friction and by rotation (edging) of the ski.

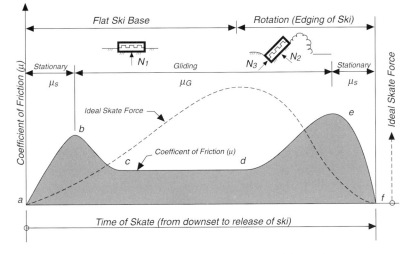

Figure A-4 *Graph of Coefficient of Friction and Ideal Skate Force Curve during Ski Skating*

Coefficient of Static Friction (μ_S)

The shaded area under the curve from "**a**" to "**b**" represents the area of the static friction coefficient "μ_S" The curve rises from 0 at "**a**" to maximum at "**b**" as the ski makes firm base contact with the snow. For the Classic stride the static frictional kick may vary from .1 to 1.0 sec.

depending on the efficiency of the skier's technique, the slope of the hill, snow conditions, etc. The author suggests that in skating a similar situation may exist, but has a smaller coefficient of friction "μ_S", depending on the downset of ski.

Coefficient of Gliding Friction (μ_G)

The curve extending from "**b**" to "**d**" represents the length of time when the skier is expected to glide on a flat ski base. The curve from "**d**" to "**e**" represents the length of time when the skier is edging (rotating the gliding ski). The edging starts at "**d**" and reaches maximum at "**e**". From the graph, the coefficient of gliding friction "μ_G" decreases immediately after the glide starts at point "**b**", and then becomes minimum at "**c**". As long as glide occurs on a flat ski base, μ remains at a minimum. As the skier starts the edging of the ski at point "**d**", "μ_S" starts to increase relative to the amount the ski rotates. It becomes greatest at "**e**" immediately prior to the final skate push-off with release of ski at point "**f**", when "μ_S" becomes = 0.

Static Friction At End Of Skate

During the final skate push-off, (curve from "**e**" to "**f**") the ski is stationary for a short time. At point "**f**", the ski is released (no contact with the snow). The edging of the ski creates turbulence of the snow and rougher contact between the side of the base and the snow, which explains the higher coefficient of gliding friction from "**d**" to "**e**". The higher coefficient of stationary friction at "**e**" is particularly noticeable in steeper uphills. The friction of ski contact with the snow will vary according to the reaction forces N_1, N_2, for the base and N_3 for the side of the ski.

Ideally, to skate efficiently, the skier should maximize the effect of the skate between "**c**" and "**d**", where there is gliding friction, and apply less weight (force) to downset of the ski ("**a**" to "**c**"), and edging of the ski ("**d**" to "**f**") where stationary friction occurs on both sidewalls of the ski (N_2 and N_3). The **Ideal Skate Force Curve** suggested in Figure A-4 complies with such a condition. Video analysis of world champion ski skaters, indicates that the distribution of Skate Action Forces is in agreement with this graph.

II. INERTIA

The effect of rotational inertia during the recovery phases of poling and skating in cross country skiing has been ignored in the past. The author's conclusion, from much study, is that the effect of rotational inertia in producing higher speed of skiing movement is significant.

Rotational inertia is defined as the resistance of a segment of the skier's body to a change in *state* of motion. The term rotational inertia, in the following, applies to the skis and the lower limbs, whose relatively large mass is involved in independent rotary motion about the hip joint (axis), and the swing of the arms and poles around the shoulder joint (axis). This rotational inertia occurs independently, while the COG for the entire body is moving in a linear direction. In the following discussions, the term "inertia" will mean rotational inertia, unless otherwise specified.

Inertia depends on how much mass is involved and the type of movement. Inertia during movement of an arm and pole is less than inertia of a leg and ski, because of the difference in their masses. The greater the mass, the greater the inertia. Inertia is also affected by the distance (radius) from the joint of rotation to the COG of the mass involved, speed of movement, and acceleration. The faster the rotary or linear movement of a limb, the greater is the effect of inertia.

Rotational inertia, as defined in this section, is not caused by external forces, i.e. poling and skating actions, but is due to internal muscular action and action of gravity forces on the limb and equipment involved.

In order to explain inertia and its effect on cross country skiing movement, it is beneficial to understand and interpret some of the basic expressions from physics and mechanics. Skiers and coaches who understand and have a feeling for how inertia physically effects skiing movement should not be overly concerned about not being able to interpret physical and biomechanical expressions. What is important is to know how inertia increases or retards skiing speed when evaluating skiing technique and use of energy.

A. FORCES CAUSING LINEAR SKIING MOVEMENT

The following two expressions are a review of the forces that cause linear movement, which were discussed at length in Chapter 11.

1. EXPRESSION FOR WEIGHT OF BODY SEGMENT AND SKI EQUIPMENT

In a stationary position, during downhill skiing, the gravity force $W = m(g)$ is the only one that causes downhill movement (Ch. 11, Sec. II-C-5).

$W = m(g) =$ Mass times gravity acceleration.

$m =$ Mass (remains constant; it is assumed to act at COG of the involved material, limb or item of skiing equipment.)

$g =$ Gravitational acceleration. This changes with elevation. When (W) changes with elevation, it is (g) that changes, not the mass (m).

2. EXPRESSION FOR MUSCULAR FORCES

Cross country ski skaters use muscular forces applied to poles and skis for forward propulsion in mild downhills, on the level, and in the uphill. The muscular forces are expressed by:

$F = m(a_L)$

$m =$ mass

$a_L =$ acceleration in a linear direction created by a force (F).

$F = m(a_L)$, an expression for linear movement (Ch. 11, Sec. II-B-9), is applied to how the skier's body (COG) is moved forward by leg forces in Classic and Skating, and by poling forces in most techniques. It is a *linear* expression only, and does not apply to independent *rotary* motion, which is discussed in more detail in the following sections.

B. EXPRESSIONS FOR INDEPENDENT ROTARY MOVEMENT BY LIMBS AND SKI EQUIPMENT

Rotary motion takes place independently from the forward linear movement of the skier's COG, as explained in the preceding section A. It occurs when a leg and ski is swung forward during the recovery phase in Classic and skating techniques, and during the forward arm swing of a pole recovery. A segment of the body and/or equipment rotates about a fixed axis, which may be the hip joint for skate action and the shoulder ball/socket joints for pole action *(Fig. A-5 and A-6)*.

This movement by independent segments of the body and equipment causes **rotational inertia,** which effects skiers movement and speed.

During such rotary motion the mass (m) of a body limb, segment or skiing equipment has a COG that is centered a distance (*r*) away from the axis of rotation. In the following expressions, these symbols are used for rotational inertia:

$I = mr^2$ = Rotational Moment of Inertia

m = Mass of a limb and/or equipment

r = Radius from axis (joint) of rotation to COG for m

t = Time in seconds of rotation

ω = Rotational velocity (Unit = radians / sec)

$a_R = \dfrac{\omega_2 - \omega_1}{t}$ = Rotational acceleration (Unit = radians / sec^2)

ω_1 = Initial rotational velocity

ω_2 = Final rotational velocity

a_L = Linear acceleration

1 radian = $\dfrac{360°}{2\pi}$ = 57.3°, also

1 radian = $\dfrac{Q}{r}$ Where Q is distance of the arch rotation of COG for (m)

According to this expression for inertia, if the distance (*r*) from the axis of rotation to the center of the mass (m), of a segment or equipment doubles, the Rotational Moment Inertia (*I*) accordingly increases fourfold. A skier can vary (control) the distance (*r*) to some degree to advantage when the effect of inertia has a *positive* effect in the direction of skiing movement, as will be discussed in the following sections C and D.

C. INERTIA IMPULSE AND MOMENTUM FROM ARM AND LEG MOVEMENT

The acceleration or deceleration from independent rotary movements of limbs and equipment is transferred to the COG of the entire body, having an effect on skier's speed and movement.

Just as the body, or part of the body and skiing equipment that is moving linearly, has an impulse F(*t*), and a momentum m(*v*) (see Ch. 11, Sec. II-B-9), likewise the independent rotating parts of the body (arm and poles, legs and skis) have Rotational Impulse and Momentum.

While the **Linear Impulse and Momentum** is

$\qquad$ F(*t*) = m(*v*), and

The **Linear Force Action** is

$\qquad$ F = m(a_L)

The analogous **Rotational Impulse and Momentum** expression is

$\qquad$ $R_O(t) = I(\omega)$, and

The **Rotational Force** is

$\qquad$ $R_O = I(a_R)$

Figure A-5 *Rotational Inertia from Forward Arm Swing*

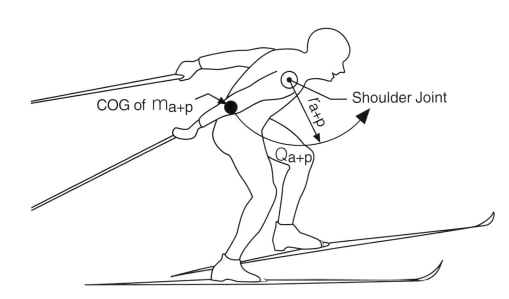

Figure A-6 *Rotational Inertia from Forward Leg Swing*

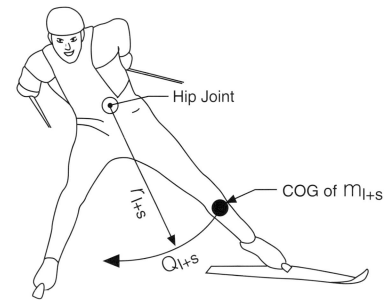

Figure A-5 illustrates the *positive* effect of inertia from the forward arm rotation about the shoulder joint during poling recovery. This contributes to increased forward acceleration (and speed).

m_{a+p} = Mass for arm and pole concentrated at COG

r_{a+p} = Average radius from shoulder joint to m_{a+p}

Q_{a+p} = Distance (path) of COG along the arch

By relaxing and extending the arms, the radius (r) becomes longer, which *increases the positive* effect of inertia.

Figure A-6 illustrates the *positive* effect (increase of speed) by inertia when leg and ski are swung forward in the recovery after the leg's skate push. The rotation takes place about the leg's hip joint.

m_{l+s} = Mass for *leg* and *ski* concentrated at COG

r_{l+s} = Average radius from hip joint to m_{l+s}

Q_{l+s} = Distance (path) of COG along the arch

By relaxing and extending the leg, with the ski following a path close to the surface, the *positive* effect of inertia during the skate recovery is increased.

D.   EFFECT OF ROTATIONAL INERTIA OF LIMBS AND EQUIPMENT ON SPEED OF SKIING

The effect of rotational inertia can be practically demonstrated using a pair of roller skates, whose wheels have very little frictional resistance. While standing still on a smooth, level surface with the arms extended backward, quickly swing the arms forward along the side of the body. The skates start rolling, and the body's COG will move forward. Likewise, with a similar quick rotation of the arms backward, the body's COG will move backward as the wheels roll backward .

During ski skating there are rotational movements for every skate stride, where the forward swing of individual body segments and equipment, independent of skier's COG, has a *positive* effect on skier's movement and speed.

While independent rotational movement forward has a **positive** effect on a skier's speed, movement in the backward direction has a **negative** effect because the action is in the opposite direction to the skier's COG.

During effective skating, the *negative* effect caused by backward movement of arm and pole, leg and ski, after the release, is smaller than the positive forward swing action, since the radius (r) to the mass (m) is shorter, and the rotational acceleration (a_R), velocity (ω), and distance of arch (Q) are all less (see previous section, C).

Likewise, keeping body elements and equipment closer to the vertical body axis and COG during the backward rotations during poling and skating action, will shorten the distance (r), and thereby reduce the *negative* effect of inertia.

In some techniques, such as in the Single Dance (Ch. 8, Sec. II), the inertia from the forward arm swings contributes more to the forward speed than the arm swings in many other techniques. Thomas Alsgård in Chapter 8, Figure 8-7, is an excellent example of a skier taking advantage of the effect of *positive* inertia.

In Diagonal Dance Skating Without Poling (Ch. 8, Sec. IV), the *negative* effect of inertia while applying the pole arm swing technique can be substantial, but can be reduced considerably by using a bent elbow with a smaller radius (r) for the backward (*negative* effect) movement and a larger radius (r) with extension of the arm during the forward (*positive* effect) swing movement.

By actively increasing the rotational acceleration (a_R) and the *positive effect*, the skier can shorten the pole recovery time. Sequentially, this could give more time for preloading prior to the pole plant. Likewise, by increasing the rotational accelerating during the leg recovery, there would be more time for bringing the legs close together, commonly neglected by many skiers.

In the many skating techniques described and illustrated in this text, the author has given frequent consideration to *maximizing the positive*, and *minimizing the negative* aspects of inertia, with respect to speed, skiing movement, and least use of energy.

SYMBOLS FOR CHAPTER 11 AND APPENDIX

Note: The page number indicates the first occurance of the symbol

INDEX OF SKIERS

Champion Skier Vignettes

BIBLIOGRAPHY

Andersen, Inge, and Nymoen, Per, *Langrenn - Trening, Teknikk, Taktikk,* Norges Skiforbund, Universitetsforlaget, Oslo, NOR , 1991.

Anderson, Robert, *Stretching*, Stretching Inc., Palmer Lake, CO, USA,1975.

Anderson, Kjell, et.al, *Bättre Skianläggningar,* Svenska Skidförbundet, Bjästa, SWE, 1990.

Åstrand, Per-Olof, and Rodahl, Kaare, *Textbook of Work Physiology,* McGraw-Hill, New York, NY, USA, 1986.

Barham, Jerry N., *Mechanical Kinesiology,* Mosby, St. Louis, MO, USA, 1978.

Bergh, Ulf, *Physiology of Cross-Country Ski Racing,* Translated by Michael Brady and Marianne Hadler, Human Kinetics, Champaign, IL, USA, 1982.

Bergsland, Einar, *Skiing a way of life in Norway,* H. Aschehoug & Co., Oslo, NOR, 1952.

Brancazio, Peter J., *SportScience - Physical Laws and Optimum Performance,* Simon & Schuster, NJ, USA, 1984.

Dalen, Magnar, and Gabrielson, Lars, *Valla rätt med Magnar*, Svenska Skidförbundet, Bjästa, SWE, 1990.

de Vries, Herbert, *Physiology of Exercise for Physical Education and Athletics,* Wm. C. Brown, Dubuque, IA, USA, 1986.

Dirix, A., Knuttgen, H.G., and Tittel, K, *The Olympic Book of Sports Medicine, Vol. 1,* Blackwall Scientific Publications, Oxford, ENG, 1988.

Endestad, Audun, and Teaford, John, *Skating for Cross-Country Skiers,* Leisure Press, Champaign, IL, USA, 1987.

Engqvist, Hans, et. al., "Skidteknik - Längd", *Träningsråd,* Svenska Skidförbundet, Bjästa, SWE, 1984.

Fisher, Arthur, et. al., *The Healthy Heart*, Time-Life Books, Alexandria, VA, USA, 1981.

Flemmen, Asbjørn, *Skileik - Skiopplæring,* Norges Skiforbund/Universitets Forlaget, Oslo, NOR, 1990.

Forsberg, Artur, et. al., *Längdåkning,* Rabén & Sjögren, Lund, SWE, 1978.

Forsberg, Artur, *Träna Din Kondition,* Utbildningsproduktion, Malmö, SWE, 1989.

Forsberg, Artur and Saltin, Bengt et. al., *Konditionsträning,* Idrottens Forskningsråd, Sveriges Riksidrotts-förbund, Farsta, SWE, 1988.

Gabrielson, Lars, and Nilsson, Jonny, "Förslag till klassificeringssystem, för olika tekniker i längdåkning", *Svensk Skidsport,* Vol. 6-91, May, 1991, pp. 62-63. CEWE Förlaget, Bjästa, SWE.

Gabrielson, Lars, et.al., "Träning på snö - Längd", *Träningsråd,* Svenska Skidförbundet, Bjästa, SWE, 1991.

Gray, Henry, *Anatomy Of The Human Body*, Lea & Febiger, Philadelphia, PA, 1985.

Hochmuth, Gerhard, *Biomechanik sportlicher Bewegungen,* Sportverlag, Berlin, GER, 1974.

Howe, John, *Skiing Mechanics,* Poudre Press, Laporte, CO, USA, 1983.

Idrottens Forskningsråd, *Kvinnor och Idrott,* Idrottens AHus, Farsta, SWE, 1988.

Karlsen, Torbjörn, *How, When, Why Training Guide for Cross-Country Skiers,* Nordic Equipment, Inc. Park City, UT, USA, 1990.

Kreighbaum, Ellen, and Barthels, K., *Biomechanics,* Burgess Publishing Co., Minneapolis, MN, USA, 1981.

McArdle, W.D., Katch, Frank I., and Katch, Victor, *Exercise Physiology, Energy, Nutrition, and Human Performance,* Lea & Febiger, Philadelphia, PA, USA, 1986.

McNaught, Ann B., and Callander, Robin, *Illustrated Physiology,* Churchill Livingstone, London, ENG, 1983.

Norges Skiforbund Langrennskomiteen, *Norges Skiforbunds Veiledende Normer for Langrennstrening,* 4. utgave, Oslo, NOR, 1984, 1986.

Powell, Mark, and Svensson, John, *In-Line Skating,* Human Kinetics, Champaign, IL, USA, 1993.

Railo, Willi, *Best Når Det Gjelder, Praktisk råd i idrettspsykologi og mental trening,* Norges Idrettsforbund, Oslo, NOR, 1985.

Rawald, Jan, "Skridskotekniken", *Träningsråd*, Svenska Skidförbundet, Bjästa, SWE, 1987.

Rohen, Johannes W., and Yokochi, Chihiro, *Color Atlas of Anatomy,* Igaku-Shoin, Tokyo, JAP, 1984.

Saltin, B. and P.D. Gollnick, "Skeletal Muscle Adaptability - Significance for Metabolism and Performance", *Handbook of Physiology Skeletal Muscle,* Sec. 10, Ch.19, pg. 555, American Physiological Society, Bethesda, MD, USA, 1983.

Scheier, Anton, et.al., *The National Guide to Loppet Skiing,* Cross Country Canada, CAN, 1985

Sharkey, Brian J., *Training for Cross-Country Ski Racing,* U.S. Ski Team/Human Kinetics, Champaign, IL, USA, 1984.

Skard, Halldor, *Lær deg Snösköyting,* Universitetsforlaget, Oslo, NOR, 1986.

Skard, Halldor, and Larsson, Olle, *Langrenns teknikk,* Universitetsforlaget, Oslo, NOR, 1981.

Skard, Halldor, and Gjerset, Asbjørn, *Treningslære,* Universitetsforlaget, Oslo, NOR, 1983.

Skiforlaget / Erling Ranheim, *Norske Skilöpere,* 5 Volumes, Skiforlaget, Oslo, NOR, 1955-1956.

Smith, Gerald Allen, "The Effect of Velocity and Grade on the Kinematics and Kinetics of V1 Skating in Cross Country Skiing", UMI Dissertation Services, Ann Arbor, MI, USA, 1990.

Strømme, Signumd B., and Kjeldsen, Bjørn, *Spis riktig - yt mer!,* Universitetsforlaget, Oslo, NOR, 1989.

STUI / Norges Skiforbund, *Skianlegg - Langrenn,* Universitetsforlaget, Oslo, NOR, 1988.

Svensson, Einar, "The Significance of Lateral Movement and Weight Shift for the Diagonal Stride", *American Ski Coach,* Vol 11, No.3, pp.12-15, Jan. 1988, US Ski Coaches Assoc., Park City, UT, USA.

Torgersen, Leif, God Glid, H. Aschenhoug & Co, Oslo, NOR, 1983; translation by Michael Brady, *Good Glide, the science of ski waxing,* U.S. Ski Team/Human Kinetics, Champaign, IL, USA, 1983.

Trozzi, Sergio Fucci e Vincenzo, "Analisi biomeccanica del passo alternato dello sci di fondo", Scuola Sport, Federazione Italiana Sport Invernali, Rome, ITA, 1981.

Van Ingen Schenau, G.J., and Cavanagh, P.R., "Power Equations in Endurance Sports, *Journal of Biomechanics,* Vol.23, No.9, 1990, Pergammon Press, Oxford, ENG.

Wirhed, Rolf, *Athletic Ability, the Anatomy of Winning,* Harmony Books, New York, NY, USA 1984.